Parenting Mindfully

Parenting Mindfully

101 Ways to Help Raise Caring and Responsible Kids in an Unpredictable World

Catherine DePino

ROWMAN & LITTLEFIELD
Lanham • Boulder • New York • London

Published by Rowman & Littlefield
An imprint of The Rowman & Littlefield Publishing Group, Inc.
4501 Forbes Boulevard, Suite 200, Lanham, Maryland 20706
www.rowman.com

Unit A, Whitacre Mews, 26-34 Stannary Street, London SE11 4AB

British Library Cataloguing in Publication Information Available

Library of Congress Cataloging in Publication Information

Name: DePino, Catherine, author.
Title: Parenting mindfully : 101 ways to help raise responsible and caring kids in an
    unpredictable world / Catherine DePino.
Description: Lanham : Rowman & Littlefield, [2018] | Includes bibliographical refer-
    ences.
Identifiers: LCCN 2018011769 (print) | LCCN 2018012486 (ebook) | ISBN
    9781475843224 (ebook) | ISBN 9781475843217 (cloth : alk. paper)
Subjects: LCSH: Parenting. | Parent and child. | Caring in children. | Responsibility in
    children.
Classification: LCC HQ755.8 (ebook) | LCC HQ755.8 .D458 2018 (print) | DDC 649/.1—
    dc23
LC record available at https://lccn.loc.gov/2018011769

∞ ™ The paper used in this publication meets the minimum requirements of American National Standard for Information Sciences Permanence of Paper for Printed Library Materials, ANSI/NISO Z39.48-1992.

Printed in the United States of America

To my daughter and son-in-law, Shayna and Len,
who love spending time with their children while helping them
become smart, caring, responsible human beings.

"The family is the salt of the earth and the light of the world. It is the leaven of society."—Pope Francis

Contents

Acknowledgments

At Rowman & Littlefield, I'd like to thank Carlie Wall, managing editor, for her help and kindness and Dr. Tom Koerner, vice president and editorial director, for his constant support and encouragement. I also want to thank Sheree Bycofsky, a caring literary agent.

Introduction

How Can Mindfulness Help You Raise Smart, Caring, Responsible Kids?

More than ever, life in our world, nation, and communities appears insecure and unpredictable. Every day, new and disturbing incidents pop up on the news that feed this sense of unrest. In our communities, people don't attempt to understand each other's points of view, causing compromise to give way to discord and conflict. Politics, lifestyles, and religion are all fair game for fomenting conflict in our divided society.

Many of us live with a sense of tension and alienation because of our uncertain, unpredictable world. This unremitting stress, in turn, filters down to the way we raise our children and the way our kids respond to accepting the values we work hard to impart.

Schools feel the fallout from this sense of insecurity and unpredictability in the form of increased conflict within the school community and increased incidents of bullying. Children of all ages, especially elementary and middle school kids, experience more anxiety these days than kids growing up in their parents' generation. They feel the relentless push for academic excellence in which they're measured against an arbitrary standard rather than against their own abilities. Furthermore, pressure to fit in with peers abounds, often at the expense of nourishing children's unique sense of individuality and self-worth.

Parenting mindfully can help you provide your kids with a buffer against an insecure, unpredictable world and the stresses associated with it. Following the principles of Mindfulness can help you raise kids who become school smart, street smart, caring human beings. If you want to help promote character traits in your kids like compassion, kindness, and respect for you and others, using mindfulness techniques can help jumpstart these traits in your children. Moreover, raising kids the mindful way can help them navigate an increasingly complex world where uncertainty and insecurity reign.

Stop for a moment. Imagine what it would be like if you could begin to find a way to parent your kids successfully despite the growing negativity in the world. Parenting mindfully can help both you and your kids discover a new and rewarding way of living, and that's a promise.

Many school districts are incorporating Mindfulness programs, and parents are studying its precepts to help them raise happy, well-adjusted kids and to help themselves in the process. Mindfulness, popularized by the Buddhist monk Thich Nhat Hanh, and brought to this country by Jon Kabat-Zinn and his Mindfulness-Based Stress Reduction Program, helps people of all ages live satisfying and fulfilling lives by encouraging them to live in the present rather than in the past or the future. Although meditation is an important component of Mindfulness programs, *Parenting Mindfully* focuses on using the principles of Mindfulness to help kids ages 6-14 live their best possible lives.

You probably know that once kids get older, it's harder to change their way of thinking. That's why this book targets parents of elementary and middle school kids. You, as their parent and main teacher, are the best person to show your kids how to maximize their talents and potential for happiness while minimizing the stresses and tensions that characterize our frenzied lifestyles.

WHAT ARE THE BASIC PRINCIPLES OF MINDFULNESS?

Using the principles of Mindfulness not only helps you raise strong, resilient kids, it also helps you improve your own physical and emotional health. As you begin to use these techniques to help your children grow and flourish, you'll help yourself become more patient, tolerant, flexible, and compassionate. Because you're willing to be an active listener, your children will listen more when you talk and will talk back less. Since you're willing to speak assertively rather than aggressively to your kids, they'll reciprocate by speaking to you in a more polite, respectful manner.

You will find threads of Mindfulness woven throughout all the activities in this book. In a world that stresses perfection in outward appearance and intelligence, Mindfulness assumes that your children are fine exactly as they are, a concept many children struggle with in their interactions with peers. Another characteristic of Mindfulness, acceptance of what happens in the present moment, but not necessarily agreement with it, helps children cope with the many uncertainties they face each day.

It's equally important that kids demonstrate curiosity, another hallmark of Mindfulness, when problem-solving or interacting with other children during mild disagreements or heated disputes. They need to fully understand the other person's message before becoming needlessly upset. Curiosity helps kids ask the right questions to find the best answers. Being curious and asking questions also helps promote better communication. When you're gently curious while talking with your children about their concerns, you can pinpoint problems they're facing and help them find answers.

Mindfulness in communication helps diffuse arguments and promote understanding. Mindfulness asks us to pay attention to Metacommunication when interacting with others; in this case, our kids. This simply means listening to the messages that go beyond the words we use with one another. Body language, eye contact, word choice, and pitch often reveal the true messages that words don't convey.

In line with this, it's important to become sensitive to the right time to talk with kids about your concerns. Look for the teachable moment rather than asking your child to change a behavior when both of you are upset or in the throes of a disagreement. To capture your child's attention, say something like this: "I'd like to tell you more about my feelings on this subject. Would you like to talk now, or would you feel better waiting a little while?" Needless to say, this doesn't mean postponing the talk indefinitely, but rather taking cues from your child about a time she'll be more receptive to what you have to say.

Mindful listening asks kids to respond rather than react, to hear what the other person has to say and to listen respectfully, whether they agree or not. Rather than shoot from the hip during potential temper flare-ups, it helps to pause, relax, and be open to what the other person is saying. Kids and adults alike often react before speaking, which leads to misunderstandings and disagreements.

The way children communicate with others becomes especially important in helping them get their ideas across to family, friends and classmates. Mindfulness stresses assertive, rather than passive or aggressive, communication. It's important for kids to learn how to talk to others without being vague and timid or pushy and confrontational. Talking assertively helps them communicate so other people listen and respond favorably. Mindful speaking also includes using "I" messages, which relate how the speaker feels, rather than employing "you" messages that can sound negative and accusatory to the person on the other end of the conversation.

Similarly, it's important for kids to learn to frame requests positively and assertively to promote harmony and derail conflict. For example, if your child experiences bullying, he needs to get the point across briefly and emphatically that he will not tolerate the harassment. Whether or not the bully listens, your child has given fair warning that he will not accept this treatment.

Putting oneself in another person's position is another characteristic of Mindfulness that contributes to being an empathetic listener and thoughtful speaker. Model this behavior for your children so that they, in turn, will use it when a friend or family member needs someone to truly listen and understand.

Another important part of Mindfulness is granting loving kindness to oneself and others. Many kids these days are too hard on themselves, always trying to measure up to impossible standards. When a child gets in the habit of showing loving kindness, she's gentle and caring with herself and cuts herself some slack because she knows it's unrealistic to be perfect in every way. Demonstrating loving kindness also makes kids more compassionate toward others.

If you incorporate Mindfulness into your daily dealings with your children, it's highly likely they'll turn out to be smart, caring, and responsible kids who know how to deal with all the problems that come their way. Moreover, they will experience greater joy each day by living in the moment, the only moment that all of us truly have, the Present.

HOW TO USE THIS BOOK

This book is divided into twelve chapters that offer specific ways parents can help children, ages six to fourteen, raise their kids to be smart, caring, and responsible human beings. The first section of each chapter, Think About This, gives a comprehensive overview of the topics covered in that chapter.

Model a Conversation, the second section of each chapter, offers parents sample conversations about topics in the book between parents and children of varying ages. You can model the behavior listed for each situation, modifying it to your individual scenarios.

You've probably heard that psychologists see modeling as one of the major factors in influencing children. The time-tested adage "Children learn what they live" brings home the fact that if your children see you acting and responding in certain ways, they're more likely to embrace these methods for coping with a variety of challenging situations throughout their lifetimes.

Try This, the third and final section of each chapter, offers activities that target all the topics in this book. Try the activities as they are, or use your own creativity and ingenuity to tweak the activities to suit your own family situations and issues. You'll find activities listed for each different age group, six to nine and ten to fourteen. You can also use all of the activities for age groups different from the ones listed, depending on the unique situations your child faces and his maturity level.

Chapter One

Bolster Confidence

THINK ABOUT THIS

Confidence helps kids build meaningful friendships, achieve in school, and make wise choices. Children who have confidence are not afraid to step outside their comfort zones because they trust their judgement to do what's best for them, even when peers try to put doubt in their minds or ridicule them about their opinions or choices.

How can you help your kids gain the confidence they need to accomplish their goals and weather challenging situations that pop up in their lives, such as problems in school, conflicts at home, and bullying? How can you impart a sense of confidence in them so that no matter what challenges they face, they can emerge confident in knowing they can handle many of their own problems? One way is by instilling a sense that they are okay exactly the way they are, that they already have inside them the qualities they need to show resilience and perseverance despite the struggles they sometimes encounter.

One simple thing you can do to bolster confidence is to present your children with tangible evidence that they are talented, smart, and caring individuals with their own special abilities. The first activity in this chapter involves giving your child an award certificate. Another involves having a family dinner in your child's honor in the comfort of your own home. You can recognize your children in many different ways. All you have to do is use your imagination.

Another project that helps build confidence, especially in younger children, is building a scrapbook or photo album highlighting special events in their lives. This special album or scrapbook, unlike a family photo album, belongs to one child.

Children, particularly in their pre-teen and early teenage years, can experience issues with self-confidence because of body image, such as excess weight, complexion problems, and dental issues like braces. You, as a parent, can help resolve these concerns by being there for your child, by using Mindful listening and talking, and by seeking medical help when necessary.

Disappointments and setbacks can also put a dent in a child's self-confidence. Mindful listening on your part can help your child recover faster from a small or large disappointment, such as getting sick the day of the school trip or not getting a part in the school show. Allowing your children to express disappointment freely and to come up with solutions and alternatives can make them more confident people, who realize they can overcome setbacks and that their problems will improve in time.

Another problem that affects confidence in kids involves personality differences between them and an adult authority figure, such as a teacher or coach. In the interest of boosting confidence, you wonder whether you should encourage your child to adjust to the teacher's class or to try to have the class changed. In this case, you may want to think about what is best for the long term, since your child will have to face situations in the future when he doesn't have a good rapport with someone, such as an employer, because of personality differences, or a spouse because of minor marital squabbles.

Finally, your children coping with not getting what they want, like an invitation to a party or acceptance into a certain group of kids, requires strength and confidence. When you listen and respond mindfully, you'll help your child learn to cope constructively with many of life's disappointments.

MODEL A CONVERSATION: BOLSTER CONFIDENCE

1. Being Left Out Is Not Fun

Here's a conversation between Mandy, a twelve-year-old, and her mother Sarah. Mandy, a sixth grader, finds out she's not invited to a birthday party by a girl she thought was a good friend.

Sarah: I'm wondering why you're so quiet lately. You're definitely not your usual chatty self. I see you've been spending a lot of time in your room and you didn't eat much of that cherry pie I made last night.

Mandy (lying on the sofa texting): I don't feel like talking now.

Sarah: I can see that, but when you're ready, I'm here. I can tell something's wrong, and I want to help.

Mandy doesn't look up and keeps texting on her cell phone. Sarah goes in the kitchen and searches the fridge to gather food for a cook out.

Mandy (getting up from the sofa): I know you'll keep bugging me until I tell you, so here's what happened. Jessie didn't invite me to her party. (Looks away) I didn't want to go anyway.

Sarah: Jessie and you have been friends since first grade. I can understand how that must hurt.

Mandy (starts to cry): Why wouldn't she invite me? We've been friends forever.

Sarah (touching Mandy's arm): Sometimes there's no reason people do things. Did you talk to her about how not inviting you made you feel?

Mandy: I told her I thought we were friends and that I felt left out. I said I didn't want to be friends with her if I wasn't good enough to be invited to her party.

Sarah: What did she say to that?

Mandy: She said, "Sorry you feel that way, but I want to start hanging out with a different crowd. I met some new kids since you and I are in different classes this year. I want to get to know them better."

Sarah: So, there's your answer. Now here's a question for you: How do you feel about having a friend who feels that way?

Mandy: When you put it that way, it makes me think I deserve better. I'd probably be better off spending time with kids who care about me, kids who don't worry about being in the popular crowd.

Sarah: It's good you told her how you feel. It's also important you know how what you think about yourself doesn't depend on one person's friendship. You have a couple of good friends who care about you and enjoy being with you.

Mandy: I guess you're right. I feel good about things most of the time, and I have friends who like me for myself, not because I'm part of a certain group.

Sarah (hugging Mandy): You know how to handle tough situations. You can be proud of yourself for that. You're a pretty strong young lady, if I do say so myself.

They leave the kitchen together, carrying trays of food outside to cook on the grill.

TRY THIS: ACTIVITIES TO HELP BOLSTER CONFIDENCE, AGES 6–9

2. Boost Self-Confidence with Tangible Rewards

Your child did something noteworthy in school or scored in his favorite sport. Reward him with a homemade award certificate. Print it from free Web templates, or create your own award certificates. Write short messages on the certificate to boost confidence in your child's special talent or ability. Example: "You aced that science test yesterday. I know how great that made you feel"; or, "You can be proud of yourself for how you scored in the game last night." (Stress confidence and pride the student has in his own abilities rather than pride coming from other people's confidence, even your own, in the child.) Leave the certificate in your child's room or backpack where he can easily find it.

Planning an award dinner is another tangible way to boost self-confidence. Simply prepare your child's favorite dinner or dessert at home to recognize one of his achievements. After the dinner, you can say a few things to honor your child and his accomplishments, whether it's a small one like student of the month, or a larger one like an appointment to student council. Again, focus on his pride in his own ability rather than external praise. ("I can see how happy you felt when you got up there on the stage," or "I know how excited you are to be elected to student council.")

Be sure to distribute award dinners evenly among siblings to avoid hurt feelings. In both activities and in ones you create, loving kindness among family members rather than elaborate solutions and expensive rewards go a long way toward boosting your child's confidence.

3. Encourage Your Child to Make Good Choices

Making choices is something your child faces from an early age in school, at home, and in the neighborhood. She chooses how much time to devote to doing her best in school by paying attention in class and devoting time to homework. At home, she chooses whether to cooperate with your rules and chooses to what extent she makes the effort to get along with her siblings. In the neighborhood and in school, she makes friendship choices, for better or worse.

Imagine that your child has to make one of these decisions: to try out for the softball or track team; what to wear for a party she's going to; or whether to befriend a child in the popular crowd that she has questions about because she saw the potential friend treating another child unfairly. In the case of choosing a sport, help her map out the positive and negative points of choosing one sport over another. Encourage her to make the right decision herself, rather than relying on family members or friends to make it for her.

Choices like deciding what to wear to a party should also be her call, unless you feel her choice is inappropriate for the occasion. In this case, you can gently lead her to a better selection by asking what she thinks would be a suitable choice for the occasion and why, or by eliciting her sister or another trusted family member's help.

In the case of choosing a friend, have an on-going discussion with her about what traits are important to her in a friend, like kindness, consideration, honesty, and treating other kids fairly. Ask: What it would mean to have a friend who didn't possess these qualities? Why are the positive traits listed important in a friendship?

The choices your child has to make when she is growing up pave the way for her to make important choices throughout her life, such as what to study in college, where to live, and what to look for in a prospective partner. It's important to discuss issues surrounding her choices ahead of time so she's better prepared to choose the best path for herself in all areas, during her formative years and for the years to come.

4. Strengthen Confidence with Visuals

Taking the time to be with your child in a mindful way helps him feel reassured and confident. Working with your child on a photo album or scrapbook requires a few spare moments on a weekly basis. The project can be very simple. It doesn't take much time to download and print pictures and create brief captions. Parents or grandparents and a child will enjoy doing this activity together. This project differs from a family photo album in that it belongs to one child alone; it is his unique story. This special album or scrapbook, unlike a family photo album, makes your child feel honored in his uniqueness.

Here's another added benefit to creating an album or scrapbook: Whatever your child's learning style is, you can address it with this project, ensuring that this activity will make a strong impression on his sense of confidence. It's easy to see that making a photo album or scrapbook brings into play all the learning styles, such as visual (sight), kinesthetic (touch), and auditory (hearing).

The visual part of the project includes all the pictures gathered and how your child chooses to arrange and describe them. The touch component of the project involves your child using his hands to gather pictures and write descriptions under each of the events. The project includes auditory elements because you and your child constantly interact with each other as your child

picks and chooses pictures and writes captions to create his album or scrapbook. Because this project appeals to every type of learner and uses all the
senses, its benefits will stay with your child and leave its strong imprint on
him and his sense of confidence.

Here's how to strengthen confidence by making a scrapbook or photo
album: Help your child build a scrapbook or a photo album marking special
occasions, such as making the honor roll, getting recognized for a talent,
making the team, or reaching a milestone in his faith. Ask him to write brief
captions, explaining how the events brought happiness to his life and made
him feel confident. Encourage him to share his scrapbook or album with
relatives, such as grandparents, aunts, uncles, and friends. It will boost his
confidence even more to help a friend create a photo album or scrapbook for
himself.

5. Spark Your Child's Unique Interests

Your child shows an interest in a sport or talent, like art, music, or writing.
Be active in helping her explore her talent. Attend games with her, encourage
her talents by keeping up with her progress and assisting her in finding
outlets for her interests. Help her research people who achieved satisfaction
and success by using talents like the ones that interest her. Help her think
about what they did specifically to help nurture their special talents. How did
their interests carry over into a hobby or career?

Point out that the good thing about talents is that they can turn into a
lifelong career or can contribute to practicing a related career. For example,
love of sports can turn into a career as a physical education teacher or a
personal trainer. An affinity for art can contribute to a graphic artist's or
illustrator's profession. Love of music can help a person start a business
performing at weddings or teaching music. Love of writing can benefit an
aspiring lawyer, speech writer, or English teacher.

Another thing you can do to encourage your child's talents is help her
find outlets to showcase her talents. In the areas of art, music, and writing,
there are organizations that promote children's works. Google them and see
if any are right for your child. Be sure to google something like "reputable
publishers that accept children's writing or writers." There are many scam
artists out there who are ready to take your money in exchange for their
services, so let the buyer beware. A few reputable publishers accept children's writing, while others are open to receiving illustrations from children.
In the area of sports, organizations, including universities, offer summer
camps for children. Local communities and private organizations also sponsor sports camps for kids.

Here's the bottom line: Encouraging special talents and abilities goes a
long way in boosting confidence in children. When your child has a unique

talent, it can carry her far in life. That's why it's important to nurture it in childhood. Your influence can be a prime factor in helping her talents grow and develop.

TRY THIS: ACTIVITIES TO HELP BOLSTER CONFIDENCE, AGES 10–14

6. Back Your Child Against Bullies

Bullying is one of the worst confidence killers. When someone bullies your child, he may begin to question why he was singled out and experience a sense of inadequacy and depression that can seep into every area of his life. If you child is bullied, deal with it aggressively, not stopping until you get assurance from the school that staff members are doing everything in their power to stop the bullying.

At the same time, you'll want to offer your child unwavering support and build up his confidence. Keep in close contact with the school counselor to determine ways to help your child cope and overcome the after-effects of bullying. If the bullying is severe or continues, seek counseling for your child as bullying can precipitate severe depression and, in some cases, suicide.

Here's a case in point: Your child comes home from school in a terrible state but won't tell you why. The teacher calls later that day to tell you that two classmates bullied him in the lunchroom, surrounding him and chanting, "fat, ugly pig" and some other choice epithets you wouldn't want repeated. You learn from the teacher that this has happened once before, but this is the first you've heard of it. Your son tends to keep things inside.

In this case, since it's the second recurrence of bullying, it's important to ask the teacher to call you if it happens again. The teacher tells you the principal suspended the perpetrators, who have to bring their parents in before they can return to school. The assistant principal assures you they'll do their best to ensure it doesn't happen again. However, you've heard from another parent whose child was bullied by the same students that they didn't stop bothering her son even after a suspension. That makes you decide that if the problem isn't solved at the school level, you'll follow up and call the district office to gain more assistance. If that doesn't work, you'll go all the way to the top to the superintendent's office to solve the problem.

When your child is ready to open up, listen mindfully to what he tells you. Buoy his confidence by reminding him that he's a super kid with many talents. Talk to him about why it's important to discount the bully's senseless comments and to concentrate on the rewarding relationships he has with his close friends.

If he doesn't have any close friends, work with him to find ways of making new and lasting friendships. Also, stay in close touch with the teacher, counselor, and school administrator to find ways to function together as a team to put an end to the bullying.

7. Counter Poor Body Image

Your child is self-conscious and socially withdraws because she's over-weight, wears braces, and has problems with her complexion. She spends most of the time in her room alone, playing loud music and tuning in to social media on her computer. Although you've installed safeguards on her computer, you know it's not good for her to have mostly virtual and few real friends. Do your best to encourage her to invite a friend or schoolmate on a family outing to a place she likes, such as the beach, mountains, or an amusement park.

If she doesn't have friends, encourage her to join a club at school. Since she's interested in computers, a computer club would be a good one to join. If she goes to a church, a youth group would be a good place to start making friends.

If she refuses to go on a family outing with a friend or to make an effort to find friends, ask her what would help her want to get out of the house. Listen without interrupting, and take your cues from her. If she insists on staying in her room avoiding all social contact, make an appointment with your family physician, and then, if the isolation persists, take her to a recommended counselor.

Discuss her feelings about wearing braces and remind her that the day will come when she won't need them. Also, find a dermatologist who has a good rapport with kids and begin a course of treatment. Discuss weight issues with her physician, and encourage her to go on a diet. Be sure to give her input into what type of weight loss plan she thinks would suit her best. The more autonomous and independent she feels about health issues, the more confident she'll eventually feel in carrying out a successful plan to improve her body image.

8. Deal with a Student/Teacher Mismatch

Your son constantly complains about his eighth-grade English teacher, Ms. Reynolds. He claims she bores him and the rest of the class with long lectures and little student interaction. He says Ms. Reynolds singles him out because he talks back to her in class and doesn't do his homework. The teacher says that in addition to his behavior problems he also entices the other students to act up in class. Recently, Ms. Reynolds sent your son to the dean's office and wrote a pink slip because he talked back, screaming that he hated her class and everyone else did too.

Before the required parent conference to discuss the pink slip and remedy the situation, you thought about how to help fix the problem. Would requesting a class change because you believed your son and the teacher had a personality conflict be the best thing to do? Possibly, it would prove a quick fix to solve the problem, but what would the long-term message be to your son? Added to this, with the school schedule carved in stone at this point in the semester, would a transfer to another class even be an option?

Throughout your son's life, he's going to have to deal with people he's not fond of, so possibly it would be helpful to view this student/teacher clash as a learning experience for him. After careful consideration, you decide that maybe your son should stay in the class and do his best to adjust to an uncomfortable situation, trying to meet the teacher halfway by showing her respect and making a strong effort to cooperate. He also needs to promise to stop involving other students in his personal battle with the teacher.

Once you make your decision to keep your child in the class, your son agrees to cooperate. The main thing that drives his decision is not getting a bad record in the discipline office, which may disqualify him from playing JV football. After he makes his commitment to cooperate in class, the school counselor says she'll check in with him periodically to see if there's an improvement in the student/teacher relationship. The counselor keeps in touch with the teacher, who writes a short daily report about your son's subject and behavioral progress, forwarding it to you each day for your signature.

Ms. Reynolds will probably never be your son's favorite teacher, but she too has learned to compromise by accepting his apology. You tell your son to stop and take a deep breath when potential conflicts look like they're going to escalate between him and the teacher. Your child learns that dealing with problematic relationships is better than seeking the easier solution of trying to make things better by looking for a quick fix, like a class change, and not dealing with the issues at hand. Of course, in this case, if your son was not willing to stop disrupting the class and the teacher was not willing to make a fresh start, a roster change would most likely be the best way to deal with the mismatch.

9. Listen with Your Heart

Your daughter feels extremely disappointed about not getting a part in the school show after she's spent hours polishing her act. She studied singing and dancing since first grade and performed in community theater to rave reviews. Your child pretends that not having a part in the show doesn't bother her, but you can tell it does because whenever you bring up the topic she gets testy. She also said she wasn't hungry even though you made shrimp stir fry, her favorite dinner. She's irritable and sulky and can't let it go.

Find a time she seems to be in a good mood. Listen mindfully without interrupting when she's ready to talk, and try putting yourself in her place as she tells you how she feels. Be curious and ask questions about what her feelings are and what she can do about them. Listen, and accept what she says even if you don't agree. Feel free to tell her if you disagree, but wait until she's finished talking, and by all means, say it gently and give her time to respond.

At some point, ask if she'd like to be more involved in community theater or to seek other outlets for her talents. Reassure her that even the best entertainers don't get every part they try out for, and, after researching the topic, give specific examples of actors, artists, or writers who have faced rejection and overcame it.

Discuss instances when you or other family members experienced disappointment because they didn't get what they wanted in life. Maybe you worked hard to get a promotion and were denied it because the company wanted new blood, resulting in a person who hadn't been with the firm long landing the job. Possibly, your husband wanted to play a sport in college but didn't make the cut. Discuss your or another person's sense of disappointment, how it affected the person involved, and how you, or someone you know, ultimately coped with the sense of not seeing what you wanted materialize. Let this discussion act as a springboard for your child to voice her feelings about dealing with rejection without sacrificing her sense of confidence in herself.

Chapter Two

Encourage Responsible Behavior

THINK ABOUT THIS

We all want our children to act responsibly toward themselves, us, and everyone they encounter. Responsibility is one of the main character traits a person needs to live in loving, stable relationships, hold down a desirable job, and maintain lasting friendships. If parents reinforce responsibility in childhood, children will have a better chance of living a satisfying, fulfilling life when they become adults.

One way parents can instill a sense of responsibility in children is to help them gain independence in making decisions. If parents don't give kids the chance to evaluate and decide what's right for them in a given situation, they won't be able to solve their own problems or have a good grasp of what's right and wrong for them personally.

Kids love using electronic devices, but as you know, using these and social media excessively can hamper effective communication. In fact, many kids feel more comfortable using text messaging and social media than talking one-on-one with parents and peers. Parents can model using these devices judiciously so kids can strike a balance between staying in touch with their friends and family members electronically and communicating with these same people in person to form closer bonds.

Parents can also instill responsibility by making kids own their mistakes and learn from them. Smoothing things over and making excuses for your children when they do something that leads to a poor outcome will not help them learn and grow, but will turn them into adults who tend to rationalize mistakes and who lean on others rather than on themselves for support.

Another way to instill responsibility in children involves encouraging children to develop a sense of organization when it comes to studying for tests and homework. Kids who get their work in on time and come to school prepared feel more relaxed and less harried than those who scramble around to complete assignments or cram for tests at the last minute.

Also, kids need to learn the importance of keeping a neat room without expecting their parents to clean for them or pick up their dirty clothes from the floor. They need to learn to pitch in with household chores without expecting to be paid. Related to that, teaching responsible behavior involves learning skills like cooking simple meals or running a load of wash so they're not completely dependent on you.

Teaching kids to handle money wisely is another way parents can encourage responsible behavior. When someone gives your children monetary gifts, spend time discussing the advantages of saving some of the money and spending some, rather than using all the money on a gadget that may not hold their interest for long.

Responsible behavior includes showing concern for family members when they're in need of companionship or comfort. It's particularly important for kids to spend time with older relatives, such as grandparents, so they can learn from them and show love and compassion to them, whether they are well or sick.

Being responsible means kids keeping parents informed about their friendships and whereabouts. In most cases, parents have to emphasize the importance of open communication about these issues with their kids. Especially with middle grade kids, parents need to know where they are at all times and who they're choosing as friends.

To ensure knowing about your children's friends, open your home to these friends and get to know their parents. Observe your kids' interactions with these friends, and be sure they're healthy ones. Create a workable system for having your children keep you informed about where they're going and how long they'll be in a certain place. Be sure they know to call you if they change their plans.

Finally, think about the importance of helping your children become responsible users of electronic devices like smartphones and playing video games online. Consider their use of social media and how it and the various devices they're depending on for communication and entertainment often dominate their lives to the exclusion of meaningful conversation and interaction with family and friends.

As you've probably observed, it's come to the point that many children feel awkward conversing with people in person because they're so used to texting or relating to friends on social media. Because of a lack of authentic one-on-one communication, a sense of loneliness and alienation sometimes prevails.

MODEL A CONVERSATION: ENCOURAGE
RESPONSIBLE BEHAVIOR

10. Curb Electronics Overuse

Carrie, a neighbor, complained to me that her fourteen-year-old stepson Lamont spends hours texting on his phone and playing video games on his TV. He brings his smartphone to the dinner table and spends the entire time hunched over it. He rarely talks to his parents about his friends or school. If they try to engage him in conversation, he responds by saying, "Stop bugging me," or "I'm not a little kid."

Carrie invited me to her house for dinner with her, Lamont, and her husband. She wanted me to observe the family dynamic to see if I could give her any insights and advice about what she considered a budding problem. The first thing I noticed when I sat down at the table was her husband Will texting a business associate. Apparently, Carrie was oblivious to the fact that her husband was preoccupied on his phone, or maybe she thought a double standard between what parents and kids do was the norm.

When I asked her about it later, she said that both she and her husband routinely text during meals. It stands to reason that when kids see parents texting at home or at a restaurant, rather than talking to each other, they'll see this behavior as perfectly acceptable. Carrie mentioned that "Do as I say, not as I do," was a rule they both grew up with, and they saw nothing wrong with that.

Here's what the conversation at my friend's dinner table looked like:

Carrie: Lamont, can you put your phone away and join the conversation with our guest, Miss Catherine?

Lamont: (frowning) Why is Dad allowed to text and I'm not?

Carrie: He's doing a business text. It's part of his job.

Will: (putting his phone in his pocket) Remember, son, sometimes there are different rules for kids and adults.

Lamont: That's dumb. I don't buy it.

Carrie: (ignoring his remark) Lamont, how about telling Miss Catherine what's happening with you? Making the baseball team must be exciting for you.

Lamont: It is, but I don't feel like talking now. Why can't I finish this text and talk later? My friends and I are making plans to go to a concert this weekend.

Carrie: What about the people here you're with now? Don't they count for anything?

Lamont: Cut it out, mom. I'm sure your friend doesn't want to be part of a family fight.

Me: I'm here to help, Lamont. From what I can see, your mom wants you to spend more time talking with her and your dad. She's not saying to stop texting your friends. She's asking you to spend some time enjoying your family's company.

Lamont: She and Dad both text at the table, even when we go out to eat. Why is it okay for them and not for me?

Will: I'm beginning to see how what we're doing isn't a good example for you. What do you think, Carrie?

Carrie: I think you may be right. I didn't give much thought to how it could be wrong for us to tune you out by texting when we expect you not to do it. Your dad and I grew up believing in one set of rules for parents and another for kids. That's the way it was back then, but that doesn't mean it's right.

Me: There's nothing wrong with texting friends or business associates if it's done at the right time, Lamont. Without technology, where would we be? However, I'd like you to consider this: When we talk to people we care about, it's helpful to look at them and give them our full attention. That way, they'll hear us, and we'll hear them. We can agree or disagree on things, but when we give those we're with our full attention instead of being wrapped up in our electronic gadgets, it shows we care about them and want to be present for them. What do you think?

Lamont: (pausing for a moment before answering) I guess you have a point. I'm so used to texting all the time, I never thought about how it could affect the people I'm with like dad, mom, and even my friends.

Me: Yes, everybody texts and it's become a new way of communicating.

Carrie: Sometimes it's at the expense of experiencing true communication with give and take. You can't see other people's reactions, and they don't know how you feel about what they're saying when you text. Nothing can ever replace a good in-person conversation. That's all I'm trying to say.

Will: I'm not sure if this will work, but I'll try to keep my texting private, when you guys aren't around.

Carrie: (looking at Lamont) So, you're saying you're okay with giving some time to us without having your cell in close reach all the time?

Lamont: (laughing) I guess we could try it as long as you don't expect me to tell you every detail of my life like you usually do.

Carrie: (smiling) Stop and think for a minute. How could we ever expect to learn all your secrets, and why would we even want to?

Will: (making eye contact with Lamont) How are we going to work this so we're all okay with it? We're ready to listen to what you have to say.

Lamont: I won't bring my phone to the table so I'm not tempted to text, but you two have to promise not to ask me too many questions, okay? I'll talk and listen to you, as long as you don't get carried away.

Carrie: It's a deal.

Will: Count me in.

Me: Sounds like a good solution to me. Not to change the subject, Carrie, but can you bring on your famous roast beef and mashed potatoes? I'm starved.

TRY THIS: ACTIVITIES TO HELP ENCOURAGE RESPONSIBLE BEHAVIOR, AGES 6–9

11. Inspire Your Child to Pitch in with Chores

Many parents argue with their kids about keeping their rooms habitable and pitching in with household chores like sweeping, clearing the table, or emptying the dishwasher. Even when kids get an allowance for doing chores, some kids don't follow through by keeping their part of the bargain.

Picture this: your eight-year-old son's room is a disaster area with clothes and food, like half-eaten plates of ice cream, cookie crumbs, and candy bar wrappers covering every surface. When you ask him to clean up, he says the mess doesn't bother him, and besides, he doesn't have time to clean up. You've tried everything to get him to keep his room presentable, and nothing works. Now it's time for a serious talk. When you catch him in a receptive mood, ask him what would make him want to have a decent (or halfway decent) room.

He says, "Simple. If I don't have to do it your way, I'm cool with it." This is a revelation to you because you're not sure what "your way" means. When you ask him to tell you more, he says it means perfect like everything else you expect of him and everyone in the family. This revelation on his part, disturbing though it is to you, leads the way to a discussion of what you'd both be able to accept in room cleanliness.

You listen to what he has to say without sounding accusatory, even if you have to hold your hand over your mouth to keep yourself from talking. Then you say it's your turn, and ask him to give you the same courtesy by listening without saying anything until you finish presenting your side. You tell him your expectations include his picking up clothes from the floor, throwing them in the hamper, and clearing away the food items he's left behind.

Since he feels he has some input, he agrees to do a few things to keep his room presentable. He says okay to the spoiled food but can't promise that he'll pick up all his dirty clothes. You tell him it's okay to leave his clothes for the next day on his bureau if he picks up the clothes on the floor. He grudgingly agrees. After a week of the new regime, he admits he feels better living in a clean room. He doesn't clean to your standards, which may be a little high, and backtracks more often than you'd like, but with a few friendly reminders, he seems willing to try again.

Here's another example of a child who balks at household chores and what you can do to help change her behavior. Your daughter, age nine, refuses to cooperate in doing household chores. She gets a small allowance but doesn't think she needs to help around the house because none of her friends do. She complains if you ask her to clear the table or empty the dishwasher because she's "tired from being in school all day."

You know it's important to teach her responsibility by doing a few simple chores around the house, but you want her to do it because it's an important part of living in a family, not because you need to win a power struggle. Schedule a time you think your daughter will be receptive to listening to your concerns.

Use "I" messages like this: "I know how you feel about helping around the house, but your dad, brother, and I all pitch in to keep the house running smoothly, and I'm hoping you'll do your part to make it a comfortable place for all of us to live." When she protests, respond in an assertive yet non-aggressive manner by telling her it's important for both of you to have this conversation, and that you want to get her ideas about how she'll be willing to help more around the house.

Your child says she gets what you're saying, but she hates housework. That's why she's going to get a high-paying job that will let her have someone take care of the stuff she doesn't want to do, like cleaning the refrigerator or the bathroom. You impress upon her that no matter how much money she makes there are still certain things she'll have to do for herself.

You ask her what chores she'd be willing to help her brother with on a rotating basis if she was able to choose. She says she wouldn't mind emptying the dishwasher or clearing the table after dinner, but toilets are off limits. She says maybe she can convince her brother to do latrine duty it if she takes two of his jobs. You tell her you think that's fair and that you're thankful for her cooperation. She keeps her end of the bargain, but when she slips up, her brother doesn't hesitate to remind her. After all, he's stuck with the worst job in the house.

12. Help Your Child Handle Money Responsibly

Luis, age seven, frequently receives gifts of money from family members for his birthday and other holidays. Every time he gets a monetary gift, he immediately wants his mom to take him out to buy a new toy. He isn't happy until he spends all the money on things he forgets about after a few days, leaving them strewn about his room.

Maria, his mom, wants to help him learn to be more responsible with money. She takes the first step by showing him how she divides up her paycheck she earns as a nurse at the local hospital. Part goes to rent, part to food, part for entertainment, like the videos she and Luis enjoy watching, and the rest goes into a savings account she plans to cash in for a family vacation at the beach.

Luis seems surprised she has to make her paycheck stretch so many ways. "I knew you had to pay rent, but I didn't know you had to buy so many other things with it."

"If I spent it all on videos and eating out, we wouldn't have any money left for other things. We wouldn't be able to go to the beach if I didn't put some in the bank to save for a vacation."

Luis says he'd like to think of a good way to divide his money so he'd have some left in case he wanted to save for a big item like a video game instead of spending all on cheaper toys that break easily or ones he tires of after a short time. Maria sees this as a teachable moment, especially since Luis has initiated it.

"Can you think of some ideas to help you with your new money plan?" she asks.

"Maybe I could spend part of it and put some in the bank like you do. Then, after I've saved enough, I could buy something I really like that will last, like that new video game."

"Good idea," Maria says.

"I could put a little aside to buy birthday gifts for you and dad."

"That's very thoughtful of you, Luis."

The next time Luis gets money from his relatives, he carries out his plan. After a few months, he finds he's saved enough money to buy that video game he's had his eye on. He also buys small gifts for his parents, which, he finds, pleases him more than spending all the money on himself.

13. Foster Organizational Skills in Your Child

Emma, a nine-year-old, earns fair grades in school, but Jessica, her mother, and her teacher, Mr. Taylor, believe she can do better, especially in English, which she nearly failed. Her main problems lie in studying for tests and getting homework in on time. She waits until the last possible minute to study for tests and work on book reports. Emma starts her homework late at night, after the rest of the family's asleep, because she wants to spend time texting her friends.

The first thing Jessica does is set up a conference with Emma and Mr. Taylor to discuss the problem and offer ideas to remedy her organizational issues. She makes sure her daughter knows ahead of time that she's the major contributor to this conversation since she has to come up with ideas she'll be willing to carry out. Her mother believes if she makes her own decisions about solving her difficulties with English and her other subjects, she'll be more likely to follow through with her plan, and she'll learn to be more self-reliant, and ultimately, more responsible.

Jessica asked Mr. Taylor to give her a progress report every two days for the first couple of weeks. Keeping the teacher's time limitations in mind, she asked the teacher to give a simple letter grade (*a, b,* or *c*) or *E (excellent), S (satisfactory),* or *U (Unsatisfactory)*, whichever he found convenient, for homework and classwork each day. She also asked the teacher to call her for a weekly update on Emma's progress until she felt satisfied her daughter's grades had improved. With Emma's input, she decided which areas of the subject most needed work, and in concert with Emma and the teacher, developed an action plan.

When they got home from the conference, Jessica asked Emma what she could do to help herself perform better in school, emphasizing that her input was crucial at every point in implementing the plan. Her mom listened to her ideas and supported the ones she believed would help her become more organized in studying her school subjects and improving her performance in all of them, especially English.

Jessica reinforced what Emma decided to do by helping her keep her resolutions. If Emma said she'd write down her assignments and check them off as she did them on a daily basis, Jessica asked Emma to show her the assignment book she kept to ensure she'd followed through. If Emma said she had to read a book for English, her mom periodically questioned her about how far she'd progressed in the book and asked for a brief summary. When Emma told her about an upcoming test, Jessica offered to quiz her on the material, highlighting the sections she needed to study more. She expected her daughter to do the work on her own, but she committed herself to being there for Emma whenever she needed her assistance or advice.

If she found that problems persisted, she'd set up an appointment with the school counselor with the teacher in attendance. If she needed further help, she'd determine what additional services the school offered, and use them.

As it turns out, because of Jessica's determination to help Emma and her resolve to help herself, the action plan proved successful. Emma improved her grades in all her classes that semester and told Jessica she hoped to make the honor roll by the end of the school year.

14. Advise Your Child to Own Mistakes

Kayla frequently blames her older sister for starting arguments when she's the one who always instigates them. Kayla's mother Renee has seen it happen more than once. At first Leah, Kayla's thirteen-year-old sister, showed patience and chalked it up to Kayla's age and the fact that she just started first grade and had a difficult adjustment after attending half-day kindergarten. As the days turn into weeks, Leah's beginning to lose patience with Kayla and refuses to take her to the movies or to the coffee shop for hot chocolate, Kayla's favorite things to do because they make her feel grown up.

When Renee talks to Kayla, she's reluctant to tell her why she lies about her sister starting arguments. However, after two weeks of no movies or coffee shop outings, she finally admits she's jealous of her big sister because Leah can do a lot of things she can't. Kayla also thinks her mom and dad prefer Leah to her because she's the "perfect child."

Despite Renee's reassurances that she and her husband love both Kayla and her sister equally, Kayla keeps making excuses for her behavior by saying, "You like her best," and continues showing negative behavior toward Leah, accusing her of starting fights although the opposite is true. The facts are obvious to Renee: As long as Kayla continues to justify her behavior by making excuses, the two girls will find it hard to reconcile.

After giving it a lot of thought, Renee comes to the conclusion that the first step in solving the problem is to talk with Kayla about how her decision to lie about her sister starting arguments is harming their relationship. She also wants to stress the importance of the whole family enjoying one another's company. When everyone's in a bad mood, people can't have fun together, let alone get along.

Renee takes the first step and asks Kayla to tell her when she's ready to stop arguing with her sister and blaming her unfairly for being the cause of their fights. She believes that once her younger child decides to own the responsibility for the sisters not getting along, they can begin to heal the rift between them. When Kayla acknowledges to herself that she's treating her sister unfairly by saying she's starting the arguments, Renee believes the relationship will improve. However, she believes Kayla has to be the one to set things in motion.

Renee does her best to impress upon Kayla that she has to want to own up to her role in causing the rift, not because her sister won't take her to the movies or the coffee shop, but because she's genuinely sorry for her actions.

After thinking it over, Kayla decides to apologize to her sister for blaming her unfairly for something she didn't do. She admits she can't stand the fighting either. Her sister starts taking her to events they both enjoy. Kayla occasionally shows signs of jealousy, but she knows that getting her sister in trouble isn't the answer.

Renee believes that even a young child like Kayla can own her mistakes and begin to find a good solution to ending their arguments by taking steps to make things right again with other family members, in this case, her older sister.

TRY THIS: ACTIVITIES TO HELP ENCOURAGE RESPONSIBLE BEHAVIOR, AGES 10–14

15. Promote Individuality

The desire to fit in is the main reason peer pressure figures strongly in the youth culture. Children, especially in their pre-teen and early teenage years, have a strong desire to be accepted, to conform, so that other kids in the group will see them as one of their own and embrace them. Kids who don't conform to group norms often experience a sense of loneliness and alienation, and, in some cases, suffer bullying at the hands of their peers.

Promoting and modeling a sense of individuality for your children can help them weather the perils of following the crowd. Being an individual means having the courage to say *no* to dangerous behaviors such as smoking, drinking, taking drugs, or engaging in premature experimentation with sex. It also means your children will stand up for what they believe and not compromise when it comes to values they cherish.

For example, if a classmate asks your child to help him cheat on a test and your child believes cheating is unacceptable, he'll refuse to cooperate. If a friend offers him a drink at a party and your son believes it's wrong to drink when he's underage, he'll have the courage not to go along with the crowd. Similarly, if a classmate encourages him to watch a video on his smartphone of another student who's scantily dressed, he'll decline. Your child doesn't have to give a reason for refusing to involve himself in any of these activities.

Simply saying, "I don't want to," or "No," is enough. The less he says, the better off he is, as long explanations often invite stronger persuasions by the person asking him to go against his principles.

You can model individuality by letting your ten to fourteen-year-old in on conversations between you and your neighbor or a relative who embrace different opinions than you do in the political arena, or even in less complex issues, such as preference in TV shows or movies.

Also, try talking with your child about times you didn't go along with the crowd, and explain how it paid off. Maybe your friends picked on a class-mate because she was shy and unattractive by your friends' standards. You didn't go along with them because you felt it was wrong; however, you honestly liked the girl and saw her as funny and smart. The upshot was that your friends got suspended for bullying. You were happy you could do your part as a caring bystander (before the term became popular) who supported the girl by talking privately to the school counselor about how the bullying played out.

When you were in ninth grade, a boy offered you drugs from his parents' medicine chest. You refused because you knew taking drugs was harmful, especially when you didn't know what types of drugs they were. A couple of the kids in your crowd took the pills, which turned out to be heavy-duty painkillers. They both ended up getting sick and had to go to the ER. They faced the ire of their parents after the police were called to the scene to determine what charges they might levy against them.

Luckily, for them, the police dismissed the charges after giving the kids a heavy-duty lecture and releasing them in their parents' custody. Here's the bottom line: Tell your child your stories about when you were growing up and how you handled the situations. Your child will relate better to a retelling of your first-hand experiences than to any headlines he reads in the paper or hears on the news.

As you can see, it's important to talk to your child ahead of time about drugs and what can happen when kids get together in a setting where they're readily available. Warn your kids about "pharma parties" where kids raid their parents' medicine cabinets, throwing all the medicine into a bowl and choosing pills at random. It goes without saying that taking part in these parties can end in fatal consequences.

Talk to your child about the advantages of being an individual and a leader rather than a follower. Praise his unique talents and his mature way of handling problems that come up, and offer positive reinforcement when you catch him being his own person.

16. Have Your Child Keep You Informed

Use teachable moments with your ten to fourteen-year-old to help her think about the importance of discernment in choosing friends, how to tell if someone's a true friend, and how to initiate and maintain friendships. Share your own experiences with friendships over the years, and talk about what you learned from them. Ask your child what she thinks is important in a friendship, and take it from there. Discuss an experience she's had or heard about where a friendship came to an end because one or both parties had a falling out.

If she has trouble making friends, suggest ways she can meet them by joining school or community activities or through other friends. If she's had a problem with a friend, use that as a springboard to initiate a discussion about what makes a true friend and how to tell if the friendship is a positive thing. Be mindfully curious and ask your child questions like these: Does being with this friend make you feel happy and uplifted? Do you feel you always have to compete or be on guard? or Do you feel intimidated in any way? How the friendship makes her feel is a good barometer of whether she should continue or dissolve the friendship.

An important part of showing responsible behavior involves your children letting you know who they're with and where they're going every single time. You need to know all their friends, what kind of supervision they have at home, and meet their parents whenever possible. This definitely holds true if a friend invites your child to a party at home.

If you know the child's parents well and find them dependable, you can rest assured your child will be safe. However, if you don't know the family or you've heard negative things about how the parents supervise their kids, it's important to touch base with them before your child goes to their house. You'll want to ensure that there's adequate supervision at all times. Every time your child meets with a friend, have her tell you where she'll be and how long she'll be there. Insist on a phone call or text if she's delayed. It's not being overprotective; it's smart and can save your child from finding herself in a precarious situation.

If you suspect your child made friends with someone whose character you question, talk to her and ask why she finds herself attracted to this friend. Encourage her to make friends with kids who share the same values you and your family espouse. That doesn't mean your child should avoid befriending children who come from different backgrounds. Some of the best friendships are forged between people of diverse cultures and ethnic groups.

Kids these days find friends on social media, which brings up the fact that you need to monitor your child's social media account no matter how much you trust her. Kids are signing up for social media accounts at younger ages even though these venues stipulate age limits. You must be thirteen to be on

Facebook, Twitter, What's App, and Snapchat, but many kids know how to get around this requirement.

The main problem with kids using social media to find and relate to friends is that using it could open them up to inappropriate content and expose them to people and ideas for which they're not psychologically ready. Therefore, it's important for parents to have discussions with their kids about using social media responsibly and to learn how to monitor their social media accounts.

17. Strengthen Basic Life Skills

My friend Ashley recently told me about the time her twelve-year-old son Darren called her at work and asked her to come home right away to make him a sandwich because he was starving. School was out for the summer, so Darren was home when he wasn't out with his friends, and Ashley worked each day as a nurse in the local hospital ER. When her son called, Ashley told Darren there was lunchmeat in the fridge, the bread's where it always is on top of the counter, and to help himself. This made my friend think about how she'd enabled Darren over the years by not encouraging him to learn simple life skills, like short order cooking.

Ashley also cleaned up after Darren when he left the remnants of his after-school snacks, like yogurt containers and cheese curls, on the family room floor. On a daily basis, she also gathered dirty clothes from Darren's room and the bathroom he and his brother shared, and ran a load of wash each day to keep up with the large pile of laundry Darren left for her. When Ashley offered to show her son how to use the washer and dryer so he could do his own wash, he said it wasn't his job, and none of his friends had to do the wash.

The day Darren called Ashley at work provided the impetus to make some changes that would make her son more self-sufficient. She knew it was important for Darren to learn responsibility if he was to grow up to be a self-sufficient, independent adult. After dinner that evening, Ashley asked Darren to join her in the family room for dessert, his favorite fudge cake, and a talk. Naturally, Darren became suspicious because his mom only made fudge cake for special occasions like his birthday. However, he was also curious. Could it have something to do with that phone call he made to his mother at work about coming home to make him a sandwich?

At this point, he didn't care because he wanted the fudge cake. Mother and son dug into the fudge cake, which tasted especially delicious this time. Ashley decided ahead of time that she'd use assertive language and "I-messages" when talking with Darren about the importance of becoming more self-sufficient. It annoyed her that Darren expected her to be a short order cook and clean up after him, although Ashley was willing to take responsibility for her part in not insisting Darren start doing things for himself. He'd start middle school in the fall, so it was important she forget about the past and start encouraging him to take the first steps now toward learning basic life skills.

Ashley began by telling Darren that she'd gotten to the point where his not doing things for himself had upset her greatly. She reminded Darren about how she was grateful they had a good relationship and could talk about anything, unlike what some of his friends' mothers had shared with her about their kids, who often disobeyed them or talked back. Because Ashley set a positive tone for the conversation and didn't judge him, Darren seemed more willing to listen.

When Ashley got to the main point of the discussion, her desire to see Darren become more self-sufficient, she framed her requests in an assertive, yet positive manner. She told her son it was important for him to know basic survival skills, like short order cooking and taking care of his own laundry when there was an overflow. If Darren left her a reasonable amount of clothes to launder, she'd be willing to wash it along with the family laundry, provided Darren left his clothes in the basket and not strewn on the floor.

She also emphasized the importance of Darren cleaning up after himself to avoid a rodent problem, which the family had experienced once before due to Darren's leaving food out in the family room. Darren laughed and said he wouldn't mind having a mouse for a pet, but Ashley didn't pursue it since rodents were one of her worst fears.

Because Ashley discussed the problem with her son in a straightforward assertive manner rather than in a weak, passive, or negative, aggressive one, she got her point across. Ashley started to put the plan in motion by asking Darren to make a list of sandwich ingredients she'd buy at the store, so he could make his own lunch each day when she was at work.

To Ashley's surprise, Darren began to enjoy choosing the ingredients and coming up with unusual sandwich combinations, such as peanut butter and bacon on raisin bread and grilled macaroni, cheese, and tomato sandwiches on focaccia bread. One night, Darren asked Ashley if he could make dinner for the family, and Ashley was happy to oblige. He found a simple recipe for shrimp tacos online, and everyone loved the meal.

Darren backtracked occasionally by forgetting to clean up after he ate snacks, and his mother playfully reminded him by putting a realistic-looking plastic mouse on the couch where he had his snacks. On the bright side, Darren also minimized the amount of clothes he used and dutifully tossed them in the family laundry basket so Ashley could launder them with the regular wash. However, when Darren had an occasional overflow, he found it no trouble to do a small load of wash himself because his mother taught him how easy it was to operate the washer and dryer. As it turns out, Darren started to enjoy his newfound independence and, to his mother's delight, began cooking more simple and delicious family dinners on a regular basis.

18. Foster Concern for Family Members

One important part of encouraging responsible behavior involves treating family members with care, compassion, and concern. Many kids give a quick greeting to older family members, like grandparents, and then race off to meet friends or spend time texting on their smartphones. However, that's not unusual behavior for kids of any age as friends often take priority. What can your children learn by spending time with older relatives, and how can you encourage them to spend more time with them in meaningful and pleasant conversation?

For one thing, you can include older relatives in family activities, such as dinners or outings, where they'll have the chance to mingle with younger family members like your kids. A picnic or a trip to the beach, mountains, or even the local swimming pool would be ideal because the wide, open space would provide a pleasant backdrop for helping the young and old get to know each other better.

When you've invited an older relative and your child starts to jump up from the dinner table, encourage her to sit a while and join the discussion. Talk to the older relative ahead of time and have him encourage your child to stay and talk and to take a special interest in what your child has to say. The family member (in this case, a grandfather) can break the ice by making eye contact and saying something like this: "Let me ask you a question: What do you like to do best in your spare time? What's going on with you in school lately? or, If you could have one wish right now, what would it be?"

The grandparent can make the question as ordinary as the first two listed, or become more creative and ask a more thought-provoking one similar to the last one. The grandparent may find it easier to start with a simple question and move up to a deeper one, depending on the child he's addressing. The content of the conversation doesn't count as much as the genuine interest on the part of the relative, the eye-contact, body language, and the level of engagement.

Another way for kids and older relatives to bond involves sharing knowledge. As you know, kids this age are usually computer experts who love to share their skills. You or an older relative can tap into that knowledge to help yourselves become more technologically proficient. This leaves the younger relative with a feeling of helpfulness and generosity in sharing knowledge. Obviously, curiosity in learning anything, a Mindfulness quality, leads to asking questions. Be curious about what you're learning from your child or grandchild, and encourage her to show the same curiosity since curiosity is the golden key that opens the door to all knowledge.

Similarly, a grandparent can share his knowledge of history and books he's enjoyed reading over the years. Instead of choosing the topic, he can let the child take the lead to ensure it's a topic she enjoys. Using clear, colorful examples and adding humor in descriptions helps keep a child interested and engaged in the conversation. Kids also enjoy hearing about the social scene when grandparents were their age. The grandparent can talk about his friends and adventures growing up, how school differed from the way it is today, what dating was like in those days, and what hobbies he enjoyed most in his younger years. In turn, grandkids can reciprocate by sharing their stories on these topics.

Fostering concern for older family members has a ripple effect in that it helps kids develop a sense of responsibility and loving kindness toward others.

Chapter Three

Boost Emotional Intelligence

THINK ABOUT THIS

Emotional intelligence is an important trait you'll want to encourage in your children. Most experts think of emotional intelligence as including these skills: being aware of one's emotions, the ability to use emotions to help with important traits like thinking and problem solving; and, most importantly, the ability to be in charge of one's emotions. If a child has emotional intelligence, she can control her own emotions and display the ability to help other people learn to manage theirs.

You can help your child gain emotional intelligence by teaching him to feel comfortable talking openly about his emotions. Practicing the Mindfulness technique of using "I-messages" to identify feelings is a good place to start. The ability to discuss how your child feels proves particularly helpful when he faces problems in school. If your child feels stressful because of school pressures, such as fear of a certain subject or test anxiety, you can teach him skills, such as meditation and breathing techniques, to help him deal with the stress.

Similarly, if your child finds himself in arguments with classmates, Mindfulness techniques like these can help him acquire traits that come with emotional intelligence, such as willingness to compromise. Sometimes problems at school show up in physical ailments like stomach aches or headaches. Being conscious of emotional intelligence within the context of Mindfulness will help your child deal with school stress in the classroom and on the playground.

It's equally important for you to show your child by example that you possess emotional intelligence. It's a good lesson for your child to see that you're able to say you're sorry when you lose your temper with her or make a mistake and say something you don't mean. Modeling this behavior gives your child a way to learn to make her own apologies if she finds herself in a similar situation with family members or friends. Having good emotional intelligence helps children learn to control how they react to emotions with parents, family members, and peers, whether things are going their way or not.

If children possess emotional intelligence, they'll be more likely to speak up when others mistreat them by knowing how and when to talk to a child who teases or bullies them.

Building friendships can be a challenge for many kids, and it's easier if you and the school work together to help your children use emotional intelligence skills to help them build and maintain friendships.

Lastly, possessing emotional intelligence also means your child will display the ability to read and use body language. Body language tells a child what others are thinking before they begin to talk and gives helpful clues about how to communicate with people while conversing with them. Kids will get along better with their peers if they can read their body language because they can gauge their moods and respond accordingly. They will also know how to interact with kids and adults alike to get their message across successfully. Even the youngest child can learn meanings of the most common body language and learn to read and apply it.

MODEL A CONVERSATION: BOOST EMOTIONAL INTELLIGENCE

19. Model an Understanding of Body Language

Kia, mother of thirteen-year-old Chloe, believes that a knowledge of body language will help her child grow in emotional intelligence. She turns learning about emotional intelligence into an educational game by demonstrating body language and seeing how Chloe interprets it. Mother and daughter also discuss under what circumstances people often use different types of body language to get their messages across.

As her mother helps Chloe gain proficiency in identifying and interpreting body language, she demonstrates different gestures and asks her mother to state their meanings. Here is a transcript of one of their sessions:

Kia: Chloe, we've discussed how knowing about body language helps us figure out what others are trying to tell us before they even begin to speak.

Chloe: We also talked about how I can use it to help people understand the way I'm feeling about things. I've tried it already with my friends, and you're right, it really works.

Kia: That's great. Now we'll take turns practicing body language, so you can use it to figure out the meaning behind the words and how you can back up your words so someone will clearly understand your message. Can you show me an example of using body language to reflect how you feel about something I said or did?

Chloe: (making eye contact while leaning toward Kia) Let's talk about how you feel about whether or not I should go to overnight camp this summer.

Kia: (After a brief conversation about the pros and cons of camp for Chloe, Kia responds.) It looks like you were listening to my concerns about your being away from home for the first time. I could tell by the way you looked at me when I talked about it. You nodded your head once in a while, which didn't necessarily mean you agreed, but that you were listening. After we talked, I felt like you heard me. I began to think maybe camp might be fun for you and that you'd be fine there. The way you used body language made me less concerned about your going to overnight camp. Now it's your turn.

Chloe: (Arms folded, frowning) I don't like it when you criticize my friend Amy because she talks back to her mom. Let's talk about what you said about Amy the other day.

Kia: I can see by the way you're frowning and keeping your arms folded that you don't like what I said about your friend being rude to her mom.

Chloe: You're right. Amy's a good friend, and how she acts toward her mom doesn't have anything to do with whether we should stay friends. I don't see why you have to hold that against her. Sometimes she gets emotional over things and says things she doesn't mean. I think we all do that.

Kia: That may be true, but I worry if you spend a lot of time with her, you may not see anything wrong with how she treats her mother and start acting that way too.

Chloe: (nodding and using "I- messages") I can see why you might feel that way, but you know I would never talk like that to you, at least most of the time.

Kia: Okay, fair enough, but I'd still feel better if you'd spend more time with friends who act kind to their parents and treat them with respect.

Chloe: (smiling) I hear you, mom.

Kia and Chloe continue to practice using body language with each other. It helps their relationship flourish even through rough spots all parents and kids face, like disagreements about friends, school, and chores. Sometimes Chloe, her mom, and Chloe's siblings draw slips of paper that Kia has prepared ahead of time that list various types of body language.

They take turns acting out the body language they draw to see who can identify what each instance of body language means. All participants may respond, and the person acting out the body language verifies their answers. Those identifying the body language then explain how they can use it to help better understand others and more effectively get their points across to friends and family members.

TRY THIS: ACTIVITIES TO BOOST EMOTIONAL INTELLIGENCE, AGES 6–9

20. Prompt Kids to Talk Openly about Emotions

Ms. Carey, the teacher on playground duty called home after she found Jacob, Shayna's son, sitting on the curb looking sad. When Ms. Carey asked the second grader why he looked sad, he said, "The kids won't let me play tag because they say I don't run fast enough."

Jacob, being the sensitive, quiet child he is, doesn't like to talk about his feelings, but his mother can tell he's hurting. Here's part of the dialogue she uses to draw him out and get him to talk about his feelings. She asks him to sit at the picnic table in the back yard and brings out lemonade and sugar cookies.

Shayna: Your teacher called today to tell me about what happened at recess.

Jacob (looking down): I asked her not to. It's not a big thing. Those kids are right. I can't run fast. That's why they didn't want me to play tag.

Shayna (making eye contact and nodding): I'm sorry that happened. I can tell you feel sad about it. If you want to talk about it, I'm listening.

Jacob: I felt hurt and embarrassed that I couldn't keep up with them. One of them said, "You've got to be faster or you can't play." The other kids went along with it.

Shayna: I hear you. So, what can you do if it happens again?

Jacob (looking up): I could play with another friend, or I could tell them I want another chance to show them I can keep up with them.

Shayna: Good. There's always something you can do.

Jacob (sounding more hopeful and animated): I can play tag with another group of kids that doesn't say stuff like that to make me feel bad.

Shayna: That's right. You can also choose to play another game if you're not wild about tag.

Jacob (smiling and looking up): I shouldn't let those kids get to me.

Shayna: Sometimes it's hard not to. But you can see that you have a few choices if it happens again.

Jacob: Come on, Mom, I'll race you to the house.

Shayna (putting her arm around Jacob): Whoever wins gets the rest of the cookies.

Jacob: You know that will be me, right?

They race toward the house. Guess who wins, and it was no contest.

21. Use Relaxation Techniques to Lessen School Stress

Children in elementary grades who experience school stress often do not know how to verbalize their feelings about it, so they sometimes find themselves with stress-related symptoms like stomach aches, headaches, and anxiety. Tapping into Mindfulness, parents can help calm physical and psychological results of school stress by teaching their children relaxation techniques.

One thing you can do is teach your child a simple meditation technique. Once you explain how to meditate, ask if your child is comfortable with meditating. Engaging in meditation can help your child deal with school stresses, such as tests, homework, and pressure to meet assignment deadlines. If your child decides to try meditation, start with five minutes once or twice a day, and, if your child's comfortable with it, have her move up to ten minutes.

Even a very young child can learn to meditate. Ask her to choose a pleasant-sounding word like *happy, peace*, or even a favorite flower, like *rose* or *daisy*. She can get into a relaxed position and close her eyes, but not lie down as it may make her fall asleep. Tell her to peek at the clock every so often to make a note of when she starts and stops the meditation. She can start the meditation by thinking the word she chose in her mind. Every time thoughts enter her mind, she can come back to thinking the word or mantra. When she sees that the time of her meditation is nearly drawing to a close, she can stop thinking the word and take a few minutes to stretch and get back to a more alert state.

Many Mindfulness practitioners advise using the breath as a take-off point for meditation. Your child can breathe in through the nose and out through the mouth instead of using a mantra. The breath helps her get into a meditative state, just as a mantra does. She can experiment with both types of meditation to see which one she prefers.

After your child meditates the first few times, ask how the experience went and if she'd like to continue. Ask if the time frame she chose was right for her or if she'd like it to be shorter or a little longer. If twice a day is too much, she can opt for once daily.

If your child is not comfortable sitting for a period of time meditating, you can encourage her to walk mindfully outdoors by being conscious of her surroundings. When you walk mindfully, you tune out the stresses and distractions of the day. Accompany your child on a short walk at least three times a week at around the same time. You and your child don't have to say anything. Rather, be in the moment enjoying the surroundings with your child. Afterward, share your experience by discussing these questions: What did you think about when you were walking? How did the walk help relax you? What did you learn from your walk?

Something else you can do to help your child to relax is encourage her to make room in every day to spend time doing something she loves, whether it's reading, watching a favorite TV show, or playing outdoors alone or with a friend. Just as we need time to unwind, kids can't be on call 24/7 with school pressures and social obligations. They need time to be kids and get away from it all by taking part in activities that refresh and rejuvenate them.

22. Admit When You're Wrong

As you already know, parents make mistakes. They say something they don't mean, lash out at their children in anger, or say disparaging things to their kids when they didn't mean to come on so strongly. When this happens, you could let go of your feelings of guilt and remorse and forget the words you said in anger but did not literally mean. However, words can hurt and leave lasting effects.

Conversely, you can decide to make things right with your child by apologizing for what you said or did. This provides an excellent teachable moment for your child and shows that he can show the same sense of contriteness when he says something to a family member or friend that hurts them. Listen in on a conversation between Matt and his mother Bella.

Bella (patting the seat on the sofa next to her): Have a minute to talk?

Matt: Sure, what's up?

Bella (making eye contact): I wanted to touch base with you to say I'm sorry about what I said last night. I was tired and when you talked back it got to me, I said things I didn't mean.

Matt (looking down): Yeah, like I don't appreciate the stuff you do for me and you don't know what you did to get a kid like me.

Bella: If I could erase what I said, I would. I'd try saying it differently, in a less hurtful way.

Matt (looking up and making eye contact): What would you say?

Bella: I'd use "I-messages" like the ones we talked about that time we went over good ways to communicate. I'd let you know I wasn't pleased with how you talked back to me, but I'd say it differently if I had it to do over. I'd say something like this: "I don't like how you're talking to me. Take a minute and think before you say another word. I know you don't mean to talk like this and that it doesn't make you feel good when you talk that way."

Matt: That sounds a lot better than saying the mean things you said to me. Thanks for saying you didn't mean those things, Mom. I'll try to think before I talk next time.

Bella: So will I. This was a good lesson for both of us.

Matt: It sure was. When you say something, it's important to take a breath and think before you talk, right?

Bella: It's not always easy, but it's a good way to avoid arguments. Who needs to fight when you can be Mindful and have peace?

23. Show How to Respond When Someone Uses One-Upmanship

Among other benefits, emotional intelligence helps your children deal with a variety of scenarios they'll encounter in school, the neighborhood, and on the playground. Like it or not, there are kids who will always try to top your children or outdo them by bragging about how popular they are, how proficient they are in sports, or what great possessions they own.

If your child feels belittled or intimidated by kids who display one-upmanship, ask her how she can use her emotional intelligence to respond in a calm way, while getting her point across that one-upmanship is not a polite way to treat a friend.

Imagine this conversation between Angela and her daughter Grace, who attends second grade in a neighborhood elementary school: Angela overhears Grace talking with her friend Zoe. Grace shows Zoe an old Nancy Drew book her grandmother gave her from her collection. "It was written a long time ago, but I think you'd really like it. I'll let you read it when I finish."

Zoe waves the book away and wrinkles her nose. "No thanks. My parents bought me an e-reader and some great mysteries for my birthday. I can't wait to read them. I don't like lugging books around, especially an old, musty book like that."

Remembering what Angela told her about the Mindfulness way of answering kindly but telling people exactly how you feel, Grace replies: "It might smell a little old, but it was my grandma's, and when I read it, I can picture her reading it when she was my age, and loving the book too. That makes it more fun for me."

"Whatever," Zoe says. "I can actually fit hundreds, maybe thousands, of books in my e-reader. That's more fun than reading some moldy old-fashioned book."

"It's silly to argue about stuff like this. Let's go outside on the porch and play a board game."

Zoe crosses her arms and frowns. "It's not silly to me. I know that e-books are definitely better, and I love my e-reader."

"I'm glad you do. I'm just saying both kinds of books are good in their own way."

Zoe crosses her arms. "I still say my way is best."

They go out to the porch and play board games, laying the issue of print books versus e-readers to rest. However, Grace knows she has to decide whether to keep Zoe as a close friend since lately every time they get together, Zoe tries to top her and will never listen to her point of view. Later, her mother tells her she approves of her decision.

24. Help Your Child with Impulse Control

Marla's son Liam gets into frequent arguments with a couple of his classmates and is unwilling to compromise. Ms. Alba, the school counselor, calls and suggests that Marla try Mindfulness techniques to help Liam gain better emotional intelligence by controlling his temper. The counselor says it would help to have Liam become aware of his body signs to help make sure his anger doesn't get so strong that he finds it hard to control.

Ms. Alba meets with Marla for a couple of sessions to talk with her about helping Liam recognize his body signs when he feels angry or upset in order to help keep his anger in check so he can better control his impulses. Then he can practice stepping back and take a deep breath before reacting to what his peers say. The counselor and Liam also discuss using assertive rather than aggressive words to counter what these classmates say to him.

After the sessions with Ms. Alba, Marla asks Liam to join her for a picnic in the park. On the way, she broaches the subject of Liam's frequent run-ins with some of his classmates

Marla: I want you to know Ms. Alba and I met to talk about some problems you're having with classmates.

Liam: She said she was going to talk to you. I'm sure she told you she talked to me too.

Marla: She told me you've been arguing with a few kids in your class.

Liam (frowning and folding his arms): So? They're dumb sometimes. They make me really angry.

Marla (acting curious): Tell me more.

Liam: They say I don't know anything about sports and I act like I know everything. They tell me to shut up, and they don't want me to hang out with them at recess or lunch.

Marla: What do you do when they say these things?

Liam: I scream at them and tell them to leave me alone. Sometimes I say curse words.

Marla: Would you like it to be different between you and these kids?

Liam: Maybe, but I don't know if I can control it. Once they start, I have to keep the fight going. If it keeps up, I might hit one of them.

Marla: What would happen if you could find a different way to deal with it?

Liam (thinking for a moment): I wish I could. I don't like being angry all the time and getting upset about the things they say.

Marla: You can start by knowing the signs that show you're starting to get really angry and begin to lose control. Can you think of how your body and mind feel before you let loose on these kids?

Liam: Sometimes I start to sweat and my heart starts beating so fast I feel like I can't catch my breath.

Marla: What about how you feel in your mind?

Liam: I feel nervous and upset, like I can't control what I'm going to say.

Marla: You know what signs you feel before you get angry at these kids, and that's a start. Once you begin feeling these signs, you can try stepping back and taking a deep breath. That will help you stay in control and not get carried away with your anger so you say or do something that you may regret later.

Liam: I guess I could try it.

Marla: Even if you feel like it, don't react right away. Calm yourself down and it will help make it easier for you not to react in anger.

Liam: Ms. Alba said something about being curious about how I'm feeling when I begin getting upset with those kids. She said I should think about how I feel and ask myself why I'm reacting that way.

Marla: Being curious is a Mindfulness technique that doesn't take long to do. It gives you time to stop and think before you act, like taking a deep breath does. Another thing you can do is stand up straight and tall and look strong when you talk to these kids, instead of screaming at them, which never works. You can tell them how you feel without being angry. It's called assertive speaking.

Liam: I already practiced it with Ms. Alba. She pretended she was one of the kids who bug me and said, "We don't want to hang out with you. All you do is start fights and argue about everything."

Marla: What did you say back?

Liam: I said, "That's up to you. I was hoping we could try getting along, even if we can't be friends. How about if I don't get so angry when you say things that bother me? I'll tell you how I feel and let it go at that."

Marla: That's a good way to talk to them. What will you do if they say they don't want to get along with you?

Liam: The new me would say, "That's up to you. Let me know if you change your mind."

Marla (spreading out the fried chicken and cupcakes she bought for the picnic): Good response. Whenever you talk to those kids, make it short, polite, and to the point. That's the best way to talk to people you've had a problem with in the past.

Liam: Sounds good. Think I'll try it.

TRY THIS: ACTIVITIES TO BOOST EMOTIONAL INTELLIGENCE, AGES 10–14

25. Keep Your Cool When Your Child Says You're Annoying

"I don't have to listen to you," "You're stupid," "You're so annoying," "I wish you weren't my parents," or "Shut up": If these words sound familiar to you, you're not alone. Most parents of kids in the ten to fourteen age group have heard hurtful words like these. How do you help your child get a handle on her emotions without getting strung out yourself when she comes at you with a barrage of negativity, calling you names and saying offensive things to you?

For one thing, you can try your best to remain calm, responding rather than reacting. Most of the time, kids don't mean a lot of the hurtful things they say to their parents. They're trying to assert their independence and autonomy, even though it sometimes comes out the wrong way. You can choose to ignore the harsh words they hurl at you, unless they're blatantly extreme, like "I wish you were dead," or "I'm going to kill myself." When you feel the harsh words go in a direction you find troubling or they're said too frequently, seeking professional help is the best option.

If, however, your child's epithets for you aren't what you'd consider extreme, you could simply take a deep breath, look her in the eye, and say something like this to her when she says, "I hate you":

"I love you, and I believe you feel the same about me. You're angry and upset, so I'll just imagine you never said that." Use your instincts in responding because you know your child better than anyone and know which response will help her reconsider her words.

You can also try using assertive language and "I-messages." Here's an example: "I know you're angry but I don't want you to talk to me like that. I try my best to respect your feelings even when I'm angry with you. I expect you to treat me the same way and to think before you talk."

Kids say hurtful things to their parents all the time, so you are not alone. It's a part of growing up. We as kids did the same thing with our parents.

Most of us felt remorse for saying the things we did. In the end, we and our parents ended up making up and getting along. The same can happen with you and your children if you put their rebellious remarks in perspective and don't let them hurt your relationship, with the caveat that if they're extreme, you'll take action to remedy the situation.

The next time your child tells you "You're weird, fat, ugly, stupid," or has some other choice words for you, acknowledge it and respond assertively without giving the rant too much attention. Then move on.

26. Use Mindfulness to Quell Bullying

Aiden, short for his age, struggles to deal with bullies' unkind barbs. Two boys in his fifth-grade class exclude him from their recess teams and harass him endlessly about his height. His mom and dad, along with the school counselor, try to help him build up his emotional intelligence so he can deal with the problem effectively. The goal is for Aiden to feel strong and confident as he faces the bullies assertively and head-on, but without conflict and confrontation.

In the days following his classmates' bullying, Aiden practices assertive body language with the counselor. She impresses upon him the importance of looking confident in front of the kids bothering him and of using eye contact when responding to them. She further advises him to talk briefly to them if he feels he won't be threatened or intimidated further by interacting with them. If they call him names, he should tell them to leave him alone or to stop. He should not engage in prolonged conversation with them. However, if talking to them worsens the bullying, he should walk away and speak to a school administrator or counselor, who will advise him how to proceed.

A big part of dealing with on-going bullying in an emotionally intelligent way involves helping a child express feelings of anger and sadness to someone close to him, like parents or a grandparent. He may also want to confide in his teacher or the school counselor. He needs to name what's upsetting him and to describe it so the person he's confiding in knows exactly what he's dealing with and also so he can begin to sort things out in his own mind.

It's important for Aiden to express his fears about the bullies' actions. He may be wondering if they're going to attack him physically or if they'll try to involve other kids and gang up on him. Adult helpers can encourage him to use "I-messages" when describing his experiences and apprehensions. They can also help by being curious and asking questions, such as "What have you done so far when they bothered you?" "How is it working?" "Do you think you can handle it yourself?" or "Would you like some help?"

Facing bullying is difficult under any circumstances, but emotional intelligence can help kids deal with this type of abuse by arming kids with communication skills that help them talk about the problem openly with family members and school personnel. It can also assist them in dealing with the bully when they're confronted by one.

27. Remedy School Anxiety

Part of emotional intelligence means learning to cope with emotions, even difficult ones. One problem that's becoming more common these days is school anxiety, which manifests in physical and emotional symptoms.

Every day it gets harder for Emily to get dressed and meet the school bus that takes her to her freshman classes at King High School. Melissa, her mother, admits she's a "helicopter parent," who hovers over her, putting a lot of pressure on Emily to get good grades so she can have the chance to go to a top-notch college and enter a lucrative profession like medicine, as she did. Her constant refrain to Emily is "You have to start your climb to success in high school. If you don't, it will be too late." Due to her mother's constant pressure and her increased anxiety from tests, homework, and grades, Emily has reached the breaking point.

For the third day in a row, Emily complains to Melissa about a stomach ache so severe that she can't make it to the school bus. On the other two days, Melissa insisted that Emily go to school and ended up driving her.

Listen to a dialogue between Emily and her mother about Emily's school anxiety:

Melissa: I know you're getting stomach pains and you feel you can't go to school. That's why I'm taking you to the doctor this weekend. We have to find out why. If you miss too much school, you'll fall behind, and we don't want that to happen.

Emily: If you want to know, I feel like you're part of the problem, Mom.

Melissa (being Mindful and acting curious about how Emily feels): Tell me more. I want to know why you think that.

Emily (looking down): You never listened before. Why should I think things will be any different now?

Emily: You're always talking about getting good grades so I can get into a good college and become a doctor like you. I don't care about being a straight A student. I just want to feel better, not stressed out and nervous all the time.

Melissa (validating): I hear you. I know I've been too hard on you, and I'm sorry. I'm going to try to look at it from your point of view. What about school is making you feel nervous?

Emily: I feel like I can't keep up sometimes. No matter how hard I study, sometimes I find it hard to understand the work.

Melissa: I can see why you feel that way. I know you're having trouble with English. I can get you a tutor if you want. Meanwhile, I'll stop saying things that make you stressful. I admit I may not have been going about this the right way, and for that, I'm sorry. I want you to feel relaxed and happy about school.

Emily: Thanks, Mom. I appreciate your saying that. Can you drive me to school in time for homeroom?

Melissa: I'll get my keys. While I'm there, I'll make an appointment with your counselor and see how we can all work together to make school less stressful for you.

In this case, Melissa and her daughter showed emotional intelligence. Melissa was willing to listen to Emily with concern and empathy. Emily was willing to tell her mother exactly how she felt. They worked together toward a solution to allay Emily's physical and emotional symptoms caused by school anxiety.

28. Teach Ways to Deal with Criticism

Among other things, emotional intelligence means the ability to be able to identify our emotions and to tell others how we feel about their words and actions. Alex, a sixth grader, has trouble responding when a family member, teacher, or friend criticizes him. When he's hurt or insulted, he retreats inside himself or gets angry and lashes out rather than expressing how he feels. This makes the wound fester and leaves him tense and upset for a long time after the event occurs. His mother Alma notices his reactions and today encourages him to use a Mindfulness technique to help him cope when someone criticizes him.

After Alma and her husband took a Mindfulness course at a University Hospital, they began to incorporate what they learned in their daily lives. Before she took the course, Alma was quick to criticize Alex if he came home with a poor grade or if she felt he didn't spend enough time on his school projects. Now she uses assertive language and "I-messages." ("I want you to do well in all your subjects. What can I do to help you pull up your math grade?") She takes every opportunity to show empathy and listens when Alex talks. Patience and loving kindness are her buzzwords now.

Today Alex came home from school in a bad mood. When Alma pressed him about what was bothering him, Alex told her he felt hurt and angry when his math teacher, Mr. Morgan, called him *lazy* in an after-school conference and said he wasn't working hard enough. While math has always been difficult for him, he felt that he was doing his best and the fact that his teacher called him a name was hurtful and wouldn't help him do better in the class.

Alex's mother agreed and said that he shouldn't take the teacher's remark too seriously because sometimes teachers get upset and say things they don't mean, but that didn't excuse what he said to Alex. Alma tells Alex he should talk to the teacher after class and explain how he felt about the teacher's remarks.

This made Alex even more upset. "I don't want to do that. He might hold it against me when he figures out my grade."

"I think it's better that you clear the air and let him know you're trying your best and that the subject comes hard for you. Tell him exactly how calling you a name made you feel."

"I'll think about it, but if I do it, it won't be easy."

Alma rests her hand on Alex's shoulder. "It may not be easy, but I think it will help. Remember how we talked about the Mindfulness way of talking using 'I-messages?' I believe it would work here. Tell Mr. Morgan truthfully how you feel about the things he said without placing blaming or being negative."

The next day, Alex tells Alma that in an after-school meeting he told his teacher that he felt terrible when he called him *lazy*. He also explained that while math was not his best subject, he wanted to improve his knowledge of the subject and his grade.

Mr. Morgan told Alex he didn't mean to call him a name and that he was sorry. He was frustrated because he felt Alex wasn't working hard enough. He didn't realize the subject was causing him such great problems. By the end of the conference, the teacher agreed to help Alex after school one day a week until he felt more confidence about learning math.

"How do you feel now that you talked to him?" Alma asked.

"Much better," Alex said. "From now on when someone says something that bothers me, I'll discuss it rather than keeping it inside and making myself feel worse. Keeping things inside or getting angry doesn't help."

"Telling people exactly how you feel in a polite, straightforward way does help, both you and the other person," Alma says. "I learned that in Mindfulness and will always remember it."

Chapter Four

Motivate Excellence

THINK ABOUT THIS

One of the most important factors in achieving excellence is your children's ability to work cooperatively with other students on school projects. It helps set the stage for their post-school and working years. When they cooperate and pool their knowledge, they'll be more likely to achieve excellence. Working cooperatively with small groups and partners also helps enhance your child's ability to get along with others and to learn compromise and respect for others' opinions.

It's important to help your child strive toward excellence so he can experience fulfillment in his life's work and satisfaction in everything he enjoys doing. Many people measure excellence by certain standards, such as standardized tests, report card grades, and admissions to competitive colleges. Naturally, we need standards to help children gauge their success in a subject and in their school progress.

However, it's also important to keep in mind that it's advisable for parents to help kids learn to evaluate how they're doing in school against their own goals and abilities. Not every child wants to be a scientist or an entrepreneur. Every child is unique and has her own innate talents. Some are talented in music, some in science or math, and some in language facility. It's up to children to nourish their individual talents and for parents to help support them in whatever talents they would enjoy pursuing. Encouraging kids to follow their own interests and, at the same time, succeed in school, which demands success in many different subject areas, presents a challenge to parents and children alike.

One thing you can do to motivate excellence in your children is to encourage them to give their best to every task they take on. At the same time, they need to strike a balance between work and play because allowing them time to unwind and relax will give them renewed energy when they need to give their attention to school work. If they find themselves spending inordinate amounts of time on assignments and studying for tests, they can feel frustration and lack motivation to perform to the best of their ability.

In line with this, it's important to instill in kids a desire to stay with a task and not give up easily, no matter how challenging it proves. To attain this goal and the previous one, giving their best to every task, children need to practice self-discipline, which is one of the main roads to excellence. While many children start a task with enthusiasm, be it schoolwork or a pet project, sometimes their excitement for it fizzles out because they don't gain the momentum to complete the task. One part of attaining excellence is the ability to follow through and finish a job to the best of their ability.

Another facet of excellence involves being street smart, knowing who to trust and who to befriend. It also involves knowing how to discern that the information a child gleans from books, the media, and other sources is trustworthy and reliable. Intellectual prowess alone does not ensure success, so kids have to use their common sense to know who and what to trust.

It's also very important for kids to meet their own standards for excellence, rather than feeling intimidated by the often difficult, if not impossible, standards that society imposes with its constant testing and evaluating. Needless to say, kids need to measure up to their schools' expectations in order to succeed in the real world. However, nourishing their own talents and interests, such as art, music, and writing is important to their emotional well-being.

Kids need to embrace what they love and follow that path throughout school and beyond to achieve job satisfaction when they leave school. A reality that many parents don't want to acknowledge is that college is not for every child. Some children would be happier and better suited to a trade. Listen when your child says she'd prefer one path over another. Every job holds its own unique value.

If we help children set realistic goals for themselves, they'll move closer to realizing excellence in whatever they set out to do. Baby steps will often help them reach their goals faster than giant steps.

Finally, if your child's having difficulty in school, be open to exploring all options to help him learn faster and more efficiently in line with his learning patterns.

MODEL A CONVERSATION: MOTIVATE EXCELLENCE

29. Encourage Working Together to Achieve Excellence

One day out of the blue, Lily, a bright third-grader, tells her mother Cara to expect a call from her teacher, Mr. Parker.

Cara: What's going on, Lily?

Lily: I told him I don't like working in groups. I want to work by myself.

Cara (making eye contact and acting curious): Why do you feel that way? What is it about group work you don't like?

Lily: The kids in my group take too long to do the work. Some of them expect a couple of kids like me do all the work and they spend time talking, but not about the project.

Cara: Maybe you can help the kids who take a long time. It may take some kids a little longer to catch on to the work, and you could make it easier for them.

Lily: I guess I could try that. I would like to be a teacher like you. But what about the kids who waste time playing and let the other kids do the work?

Cara: You and another person in the group could talk to them about it and say how it isn't fair for a couple of kids to do all the work while they mess around.

Lily: They'd laugh or complain if we said that.

Cara: Try it and see. If it doesn't work, I can talk to the teacher about watching your group to see that all the members do their fair share. When I do group work with my fifth graders, I give all the children specific tasks they're responsible for. That way I know who's working and who isn't.

Lily: I'll try talking to them first with a friend in the group. If that doesn't work, you can talk to Mr. Parker, but I don't want the kids to know you did.

Cara: No worries. Mr. Parker will go along with that, I'm sure. Do you feel a little better about group work now that we've talked?

Lily: I'd still rather work by myself. I don't like depending on other kids to get things done.

Cara (putting herself in Lily's shoes): I can understand that. I always enjoyed working independently too. I also learned as I got older that working in a group can help you do an even better job at whatever you're working on.

Lily: What do you mean?

Cara: Working together and cooperating with other kids is like working on a real job, one you'll have in the future. When people put their heads together, they can often do better than they can by themselves. In fact, it helps them do excellent work when they put their minds to it. Kids that find the subject easy can help kids who find it a challenge, and kids who find it hard can ask the other kids questions to help them understand the work better.

Lily: I never thought about it that way. Mom you're pretty smart, even though you are my mom.

Cara (hugging Lily): So are you. I love how you're always open to new ideas.

TRY THIS: ACTIVITIES TO MOTIVATE EXCELLENCE, AGES 6–9

30. Advise Kids to Do Their Best While Minimizing Stress

Eight-year-old Gavin, dubbed an over-achiever by his counselor's assessment, strives to make the honor roll for his third-grade class at Springfield Elementary. No matter how hard he tries, he earns average grades. His best friend Mikey makes the honor roll with ease, while Gavin expresses disappointment to his parents that he hasn't yet appeared on it. Besides the satisfaction of getting good grades, he'd enjoy the extra perks that come with it, such as the principal's invitation to lunch with all the honor roll recipients. He'd also like to see his name listed in the school foyer and in the local newspaper.

Tara, his mother, worries that the push for excellence in his school is so strong that kids like Gavin who don't live up to certain standards will feel left behind. Tara sees many so-called "helicopter parents" at Springfield school who hover over their children from an early age to be sure they get the best grades so they can get into the best classes, and eventually, into the best colleges.

Tara has heard of parents at the school who insist on a certain teacher for their child because some instructors stress academic rigor more than others. A few of her neighbors who fit this description structure their children's day so tightly that they don't have time to relax after school and on weekends so they can enjoy time being kids. When their children don't get top grades in every subject, they pressure their kids to perform better and give generous material rewards when they do well.

While Tara wants Gavin to work to his full potential and do his best, she believes it's also important for him to enjoy life as a happy, well-adjusted child. She makes sure he devotes some of his time after school to playing outside so he can strike a healthy balance between work and play.

Listen to a conversation between Gavin and Tara after he gets his report card for second marking period.

Gavin (handing his report card to Tara): You don't want to see it.

Tara (looking it over): Why would you say that? You brought up your social studies grade to an 85. I know you worked hard to do that.

Gavin: I didn't make the honor roll again. I thought I would this time, but that 75 in language arts is the only thing that kept me from it.

Tara: I know it's important for you to make the honor roll, but I don't like to see you so upset about not making it. I can see you study hard and do your best. You also play a mean softball game and you're great at singing. That's why the music teacher chose you for chorus. You have so many talents.

Gavin: I really want to make the honor roll, and it's not just because Mikey does and gets to go to lunch with the principal. I want to at least try.

Tara (listening, accepting): I think I can help with that. How about if we talk to your teacher about getting extra help with reading comprehension? We can spend more time at home going over your English assignments.

Gavin: I'd like that. I want to make the honor roll, but if I don't, at least I know I tried my best.

Tara: That's the important thing: to try your best but not get stressed out over it. Your best is always good enough.

31. Encourage Staying with a Task

Many children begin a task like schoolwork or a pet project with enthusiasm. However, sometimes their excitement for it fizzles out because they don't sustain the momentum needed to complete the job. We can model behavior for our children that shows how one part of attaining excellence is the ability to follow through and finish a job to the best of our ability. Examples we can model include career projects, home renovations, and following through on goals we set for ourselves.

Perseverance is a characteristic that can help your child stay with a task and gain a sense of pride in completing it. Sticking with anything we have to do requires us to have patience and be self-starters. Sometimes school requires kids to study subjects they don't particularly like or appreciate. Encourage your child to look at a subject objectively and mindfully rather than writing it off as a something that doesn't grab her interest, like learning times tables or how to write a paragraph.

Encouraging perseverance in your child, particularly when considering a subject that's a challenge for her, means conjuring up the motivation to stay with something she's studying even when it doesn't come easily to her. It means doing the best she can to break down the material into easily understandable small parts so she can master the whole.

You can encourage perseverance in your child by showing her how you tackle projects that may prove difficult or sometimes boring, like planning a multi-course menu when you expect company or organizing your closets.

Here's a conversation between a father and daughter about the challenges of staying with a task. Camryn, age seven, dislikes social studies and finds it difficult to stay with the tasks her teacher assigns for homework. They're studying family customs and traditions in her first-grade class, and her job is to interview some older relatives about their family life.

She begins the project with enthusiasm when she prepares questions for her grandparents about their family life and customs growing up. However, when the time draws near to write her report and present it to the class, she loses her momentum. In this scene, she's talking to her dad Anthony about her report which is due in a week:

Anthony (making eye contact, showing interest): Your project about Nonna and Grandpa Pete looks interesting. Would you like to tell me about it?

Camryn: I don't know why we have to do this project. I'm not interested in hearing kids talk about their relatives who grew up a million years ago. I don't think they'll care about what I have to say either. I don't feel like making up a talk about it. I also hate talking in front of the class.

Anthony (putting himself in her place): From what the guide-sheet says, I see that you'll learn about a lot of different nationalities and customs from the kids in class. I think your report will interest the other kids and theirs will interest you. Nonna and Grandpa Pete have some funny stories about growing up in their neighborhood in South Philly that will make the kids laugh. I also agree it isn't easy to get up in front of the class, but once you start talking, it won't be so hard.

Camryn: I don't feel like doing this anymore. It's too much work and I'm tired of it.

Anthony (nodding and empathizing): I can understand why you might feel that way. There are a lot of different parts to the project, like writing the interview questions and then talking to your grandparents so you can understand their stories, then putting it all together so it's interesting to the class. You've already done the hard part, writing the questions and interviewing your grandparents.

Camryn: I don't know if I can finish it in time.

Anthony: I believe you can. You're off to a great start. You've come this far, and all you need to do now is wrap it up by thinking about what you'll say to the class next week. Once you give your report, you'll be glad you stuck with it. I know the class will love it, especially the part about how Grandpa Pete had to ask Nonna's parents for her hand in marriage and he was afraid they'd say *no* because he had tattoos and a ton of facial hair.

Camryn (looking up): Maybe some kids will like my family stories. Grandpa Pete and Nonna are interesting and funny people, even if they don't know it. Want to hear my talk, Dad? I could try it out on you, and you could give me some ideas to make it more interesting.

Anthony (giving her a thumbs-up): Sounds good to me. I know you'll do a great job. We'll have a rehearsal tomorrow so you're ready for next week. You're going to ace this.

32. Stress Street Smarts

While it's important to motivate excellence in school, it's also important to help children achieve mastery in the area of street smarts. Having street smarts simply means that your child knows what to do in difficult or dangerous situations. It also means your children can discern which kids to befriend and which to avoid.

Showing street smarts includes knowing how to be safe when walking and riding a bike, and for older children, driving a car and riding in one. Having street smarts means kids will gain enough knowledge at home and in school to refuse to take drugs and drink and to avoid risky behavior. How can parents ensure their kids will demonstrate common sense when they face precarious situations or find themselves cajoled by peers to engage in activities they know are wrong?

The most important thing parents can do is teach their kids the difference between responsible and irresponsible behavior; first, by example, and next by talking with them assertively and frequently about what things they should and shouldn't do. Parents also need to be aware of their children's choice of friends and limit association with those they feel pose a detriment to their emotional well-being.

In addition to this, they need to be sure that kids know how to ride bikes and walk safely in their neighborhoods, and when they're older that they treat driving as a privilege and not an entitlement. If kids don't use their street smarts and do these things safely, parents may want to revoke privileges until they show a sense of responsibility. When a child's recklessness reaches the breaking point, parents may need to intervene assertively, and if it worsens, seek professional help.

Here's an example: Nine-year-old Dylan loves to ride his bike around the neighborhood. However, his Dad noticed when he accompanied him on his ride he showed some reckless behavior. Since there's no sidewalk, Dylan weaved around the passing cars on the small, yet busy, suburban street.

When confronted, Dylan told his Dad he knows how to ride and that he and his friend Jake often ride this way in the neighborhood. His older brother told his dad when they were vacationing at the shore that Dylan played daredevil with his friends on the boardwalk and raised the bike's handlebars to the sky as if the bike were a wild pony. Kids call it a "wheelie." When bike riders get close to walkers, they swerve abruptly to avoid hitting them.

For the most part, Dylan's a responsible kid who earns above average grades. However, he displays risky daredevil behavior riding his bike when he's with his friends, particularly Jake, who lives in his neighborhood. To make matters worse, he could get in legal trouble if he persists in riding like this on the boardwalk.

Dylan's dad decided it would help to ask Jake's father to join him in an intervention dealing with safe bike riding since he believed that if they got together with the boys, the message would get through to them more effectively. He also heard from Jake's dad that he knew someone personally who had a serious bike accident.

Dylan and Jake initially took the whole thing lightly and said their dads were treating them like little kids. However, as the meeting progressed, the boys began to change their minds. Jake's dad told the boys a true story about his college-age cousin who was severely injured in an accident when he was doing stunts on his bike on a country road near the college, and a car hit his bike. He had to be airlifted to a university hospital since the local one didn't have the expertise to care for him, and then he spent months in a rehab unit. He survived the accident but ended up with lasting physical and psychological scars.

Dylan's dad told a story he'd heard from a police officer friend about a boy his son's age who was doing wheelies and driving dangerously on the boardwalk of a neighboring beach. The officer saw them doing wheelies and weaving dangerously around pedestrians. He told Dylan's dad that he's seen kids doing dangerous stunts on bikes more frequently these days. The officer gave the boys a stern warning, saying they could face charges and would have to bring their parents to the police station if it happened again.

To wrap things up, Dylan's dad said, "The moral of the story, guys, is be street smart when you're riding in the street, or anywhere for that matter."

Jake's dad added, "It's important to do your best in school and in anything you set out to do, but it's equally important to use your common sense and be street smart."

After that, when the boys rode together, or when Dylan rode alone, they didn't take what their dads said lightly. They knew that riding their bikes was a privilege that they could easily find revoked if they didn't show good judgment when riding.

TRY THIS: ACTIVITIES TO MOTIVATE EXCELLENCE, AGES 10–14

33. Support Your Children's Talents

For some kids pursuing excellence in school may mean taking the academic path, while others may choose a different course of study. Children can achieve excellence in many different areas. While some children choose a college prep course, others may enjoy a course that leads them to work with the public in a variety of capacities, such as hair styling, sales, or restaurant work.

In the same vein, some kids work well with their hands and are talented in trades, like plumbing or carpentry. The bottom line is that while some children enjoy academic work and look forward to going to college, others may prefer going to trade school to prepare them for a future career. Whatever career your child shows interest in is a worthy profession in which she can aspire to excellence.

Case in point: On any weekend, Hailey, age fourteen, the daughter of James and Sara, two high school teachers, shows a genuine talent for hair styling. In fact, every Saturday, a few kids regularly show up at her house early in the morning to have Hailey cut and style their hair.

Hailey's expert interpersonal skills also endear her to many students in her class. Students respect her to such a degree that they elected her student council president of her eighth-grade class. She tells her parents she'd like to take the test to enter trade school next year. Although they've known about Hailey's preference for a few months, they're not sure of how to handle it because of their own preference for her taking the academic course in the high school where they teach.

While her mother, Sara, an English teacher, is ambivalent about encouraging her to follow her dream of becoming a master stylist, her father James, a science teacher, has definite feelings about wanting to see her go to college. She earns a "B" average in all her subjects, and if she maintains it, she could easily do well in the college prep class, in James' view. With one month left to decide, Sara and James sit down with Hailey to discuss her future plans for post–middle school education.

Hailey: The truth is that I have my heart set on a career as a stylist. I don't think that's any secret. I know you and Dad would like me to go to college like you did after high school, but as of now, it's not what I'd like to do. I know I like to work with people, and I enjoy helping them look their best. I think I have a gift for hairstyling and would like to study it.

James (using "I messages"): I understand that. You get along well with everyone and know how to talk so people listen. You like styling hair, but taking the college prep course would give you so many more career options to explore. I don't think it's a good idea to limit yourself at such a young age. Why not take the academic course, then if you decide you don't want to go to college, you can attend beauty school after you graduate?

Hailey: How do you feel about it, Mom?

Sara (putting herself in Hailey's place): I can understand your point, but I think Dad has some good ideas. I don't know if it's wise to decide about this at such a young age. You can always opt to go to beauty school later.

Hailey (using "I" messages): I've thought about this a long time, and it's something I really want to do. If it doesn't work out, I can always go back to the regular high school. I don't want you to be disappointed in me because I didn't choose to go to college like everyone else in the family.

James (validating, re-affirming): I would never be disappointed in you. You know that. I want you to be happy in whatever you choose to do. Why don't we think about it and come back and discuss it in a couple of weeks? You still have time to decide.

Hailey: Good idea. I'll think about what you said, and you can think about my idea.

In the next week, James and Sara discuss what they believe are the pros and cons of Hailey's desire to go to trade school instead of the comprehensive high school. They get back to her and tell her they'll support her in whatever decision she makes, knowing she's free to change her mind if she chooses.

34. Help Children Measure Up to Individual Standards

When the question of academic excellence comes up, discussions often touch upon whether we should mainly stress standards such as those set up by school districts that are measured by standardized test results and classroom assessments. Certainly, you need both teacher-made and standardized tests to help assess your child's progress in the classroom. However, each child has distinct attributes and abilities. It's also helpful to measure each child's progress in light of those talents.

Some children excel in social studies, science, or language arts, while others' talents lie in the areas of math, music, or world languages. Therefore, it's helpful when evaluating your child's push for excellence to consider his individual talents and see the ways he's working to his full potential in nourishing them in light of future jobs and his own personal satisfaction.

There are many ways your child can realize excellence, and that includes more than looking at the results of test scores. Realizing his own personal quest for excellence in a subject he loves can help nurture a lifelong love of that subject and ultimately lead to a satisfying vocation and interest that can last a lifetime.

Parents can help children measure up to their own standards of excellence by encouraging them to share their specific talents with others in and outside of the classroom. Older children can help boost their expertise in a subject such as math or writing by helping younger children who find the subject challenging. They can easily find opportunities to volunteer in a school or community setting.

Parents can also encourage children's quest for excellence in a subject by encouraging them to demonstrate it in different ways by sharing it with family members and friends. In addition to this, you as a parent can encourage your children to display their talents publicly by performing in sports, concerts, and recitals. Performing for an audience boosts confidence.

Every child has his own unique intelligences, such as school subjects, creative arts, or athletics for which he can reach his own standards of excellence. Strong encouragement on your part can make the difference in a child realizing his own personal goals and dreams or losing sight of them for lack of motivation. Particularly for children who don't possess strong self-motiva-

sense of loss when a close family member dies. During this time, coping mechanisms come into play more profoundly than during any other challenge a child faces. Parents can help their children cope by offering meaningful solace for their loss of a loved one.

Many children experience pressure dealing with changes in their lives that require strong coping mechanisms. Moving to a different neighborhood and enrolling in a new school often test children's coping skills in a big way. Family members can help a child fit in and adjust to a new living situation by showing compassion and empathy. Using Mindfulness techniques and encouraging a child to employ them to help them deal with these changes can make a positive difference in their ability to cope now and in the future.

Recovering from romantic break-ups can present coping challenges for pre-teens and teenagers. A child who shows good coping mechanisms can overcome these problems with the help of Mindfulness techniques and good listening skills on the part of parents.

When considering coping mechanisms, it's important for parents to give children the chance to solve their own problems. Naturally, you'll want to be available to listen and advise, but it's also important to help your children figure things out on their own. You'll want to foster independence in your child so she can call upon her own resources to find the coping mechanisms that will help her get through any difficult situations she encounters. With your help and knowledge of Mindfulness techniques, she'll be one step ahead.

MODEL A CONVERSATION: TEACH COPING SKILLS

36. Help Diffuse Irritability

Alyssa, who recently started kindergarten, comes home from school every day in a bad mood. When her mother Brittany picks her up from the bus stop, she starts crying and complaining. Today she wants her mother to stop for chicken wings at a fast food store near their home. She whines and complains loudly when Brittany tells her they have to get home to take her older brother to basketball practice.

As soon as they get home, Alyssa progresses to a full-fledged tantrum. Her mother tries to placate her by making her a chocolate milkshake while they wait for her brother to get ready for practice. When her mother gives her the milkshake, Alyssa's tantrum escalates because the whipped cream melted. Her demands of "I want another milkshake now," turns to a piercing wail.

Brittany's nerves begin to frazzle as Alyssa's acting out escalates. When she remembers what she learned in her Mindfulness class, she stops for a moment and takes a deep breath. She knows that for her child to calm down she has to model that behavior first. She wants her daughter to revert back to her pleasant, cheerful self, but she doesn't want to enable her by giving in. Here's the bottom line: Brittany wants her daughter to learn coping mechanisms when she feels tired, angry, and irritable because of her new schedule.

Alyssa pushes the milkshake aside, nearly spilling it on the coffee table. She curls up on the couch and gets ready to watch her favorite cartoon show.

> Brittany: I can see you're upset, and I hope you feel better. I know you want another milkshake but I'm not going to make it. If you want to freshen up the one you have, you can go to the 'fridge, find the whipped cream can, and freshen it up with some new whipped cream. It's up to you.

> Alyssa (crying loudly): I want you to make it.

> Brittany (calmly): If you want a milkshake, you need to get the whipped cream and swirl it on top.

> Alyssa: (Gets up from the sofa, goes to the refrigerator, takes out the whipped cream, and swirls it on top of the milkshake. Her mother detects a faint smile as Alyssa admires her work of art.)

> Brittany (smiling): It looks like you made yourself a new milkshake.

> Alyssa: (drinks the milkshake until air bubbles gurgle through the straw)

> Brittany: We have to drive your brother to practice soon. First, I'd like to talk with you about how you've been feeling this past week. I know you've been tired lately. You're not used to having a full day of school. That's okay, and I understand. But it doesn't help either of us if you're grumpy and act up when you get home. How do you feel about that?

> Alyssa: I can't help it, Mommy. I'm tired, and when I'm tired I feel grumpy and mean. When I feel that way, nothing makes me happy.

> Brittany: I understand and would like to help you think of some ideas to help you deal with these feelings. Would you like to hear them?

> Alyssa: Sure. I want to feel better.

> Brittany: First of all, when you feel tired and irritable, stop for a minute. Just stop everything and freeze. Then take a couple of deep breaths. Before you say anything, ask yourself if you really want to spend all that great energy screaming and saying things you don't mean. Relax, go

outside and play, have a snack you like. Do something you enjoy. Little things like this will help you feel better.

Alyssa: Okay. I'll try it. But I want you to do something for me before we go to the game.

Brittany: What's that?

Alyssa: Can I make milkshakes for everyone after dinner? I don't want to hurt your feelings, but my whipped cream swirls beat yours any day.

TRY THIS: ACTIVITIES TO TEACH COPING SKILLS, AGES 6–9

37. Soothe Fears and Worries

Isabella, age six, a bright first-grader, has developed two major fears since starting school: fear of doctors, especially when she needs inoculations, and fear of scary clowns that prevent her from sleeping soundly. Martin, her dad, is trying to help her cope with her fears by talking to her and reassuring her.

He knows from consulting with Dr. Terry, his daughter's pediatrician, that it's a good idea to validate her fears and not diminish her fearful feelings by telling her there's nothing to worry about. On the other hand, he also wants to do his best to show her fears won't control her if she doesn't give them power over her.

On the weekend, when they're out for a hike on the beach, Martin thinks Isabella will be more receptive to talking about her fears than during the school week when she's concerned about homework and there's little time to relax. Tune in to their conversation about Isabella coping with her fears and worries:

Martin (validating, using "I-messages"): I can see how worried you've been about going to Dr. Terry about getting your booster shots.

Isabella: I hate shots, Daddy. Remember how I screamed last time?

Martin: How could I forget? I couldn't hear for a week after that. I have some tips for you when you get the shots that always work for me. First, don't look. It's always worse when you look. The next thing is to take a couple deep breaths. Before you can say "peanut butter and jelly," it will be all over.

Isabella: I could try that, but I'm still afraid, and nothing you can say will make me not be afraid.

Martin (putting himself in her position, empathizing): I hear you, but take it from me, a guy who's gotten a lot of shots, it's over fast, and it's not that bad. Let me know how it goes after you try not looking and taking a deep breath.

Isabella: Okay, Daddy. I'll try not to scream next week so you don't lose your hearing. But what about those scary clowns hiding in my bedroom closet when I want to go to sleep? If I try not to look at them and take a deep breath like you said to do with the shots, they may come after me and I won't be able to run fast enough to get away.

Martin: I can see how thinking about those clowns may keep you awake, but I know of some special magic words that frighten scary clowns away. It only works on scary ones, not the funny ones we saw at the circus.

Isabella: Let's try it tonight, Daddy. If it works, I won't be so tired when I wake up for school. Did you ever see scary clowns in your closet?

Martin: Can't say I did, but I thought I saw a ghost once. It was tall and wore a big white sheet with holes for eyes.

Isabella: What did it do to scare you?

Martin: It said, "I'm going to get you" and jumped on my bed when I tried to sleep.

Isabella: What did you do to get rid of the ghost?

Martin: Your grandmother Theresa, who is a very wise woman, gave me some special magic words to scare the ghost away. I was waiting for the right time to give them to you to send that clown back to his clown family.

Isabella: What were the magic words Granny gave you?

Martin (closing his eyes): "Abracadabra, sis bam boom, I want you to go away real, real soon." Within seconds after I said Granny's magic words, the ghost disappeared, never to be seen again.

Isabella: My friends say hocus pocus like that doesn't work.

Martin: Try it and see. If you believe it will work, it will. It's not so much the words you say, but the desire you have in your heart for whatever frightens you to disappear. We all have things we're afraid of, like shots and the scary clown, but they can't get to you if you don't let them.

Isabella: I'm glad we talked about this, Daddy. I'm going to do whatever I can not to be afraid. If it works, great; if it doesn't, at least I tried.

Martin: After all this heavy talk, I think we deserve to go out for ice cream. I'm having a banana split. Do you want one too, or would you rather have an ice cream soda? In case you're interested, they also have clown sundaes with a little clown hat on top. Just kidding!

38. Help Your Child Deal with Natural Disasters

All natural disasters present a major challenge for helping your children deal with them. For example, hurricanes can quickly immobilize communities, causing residents to evacuate and seek safety in massive shelters. The after-effects can prove devastating because families face days, if not weeks, without power and supplies. Similarly, a blinding snowstorm can shut off lights and power for days, causing kids and adults alike to wonder how they'll cope and survive until power is restored and roads are passable.

Jayden, age eight, lives in an area where hurricanes threaten to strike on a yearly basis. Last year the hurricane was so severe that the family had to live in crowded quarters with family members in the next town for two weeks. The thought of abandoning their home and all their possessions set Jayden into a panic.

What would happen to their beloved cat Buttons, and how would Jayden salvage his sports equipment and toys that meant so much to him? What would he be forced to leave behind because his parents said they could only take the most important things? More important, would everyone be able to survive until the rescue workers were able to get them all out of the house? There was no electricity, and that meant no air conditioning. The water might be contaminated, and who knew how long the bottled water supply would last.

As soon as the hurricane warnings hit, Lauren and Alan, Jayden's parents, did their best to reassure him they'd be safe despite frantic sound bites from local officials and reporters that they faced a monster storm and would need to prepare to evacuate and go immediately to a hotel or shelter. This was compounded by the fact that trees and debris would soon clutter the roadways, and bumper to bumper traffic would face them as they exited the island.

Jayden's parents tried to diffuse his fears by reassuring him they'd do all they could to ensure his safety, their own, and that of Buttons the cat. They encouraged Jayden to name his fears, which he did: "I'm afraid we won't make it out," "When will we be able to come back home?" and "Will our house still be here when we get back?"

His parents started by telling him it would probably be a long, slow drive to the hotel where they booked a room for three days. If the hotel was full after that, they'd go to a shelter in the big arena where they held sports events. It would be hard not being in your own house, but it would be like an adventure, where they'd meet new people who would be going through the same thing. From the moment Jayden first expressed his fears, his parents were honest about what they'd probably encounter each step of the way. They acknowledged his fears, but didn't exacerbate them by exaggerating what they'd face during the hurricane.

As the time grew closer to evacuate their home, Alan and Lauren employed Mindfulness techniques to ally Jayden's fears and help him cope. They used assertive communication to help give Jayden a sense of security during the tensions the hurricane evoked in him: "We need you to calm down and listen so we can explain how we're going to organize what to take with us and what to leave behind." They also used "I-messages" to validate and show empathy for what he was feeling: "We know you're very upset and worried about what will happen when we leave the house. We're going to do our best to keep us all safe. We'll get everything we want to take with us together and organize the rest of our things, so hopefully, we'll come back to them when the storm is over."

Jayden's parents encouraged him to step back and pause for a moment before reacting strongly or crying hysterically. They showed him how to take three deep breaths when he found it hard to control his reactions to the storm and the prospect of leaving their home to go to a safe place.

In the end, Lauren and Alan encouraged Jayden to talk about all his fears about the hurricane and leaving their house. It made him feel comforted and reassured that they'd find safety in the hotel, and possibly in the shelter.

When Jayden fell into his worrying mode on the long ride to the hotel, his parents encouraged him to stop for a moment, relax, and take a deep breath. They also played music he liked along the way and asked Jayden to sing along with them.

As it turned out, the family had to go to a shelter because the hotel ran out of rooms. At first, Jayden felt tense and uncomfortable in the crowded conditions at the sports arena shelter, but after a day, he surprised himself by making new friends with other kids in the shelter that provided board games to keep them amused. Buttons, the cat, also made friends with an unlikely companion, a gigantic but gentle Goldendoodle named Gus, owned by Johnnie, one of his new friends at the shelter.

After a couple of weeks, the family moved back to their home. Luckily, they had minimal damage and found many of their prized possessions in good shape despite the flooding. The best part of the homecoming happened when Jayden told his parents the first night home, "That was a terrible hurricane but we got through it. I hope it never happens again, but if it does, we'll get through it like we did with this one, right? It was scary, but we made it."

39. Make Living with Change More Bearable

Gianna, age nine, is showing signs of stress, like irritability, crying, and sleeplessness because her mother and father, Carly and Evan, have argued constantly since Evan lost his construction job. Carly is finding it hard to support the family on her retail salary, and Evan is having a hard time finding a new job. At this point, they aren't sure they want to stay together.

Gianna's best friend's parents divorced last year, and she's concerned that if her parents continue fighting they too may be headed for divorce. When her friend Lucy's parents divorced, they moved out of the neighborhood, and now Gianna sees Lucy only once a month. She also worries that if her parents divorce she'll have to go to a new school and leave her friends behind.

Because Gianna's reaction to her parents' arguing is intensifying, they plan to talk with her to help her deal with changes that may come about in their family life. Knowing how important it is to wait for a moment when she'll be most receptive, Carly and Evan decide to broach the subject during the weekend when Gianna is well-rested and relaxed.

Carly: Dad and I would like to talk with you about what's been happening lately.

Gianna (looking away): We don't have to talk. I know what's going on. All you two do is fight.

Evan: You're right. We do argue a lot, and we've decided that it's not a good thing to expect you to listen to it.

Gianna: Are you two getting a divorce like Lucy's parents did? At least tell me.

Carly: The truth is we don't know what's going to happen, but we'll talk to you about it when we decide. As you know, we're going to a marriage counselor. We hope she'll help us fix our problems.

Gianna: I don't want you to get a divorce. I want us all to be together.

Evan: I know you do, and that's what we want too. That's why we're trying to work things out.

Gianna: I don't want to move or go to a new school like Lucy did.

Carly: We promise we'll tell you every step of the way what's going on. And we'll try not to argue in front of you.

Gianna: What if it doesn't work out? What if you decide you can't get along and decide to separate?

Evan: I can understand how upsetting that thought is to you. I hope it never comes to that. If it does, we'll do our best to make sure your life won't change as much as your friend's did.

Carly: We're taking it day by day and trying our best to deal with our problems. Whatever happens, we both love you and want you to be happy. You can talk to both of us about how you feel any time you want. No matter what our problems are, you are our main concern.

Gianna: You have to promise you won't get a divorce without talking to me first.

Evan: We promise we'll tell you what's happening as soon as we know it.

Carly: If you ever want to talk, we're here. We want to know how you feel.

Gianna. Thanks. I feel a little better, just a little, but that's better than before.

40. Offer Solace for Loss

Jackson, a third grader, is experiencing profound sadness due to the sudden death of his grandpop, for whom he was named. Jackson visited his grandfather three days before he died suddenly of a heart attack. They played ball and talked about how his grandfather was going to take him fishing next week. Tara, his mom, got a call the night the ambulance took him to the hospital. The nurse told her that her father recognized the signs of a heart attack since he'd had one five years ago, and he had the presence of mind to call 911 immediately. Tara's dad was alone when it struck as his wife had died a few years ago.

Tara was able to talk to her dad briefly before he died, but sadly, the hospital staff couldn't save him from the ravages of a massive heart attack. She found telling her son Jackson about his beloved Grandpop's death the hardest thing she had to do in her life. Jackson said he was too sad to go to school, so his mom told him he could stay home. She asked if he wanted to go to the memorial service with her and his dad, and they left it up to him.

Tara and Jackson's father Will sat down with their son and answered his questions in a caring, compassionate way to help him cope with this tragic, unexpected event. They approached their conversation mindfully and truthfully. They explained that he'd see all their family members and friends at the service, but that they wouldn't see Jackson's grandpop because, according to his wishes, he'd been cremated prior to the service. However, the banquet hall where they'd hold the memorial service would have a table with his ashes that would be placed inside a special container that looked like a book because his grandfather loved to read. Tara told Jackson that the family would take the book with the ashes home after the service and would place it on a special table in living room, where they would also keep Grandpop's picture that showed him playing ball with Jackson.

The table at the Memorial Service would also contain pictures of his grandfather from the time he was a small boy until the present. Awards he won from helping his community and serving in the military would also be on display, in addition to his prized fishing rod, which he'd promised Jackson would one day be his.

Still in a state of disbelief about losing his Grandfather, Jackson asked where Grandpop was now. Without hesitation, Jackson's mom said she believed he lived on in spirit, but that everyone would have to figure out for themselves where people go after they die. Will, his dad, said he believed in heaven, and that after people die, they enjoy eternal life with all their loved ones who went before.

Jackson said that even though he was confirmed in his faith, he still wasn't one hundred per cent sure what happened to people after they died. He believed that because his grandpop was such a great guy he was going to be okay wherever he ended up.

At this point, Jackson asked his mom and dad if his feeling of sadness and wanting to cry would ever go away. His mom said that in time the feelings of sadness he was experiencing would become more bearable, but that he would never forget the happy times he spent with his grandpop. The happy feelings would eventually take over the sad ones. His dad added that he would always remember the good things Grandpop taught him like how to fish, how to play ball, and how much he could learn from reading.

Jackson's parents gave him the choice of attending the memorial service. He said he wanted to go, but only if he could say something about his grandfather at the service. Tara asked if he felt he was up to it, and he said, "Not really, but I should say something so people remember him."

Tara and her husband tried to get Jackson to talk more about his feelings of sadness, but he said he couldn't because he was too upset. They told him when he was ready, they'd be there to listen.

When the family arrived at the memorial service, relatives and friends greeted them warmly. They all knew that Jackson was deeply affected by the loss and gave him special attention and a lot of hugs. They recalled that he and his grandfather were constant companions and also resembled one another greatly. After his mother spoke about her dad, Jackson approached the microphone. Here's what he said:

"I feel very sad about Grandpop. He was my very best friend. He taught me how to fish and how to play ball. He was a soda jerk, yes, that's what he called himself, when he was in high school. In the ice cream parlor where he worked, he made sundaes and ice cream sodas with a mountain of whipped cream. He made them for me too, and they were great. I could talk to him about anything, and he never got mad at me, even though I can be a real pain sometimes. I don't know where Grandpop is now, whether he went to heaven, or like Mom says, he's here in spirit. One thing I know is that he's probably here with us now and saying, 'Don't get corny, people. It's little old me you're talking about, not the King of England.' One thing I do know is that I'll always remember him, and I hope you do too."

TRY THIS: ACTIVITIES TO TEACH COPING SKILLS, AGES 10–14

41. Help a Child Fit In

Ella, a thirteen-year-old seventh grader, raised by her grandmother, Miss Loretta, is having trouble fitting in at school and her new neighborhood. Her father died recently and, due to health problems, her mother found herself unable to care for Ella. At the end of the summer, her uncle drove her from Georgia to Florida to live with her grandmother, who is now her legal guardian. Suddenly, Ella found herself going to a new school in a different state. She lives in a neighborhood of apartment houses and condos inhabited mainly by senior citizens with a sprinkling of young families scattered throughout.

Her grandmother, who is a young sixty-five, tries her best to use Mindfulness theories she thinks will help her raise Ella to cope with her new surroundings and to enjoy a pleasant school experience. She knows Ella is the new kid at school and that other kids, especially middle-schoolers, are often reluctant to let a new child into their already established circle of friends.

With the goal of helping Ella establish friendships, Miss Loretta paid a visit to her granddaughter's school early in the semester. She set up appointments with her major subject teachers and the counselor in hopes they would help monitor how she was getting along with the children in her classes. She asked teachers to talk to their classes about making new students like her grandchild feel welcome and accepted.

Since there weren't many children Ella's age living in the neighborhood, Miss Loretta encouraged her to join the local church's youth group in hopes she'd have the chance to forge friendships with other kids her age. At first, Ella was reluctant to go to the youth group. She hadn't belonged to any church when she lived with her parents, so it was a whole new experience for her. She found herself enjoying the picnics and dances the group sponsored, and the minister was warm and welcoming.

Once she started attending the youth group, she gradually made friends with a couple of kids who attended her school. Even though they were in a different grade, they encouraged her to go out for some of the activities they enjoyed, like chorus and drama. Ella found that joining these clubs helped her make a couple of friends in her own grade and classes.

Miss Loretta showed Mindful listening in helping Ella adjust to her new home. She encouraged Ella to talk about her new friends at school and in the youth group. Soon, she began enjoying an active social life, and with her grandmother's encouragement, invited friends to her new home. Her new friends invited her to accompany them to movies and the mall.

Although Ella was far from home, she kept in contact with her mother, who was undergoing a new experimental cancer treatment in another state. Despite her positive relationship with her grandmother and the new friendships she's made, Ella hopes her mother will recover so she can return to her home and familiar surroundings.

Whenever Ella becomes homesick, her grandmother practices the Mindfulness trait of Loving Kindness, reaching out to her and validating her feelings. She encourages Ella to express her feelings using "I-statements" to capture the full impact of her message: "Sometimes I'm very sad because I miss Mom and my old home. I hope Mom will get well so I can go back there someday."

Miss Loretta also encourages Ella to pause, take a deep breath, and relax when she experiences stress or anxiety because of her mother's illness and the move. Her new friends also show kindness and compassion to Ella, trying their best to help her adjust to her new school and neighborhood. Her classroom teachers and the counselor check in with Miss Loretta periodically to reassure her that Ella is adjusting well to her new school.

42. Offer Understanding During a Break-Up

Zane, who's completing his final year of middle school, is doing his best to cope with a break-up with Talia, his girlfriend of one year. They met in English class and had a lot in common, including many mutual friends and their love of football. Zane played for his middle school team, and Talia was a popular cheerleader. Every weekend they went to the movies or the school dance. Their parents delighted in their pre-teen romance and drove them to and from all their dates. In fact, Talia's parents, Stan and Ava, considered Zane part of the family and often invited him to dinner at their house.

A month after school started, Zane barged in the house in a bad mood. He snapped at his parents when they asked what was bothering him, and he refused to open up to them. Later that night after Zane had gone up to his room, his younger sister told their parents that she'd heard from one of her friends that Zane and Talia broke up.

As it turns out, a football player on the high school team caught Talia's eye and she went out with him behind Zane's back. When Zane asked Talia if it was true after hearing it from one of his friends, she admitted she did, in fact, go to a rock concert with the other boy. She apologized but said she thought it was best they break up because she thought they both should see new people. She felt they were too young to be tied down to dating one person. Zane told her he didn't want to break up, but she insisted. He tried not to cry in front of her, but he found he couldn't control it. He hated that she saw him in his most vulnerable state.

When he talked to some of his friends, they said it happens all the time: one person gets tired of the other, and they want to go out with other people. They advised him to suck it up and start dating other people. After all, he was popular in school and wouldn't have any trouble finding a new girlfriend. He responded in anger that there would never be another girl for him other than Talia, which made his friends shake their heads and walk away.

Because of his lack of desire to confide in his parents and his constant irritability, his parents told him he needed to talk about what happened "When I'm ready, which may be never," was his curt response.

Soon enough, things came to a head. A week after the break-up, Zane cut school and the assistant principal called his home. When Ava came home from work, she questioned him about his absence. He said he felt too sad to go to school and couldn't take seeing Talia in the Spanish class they took together. He served his detentions and promised his parents he wouldn't cut school again. His parents said it was very important for him to open up about the break-up.

Would he prefer to talk to them first, or should they make an appointment with a counselor since he was taking it so hard? They could tell he was suffering after the break-up and believed they had to do something to help him. They gave Zane the choice, and he agreed to try talking with them first. Here's a transcript of Zane's conversation with his parents, Stan and Ava:

Stan: We can see how upset you are about the break-up. The fact that you trusted her and she went out with someone else must have really hurt.

Zane (looking down): I thought we got along great until this happened. I still can't believe it.

Ava (validating): I can imagine how this made you feel. You trusted Talia, you were best friends, and now the worst has happened.

Zane: I don't know if I can ever get over this. She was so important to me, and I thought we'd never break up.

Stan (attempting to get Zane to help solve his own problem): I wish I could help you feel better, but nobody can do that for you. Only time will help. The times you shared will always be a part of you, but it won't hurt as much as time goes on.

Ava: Dad and I can tell you these things, but it's hard for you to believe it the way you feel now. Everyone has to go through it themselves to find their own way to come to terms with it and cope with it. Dad and I have both been through it. It happened to me when I was around your age and to Dad when he was in high school.

Zane: You can tell me it will get better, but the only thing I can think about is the way I feel now. I can't see myself ever feeling like I did before.

Stan: What mom and I are trying to say is that what can help keep you going and moving forward is the fact that you won't always feel the way you do now. Things will look up for you. They will get better. Trust us on that.

Ava: As long as you are patient and give it time. Don't be afraid of the pain. Let it come and go, like the ebb and flow of the ocean. Eventually it will even out.

Zane: What do I do meantime to keep from feeling miserable? I don't mean to take it out on you, but I can't help it.

Stan: Just live your life day by day. Go out with your friends, play sports, and don't try too hard to feel better. Just live in the moment, and you'll gradually feel better.

Ava: One thing that's very important is to talk to us if you feel you need help. Tell us if the feelings you're having now get worse or linger. We know a counselor you can talk to who can help you recover.

Zane: I'll definitely tell you. I don't want to keep feeling like this. (Making eye contact with his parents.) Thanks for listening. It helps a lot to know you're here whenever I need to talk.

43. Encourage Your Children to Solve Their Own Problems

Like so many kids today, twelve-year-old Taylor experiences stress due to her involvement in a lot of different activities, in addition to school, homework, and an active social life. She's having trouble sleeping, and when she finally gets to sleep has a hard time waking up. She constantly races from one activity to the next and sometimes skips meals. Because of this, she feels exhausted throughout the day and has a hard time functioning in school. Her English teacher called home because she fell asleep in class, and it was hard to rouse her.

Kelly, her mother, is growing tired of carpooling Taylor and her friends to band practice, softball, and drama club. On weekends, her dad drives her to practice for a children's touring choir. This is her favorite activity because the choir travels abroad to give concerts and promote goodwill for our country.

Because she's proficient in everything she's involved in, when there are conflicts between the activities, her coaches allow her to miss practice. Her mother would like her to focus on one or two activities so she'd have more down time and not be sleep-deprived. However, Taylor says she doesn't want to give up any of her activities because they're all important to her. Because of Taylor's break-neck schedule, the family rarely sits down together to eat and discuss the day's events. Ryan, Taylor's dad, is fearful that if she stays with her hectic schedule something will suffer; namely, her health and her schoolwork.

After Taylor's teacher called, her parents knew it was time to sit down for a serious talk. Using Mindfulness techniques, her parents told her she needed to make some changes in her schedule. However, they left the way she'd make those changes up to her. They wanted her to learn how to make decisions that would directly impact her quality of life. Their main goal is to make her self-sufficient and responsible for making her own decisions. Here's a transcript of their family meeting.

Kelly (using assertive communication): We need to talk about how you can make changes in your activities schedule so you can enjoy what you love to do and still have time to get the rest you need. We can see it's hard to keep up with everything because you're falling asleep in class and finding it hard to get your homework done. It's also important to eat healthy foods on a regular schedule and not grab a snack on your way out the door instead of sitting down with us for dinner at least three days a week.

Taylor: I tried thinking of a way I could fit all my activities in and still do all the other stuff I have to do like schoolwork and spending time with my friends, but I couldn't come up with one thing I could give up. I want to keep doing all those things. I promise I'll try to rest more on weekends so I don't fall asleep in class.

Ryan (validating, empathizing): I understand how much you love all your activities, but falling asleep in class is a wake-up call that you can't participate in all these activities, your demanding schoolwork schedule, and still have time for friends.

Taylor: I know you're right. I wish I could cut out one or two things, but I'm not sure of which ones because I like them all. I do know that the one I like most is the touring choir. I'm looking forward to going with them to Scotland in the spring. I can't give that up.

Kelly: That's good. You know one you can't eliminate. Now think of at least one other you can drop, maybe one you can come back to next year.

Taylor: I know it would be hard to go back to any of them next year if I left now. I might not be picked for drama, softball, or band and would have to try out all over again. I'm thinking that drama takes the most time because rehearsals run late. Trying out again for drama next year wouldn't be a big deal because I could try out for any plays I'm interested in when they come up. I don't have to belong to drama club to be in the plays. Going to those meetings twice a week takes a big chunk of time, in addition to all the play practices.

Ryan: It looks like you've made a good decision about which activity to eliminate, especially since it requires Mom and me to be in the carpool twice a week for drama club and at least one night a week for play rehearsals.

Taylor: I'm glad I made my decision. Now I'll have more time to relax and won't doze off in class anymore. It's still a lot to do, but I think I can handle it better than I do now.

Chapter Six

Instill Compassion

THINK ABOUT THIS

Webster's dictionary defines compassion as "sympathetic consciousness of others' distress, together with a desire to alleviate it." The Dalai Lama says, "If you want others to be happy, practice compassion. If you want to be happy, practice compassion." What kinds of things can parents do to help their children show compassion to themselves and others?

To help your children practice compassion with themselves, family members, and friends, model compassion by showing kindness to everyone you meet. Ask people who are experiencing problems about specific ways you can help them, and stand by your offer. Above all, let your children see you showing compassion to others.

Putting themselves in another's shoes is one way Mindfulness advises to help build compassion. If you encourage your child, even at a young age, to fully listen to someone in distress, he can understand more fully what that person is experiencing and help in a way that even some adults can't match.

One way for children to show compassion is to befriend someone who is lonely at school and include this person in activities. Often, a child who is different from other kids in some way, such as having a disability or an appearance different from others, experiences a sense of aloneness and alienation. If another child shows compassion, it can help the child on the receiving end gain self-confidence and greater satisfaction in life. Children can also demonstrate compassion by seeing the beauty in everyone, including all who are not like them physically or in their beliefs. People of different ethnic groups and races fall under this category.

Helping your children grow in compassion means reinforcing the Golden Rule, teaching them to treat others as they would want others to treat them.

Showing compassion also means helping a child care about himself, treating himself with the same kindness and gentleness he'd show another person. To take it a step further, showing compassion to oneself means taking good care of oneself, eating healthy foods, and getting enough exercise and rest.

Your child shows compassion when she's willing to speak out against bigotry and bullying in all its forms. A child does not have to jeopardize her own safety to be a caring bystander when she witnesses other children treating a classmate cruelly. She can band together with others to call out the unacceptable behavior, or she can confidentially tell the teacher or counselor what she's witnessed. Try teaching your child compassion by encouraging her to become a caring bystander.

You can encourage your child to show compassion to the elderly by displaying simple acts of kindness such as helping them with a physical task that's difficult or simply sitting there and talking for a few minutes. Also, talk to leaders of local organizations your child participates in, like scouting, after-school, and community clubs, and see if they're willing to initiate projects to help your child practice kindness and compassion.

Volunteering to help others can go a long way in fostering compassion in children. If you spend time with your child modeling volunteerism and talking about the rewards of volunteering, both he and those he helps will benefit greatly.

Modeling and teaching your children about compassion brings many rewards, one of which is helping them live lives filled with meaning and happiness as they reach out to help people along the way.

MODEL A CONVERSATION: INSTILL COMPASSION

44. Model Compassion for Others

Jada's parents, Miriam and Seth, are helping her learn compassion by modeling it for her whenever an opportunity arises. Although Jada is only nine and in third grade, they're showing her by example that displaying loving kindness and concern for others will bring happiness to the lives of others and to her own life.

One thing they do to model compassion is offer a helping hand to neighbors when they see them struggling in some way, like carrying something heavy into the house. If a friend or neighbor needs support when a family member is sick, Miriam and Seth offer to help by making meals or babysitting.

You can also model compassion by offering comfort and listening to someone who is sad or not feeling well. Bring your child along so she can see you showing compassion when a friend or neighbor needs someone to be there in difficult circumstances such as losing a job or a death in the family.

Another activity that's great for teaching compassion is taking your son or daughter to work. If you work in a service profession, you can model kindness by treating your clients with concern and empathy. If a person is upset and wants to vent, you can instantly calm him down by asking what you can do to help, and then do your best to rectify the problem. If you're a teacher and a parent starts venting about her child's poor grade in your class, you can say, "Let's talk about this. I'd like to hear what you have to say, but both of us need to remain calm if we're going to make progress."

When dealing with people who are upset, the Mindful way works well: Take a deep breath, respond assertively rather than reacting, and accept what they're saying, even if you don't agree. Try putting yourself in their place. When your child sees you handling conflicts mindfully, it sets an example for her when she's involved with someone who becomes angry or confrontational.

In addition to modeling compassion for your children, you can role-play a situation with your child like this one acted out by Jada's family. It demonstrates how showing kindness to others can help both the recipient of compassion and the person who offers it.

Miriam: We've spent some time showing you how important it is to be compassionate. In your Mindfulness class at school, your teacher asked in the note she sent home if we could role-play a time you could show compassion to a classmate. She wants the kids in your class to report back what you role-played with us and what you learned about compassion by doing it.

Seth: Can you think of a situation at school this year that may ask you to show kindness and compassion?

Jada: That's easy. There's this new girl named Annie who's hard of hearing. She's having a hard time making friends. When she's outside in the playground, she sits on the steps by herself and no one talks to her.

Miriam: You set up the scene and characters, and we'll role-play it.

Jada: We're in the cafeteria, and Annie is sitting by herself eating lunch. Mom, you can be Annie, and Dad, you can be my friend Calvin. I'll be myself.

Mom (Annie) sits at the dining room table by herself. Calvin starts to walk past her.

Jada: Wait, Calvin. Let's go sit with Annie. She's all by herself and that must not be fun for her.

Calvin: Do we have to? She can't hear us anyway.

Jada: We don't have to say much. We can just sit there with her. Come on. It would be a nice thing to do.

Calvin (reluctantly): Oh, okay. But I don't know if this is going to work.

Jada (smiling at Annie): Hi, Annie. Can we sit with you?

Annie (face brightens): Sure. I usually eat alone because people don't think I can hear and they'll have to shout at me. I have my hearing aids in, and I can hear you fine if you talk the way you usually do.

Calvin (sitting down next to her): Hey, that's cool. So, what do you think of our school so far?

Annie: I only got here a month ago. I like my classes, but as you can see, I haven't made any friends yet. I'm hoping I will once kids get to know me.

Jada (offering Annie a cupcake): You just made two. We'll introduce you to a couple of our friends and we can play basketball or tag at recess.

Annie (smiling): That would be fun. Thanks.

Calvin: I saw you shooting baskets in gym. You know how to score points.

Annie: My dad played in college, and he taught me how.

Jada: Great. Tomorrow meet us at the playground and we're on. There's the bell. We'll walk with you to class.

After acting out the scene, Marilyn and Seth ask Annie what she learned about compassion from the role-play.

Jada: I think it made Annie feel good that people cared about her and included her. I also learned that making friends with her made Calvin and me feel good about ourselves.

Miriam: So, do you think you're going to practice compassion the next time you see Annie?

Jada: A big "yes!"

TRY THIS: ACTIVITIES TO INSTILL COMPASSION, AGES 6–9

45. Teach Your Child to Walk in Another's Shoes

Mindfulness practitioners often talk about walking in another's shoes, which means showing compassion to others by using empathy. When you teach your child to think about what it means to put yourself in another person's place, he'll better understand what this person is going through. Showing compassion in this way will help him become a better listener who truly cares about people.

The ability to put oneself in another's place can also help your child experience how it would feel if he or another child hurt someone's feelings by being rude or excluding that person from activities.

Tyler's school recently started a Mindfulness program to help curb their bullying problem. One of the lessons Mr. Williams, Tyler's third-grade teacher, taught asked the students to put themselves in another's place while talking to a classmate or friend. Mr. Williams asked students to keep a journal explaining how they showed compassion by walking in another's shoes. Volunteers would write a brief report about how their project worked out.

Tyler knows his best friend Alex has been sad lately because his much-loved pet Peekapoo, Root Beer, has a serious kidney infection and needs surgery. His mother told him that the vet said he might not survive the surgery because of the seriousness of the infection. In his sadness, Alex withdrew and didn't want to go to Tyler's house as he usually did at least twice a week to play ball and watch their favorite shows.

When Mr. Williams told the class about the assignment about showing compassion by putting oneself in another's place, Tyler wondered if doing this would help his friend deal with his sadness. He remembered how he felt when his cat got seriously ill, and he wasn't sure he'd survive. Would he be able to help his friend by putting himself in his shoes?

A few days later, Alex's mother took Root Beer in for surgery. Despite Alex's protestations, she insisted Alex stay with Tyler until she returned. Here's what happened when Alex finally agreed to visit Tyler the weekend Alex's pet went in for the operation:

Tyler: I know you didn't feel like coming over, but I'm glad you did. Can we talk a little before we get to our game?

Alex: I guess so. But I may have to leave early. They're operating on my dog right now, and Mom's going to call to let me know what's happening.

Tyler: I hear you. Look, Alex, I can imagine what you're going through not knowing what's happening with Root Beer. I felt the same way when our cat got sick and the vet said she might not make it.

Alex: But Lucky came out okay. It doesn't look good for Root Beer.

Tyler: At the time, I didn't know if Lucky would get well. I can see how hard it is for you now. Not knowing is hard.

Alex (starting to cry): I don't know what I'd do if anything happened to Root Beer. He's been with me a long time. I don't want to lose him.

Tyler (patting him on the shoulder): It's okay, buddy. Let's hope he comes through it. Either way, I'm here to listen. Let's go outside for a while. I think we could both use a break.

Alex: Thanks. I guess it doesn't help me feel better to sit here feeling rotten. It's not going to change how things turn out.

The boys grab a bat, a glove, and a ball, and go out to play in Alex's yard.

About an hour later, Tyler's mother calls them into the house. She tells them that Alex's mother called to say that Root Beer came through the surgery. They're going to keep him in the veterinary hospital to monitor his progress for forty-eight hours to see if the surgery was successful. For now, the prognosis looks positive.

Alex waits on the porch for his mother to pick him up, and Tyler waits with him.

Alex: Hey, thanks for listening and putting up with me these past couple weeks. I know I haven't been much fun to be with.

Tyler (smiling widely): Don't mention it. Friends need to stick together, no matter what happens, right? I'm glad things are looking better for Root Beer—and for you.

46. Encourage Your Child to Appreciate Differences

Kaylee, aged seven, is in her final three months of first grade. Her father Justin, recently widowed, is raising her with the help of his mother, Sarah, who has temporarily moved in with him and Kaylee to help run the household. When Kaylee was three, Justin and his wife, Lisa, took a course in Mindfulness at the local university. It helped them cope with her illness and the big changes it would mean for their family. They often used Mindfulness techniques, such as active listening, assertive speech, and loving kindness while raising Kaylee. She's reaped the benefits of that training by turning out to be a caring, sensitive child.

One evening, Kaylee told her dad and her grandmother about Tanya, a new girl from India who had recently registered at Kaylee's elementary school. She said the other kids didn't talk much to Tanya because she couldn't speak much English. Some older kids in the schoolyard laughed at her and said mean things to her like, "Go back to where you came from."

When Kaylee heard what these children said, she told them to stop. It didn't bother her that they were in the fourth grade. "How would you like it if somebody said that to you?" They rolled their eyes and walked away. If it happened again, Kaylee made up her mind to say something to the principal.

Kaylee said she wanted to help the new student but wasn't sure how because the girl had trouble with the language. Sarah advised her to sit with Tanya in the lunchroom and offer her some cookies she baked on a regular basis for her granddaughter. Justin suggested inviting her to play a game in the schoolyard, like tag or catch, one that didn't require complex language skills.

"Maybe I can help her with English by talking to her," Kaylee said. "She goes to ESL class, but I think if she practices, she'll learn it faster."

"Good idea," Sarah said. "You could also introduce her to a few of your friends, ones you think would treat her kindly and accept her."

"My best friend Angel already said we should ask her to join our girl scout troop. I think she'd like that. She knows how to knit. Maybe she can teach us."

"Sounds good to me," Justin said.

"Dad, I don't understand why those girls in the schoolyard were mean to her."

"There are some people, kids and adults, who don't feel good about themselves, so they have to have somebody to pick on, and they often pick a person who is different from them in some way. Remember that Mommy and I always taught you to care about everyone, whether they are the same or different from you. Everyone has special gifts and is beautiful in his or her own way."

"I believe that too, Daddy."

"Grandmom, would it be okay if I invite Tanya over Monday when we have off school? We could play some of those new board games I got for my birthday. You don't have to speak English great to do that."

"That's fine with me. dear. It's great making a new friend. Meanwhile, start trying the other things you mentioned too. It will make your new friend and you happy. Your mom would be very proud of you. Compassion was the most important virtue to her."

47. Reinforce the Golden Rule for Your Child

Connor was a new student in Mason's second grade class. Before he started school, Ms. Kamala, the teacher told the class that a new student would arrive the next day. She explained that he had a cleft palate and sometimes had trouble speaking so people could understand him. Mason noticed that Connor looked different from the rest of the class, and that it was sometimes hard to understand him when he spoke.

It didn't take long for a few of his classmates to start making fun of Connor. One of them mimicked him when he talked, and another hid his backpack. Mason wondered how they could hurt someone they hardly knew because of the way he looked and talked. His parents had always told him how important it was to be kind to people, whether they were the same or different from you.

The teacher noticed the taunting and told the boys in no uncertain terms that they needed to stop. She also told them she would call their homes that evening about their treatment of the new student. If it happened again, she would tell the principal, who would bring their parents in for a conference.

The next day, Connor was absent during social studies because he had to leave for speech class. On other days, he had to go to the clinic for check-ups, so he missed quite a few days of school. Ms. Kamala told the class they were going to have a special lesson during social studies. She started out by telling the students about a quotation she'd heard on TV years ago. "When my children were little they used to watch a show, 'Mr. Rogers' Neighbor-hood,' on TV every afternoon. Mr. Rogers said something very important one day and we never forgot it. Mr. Rogers' mother told him to 'Look for the helpers. You will always find people who are helping.'

"I'm not going to give you any homework tonight. Instead I'm going to ask you to think about how you can be a helper in our classroom. I want you to think about what you can do to help your classmates, what you can do to always be a friend to them. I want you to think of one kind thing you can do to help another student in this class."

The students fell silent. The three students who had made fun of Connor looked downward or away. No one said anything for a long, awkward moment until Mason raised his hand.

"Mason, do you want to say something to the class?"

Mason walked up to the front of the room. Everyone stared at him, wondering what he would say. All the kids respected him, so they listened carefully. "I think we could all be helpers by being kind to Connor."

The boy who hid Connor's books rolled his eyes. The students sitting near him frowned at him.

Mason looked at each of the students who had treated Connor unkindly. "If you haven't treated Connor kindly, now's your chance. You can apologize for what you did and you can be polite from now on. But that's not enough. We all have to do something. I'm going to spend more time getting to know Connor. He's new to our class so we should do our best to welcome him. We can all do this in our own way."

"You make some good points, Mason. Thank you."

Ms. Kamala looked up at the clock. "It's almost time to pack up. Before the bell rings, does anyone else want to say anything about how we can be helpers?"

The student who made fun of Connor when he talked raised his hand. He talked in a low voice and sounded sad, like he was going to cry. "I'm sorry I was mean. I'll tell Connor tomorrow. I don't know what I was thinking. I saw a couple of other kids doing it, so I went along with them. I won't do it anymore."

"I know Connor will be happy to hear that, James. I hope you'll all be helpers from now on. I'm going to look for the helpers every day."

When he got home, Mason told his dad and mom the story about the helpers. He told them that the story his teacher shared showed how people could live by the Golden Rule, which means, treat others the way you want to be treated.

His mom and dad reinforced what the teacher said by modeling the Golden Rule and discussing with Mason how he could demonstrate it in his daily life. After he told his parents what happened in school, his mom said, "When you live by the Golden Rule and show kindness to people who are different in some way from you, it shows you're compassionate, and that's a great way to show you care about others."

TRY THIS: ACTIVITIES TO INSTILL COMPASSION, AGES 10–14

48. Help Your Child Practice Self-Care

Irina, a seventh grader at a private middle school, has a habit of staying up late on school nights, skipping meals due to her active sports schedule, and eating junk food. Her parents, Lisa and Mark, are becoming concerned because she's acting moody and uncooperative around the house and in school. Her counselor called home recently because she got into a major argument with a classmate who told her she liked her hair better long.

On a Friday night after going out with her family for a pleasant dinner, Irina's parents asked her to sit down with them in the kitchen to discuss some of their concerns about her. Here's how the conversation panned out:

Irina. Is this some kind of intervention? My health teacher told us about how people in a family get together to talk when someone is into something heavy, like drugs or drinking. I hope you don't think I'm doing any of that stuff.

Lisa: It's not an intervention about anything like that. We hope if you have any issues about any serious problems, you'll feel free to come to us. We'd like to talk with you about some things we're concerned about lately.

Irina: You told me the counselor called you about arguing with a girl in my class. Everything's cool now between us. We worked it out. No worries. Sometimes I get upset too easily when people say things and I take them the wrong way.

Mark: That's one of the reasons we wanted to talk. Remember when we told you about how Mindfulness helped us after we took the class? We talked about having compassion toward others and treating people kindly.

Irina (getting impatient): I told you I made up with that girl at school. She said she didn't mean what she said about my hair in a bad way. She was just telling me she liked my hair longer.

Lisa: Actually, we wanted to talk to you about how important it is to show compassion to both ourselves and other people. How you acted with your classmate may have happened as a result of not treating yourself with compassion.

Irina: Showing kindness to other people is something I have to work on, but why is it important to show it to myself, and how can I do it?

Mark: Good question. It's important to care about yourself, to treat yourself with kindness and gentleness. If you do that, you'll be more likely to do the same when you're with other people. It's good to treat yourself as you would treat another person.

Irina (smiling): But I shouldn't treat myself the way I treated the girl I yelled at in school, right? That would definitely make me dislike myself a lot.

Lisa: If you treat yourself with compassion, you'll want to be kind to other people, to help them more. You'll feel like solving problems, like the one you experienced, more peacefully. For example, if that student said something that bothered you, you could try letting her know in an assertive way, using "I-messages" that you didn't like hearing it.

Mark: You could say something like, "I don't like when you criticize my hairstyle. I'm happy with it, and that's what counts."

Irina: How else can I treat myself better?

Mark: For starters, you can take care of your physical health by trying to eat healthy food and going easy on junk food.

Lisa: Try to unwind before bedtime by reading a book or magazine or writing in your journal. Avoid using your electronic devices late at night. When you get enough sleep, you'll have more energy during the day to do the things you want.

Mark: Once you start treating yourself better in these ways, you'll feel less stressed out. You won't take it out on other people or yourself.

Irina: I guess you have a point. Maybe because I haven't been sleeping and eating right, I'm not as much fun to be around. Sorry I've been grumpy lately. I don't mean to be.

Mark (hugging her): Thanks for saying that. We'll do our part to help you turn things around.

Irina: And I'll do mine by doing a better job of taking care of me.

Lisa: That's great. And another thing: Whatever you do, try not to be too hard on yourself. Allow yourself to make mistakes, just as you would with another person.

Irina (smiling): I'll try, but it may take a while. It's not easy giving up chips, nachos, and using my Smartphone late at night.

49. Support Your Child in Becoming a Caring Bystander

Maxwell, a ninth grader, witnessed a serious bullying episode in the gym locker, where intramural baseball teams meet after school. Two boys, known for bullying students who were different from them, went after Cody, one of the players, who enjoyed excelling in academics but did not excel in sports. They saw him as a weird loner that wouldn't fit in any crowd, especially the jocks at school. Cody figured if he joined the team, he'd make more friends and that once kids got to know him, the bullying might let up. To Cody's dismay, the opposite happened.

When Cody showed up to gather his gear in the locker room and the perpetrators knew no staff members were around, they tripped Cody, kicked him when he fell to the ground, and forced him to eat dirt they'd brought in from outside in a pail. They taunted him by calling him a wimp and a few other unmentionable epithets.

The miscreants intimidated the other team members, so they were loath to get involved, fearing it might happen to them. Maxwell, one of the class leaders, felt guilty he didn't try to stop the bullies' mistreatment of Cody. He also felt powerless. There were more of them and they were strapping bruisers. He didn't know if the other team members would support him in standing up for Cody.

Maxwell's parents had always taught him they believed in treating everyone with compassion and respect, so he couldn't rest until he thought of a way to foil the bullies. In social studies class, his teacher, Mr. Morgan, had talked about the role of bystanders in aiding bullied kids. The teacher stressed the importance of standing up to bullying, preferably with other students for support. He also emphasized the importance of not putting oneself or other kids at risk when defending bullied kids.

Here's an excerpt from a conversation Maxwell had that night with his parents, Diana and Austin:

Diana: What's going on, Maxwell? I don't see you horsing around with the dog like you usually do. Did something happen at school?

Maxwell: Yes, and I have some thinking to do.

Diana: Can we help?

Maxwell: Listening would be good enough.

Austin: Tell us what happened.

Maxwell: Do you remember that kid Cody who's in my gym class?

Diana: I remember your telling us some kids were bullying him because he was a super brain and kept to himself.

Maxwell: Today things really got out of hand. Some mean guys hit him hard and made him eat dirt. They also called him terrible names.

Austin: What did you and the other kids do?

Maxwell (looking away): That's just it. We didn't do anything. What could we do? Those kids were big and bad. They're on the JV football team, and they're known for roughing up anyone who gets in their way.

Diana: How did you and your friends feel about not doing anything to help Cody?

Maxwell: Definitely not good. I talked to my friend Jaimie after it happened, and we plan to get together to talk about what we'll do if it happens again.

Austin: I remember your telling us about what your teacher said about how bystanders can help when they see someone being mistreated. I also recall that he told you to proceed with caution when getting in the middle of something like that.

Maxwell: When I talk to Jaimie, I'm going to suggest that we and a couple other kids who didn't like what they saw should get together and tell them to stop. If there are a few of us speaking out, it will be harder for those guys to continue bullying him. We can use assertive language, the kind of talk you said to use if you're in a bad situation.

Diana: What exactly would you say?

Maxwell: I'd say something like, "We need you to leave him alone now."

Diana: That sounds good. It's brief and to the point, yet strong and forceful.

Austin: I agree that if you all band together against the bullies, their power will lose some force, and hopefully they'll go away.

Maxwell: But I'm wondering what will happen if they don't stop and they don't go away?

Diana: Then it's time to tell an adult you trust, like a teacher, counselor, or the assistant principal.

Maxwell: They may find out we told on them. They'll bully Cody worse, and we'll be their next targets.

Austin: I don't think you need to worry. Whoever you tell will keep it confidential and hopefully will be more vigilant from now on in keeping an eye on things. That way it will look like one of the adults in charge discovered it, and you'll be off the hook.

Maxwell: Thanks. I'm going to call Jaimie now and we'll meet with some other kids tomorrow to draw up an action plan. Look out, bullies, the bystanders are on their way!

50. Encourage Organizations to Help Your Child Show Compassion

Another thing parents can do to raise their children mindfully is to encourage organizations, such as scouting, after-school, and community clubs, to sponsor activities that help their children grow in mindfulness traits such as kindness and compassion. If you're trained in Mindfulness, you may want to volunteer to speak at these venues to help children learn the benefits of Mindfulness for themselves and others.

Kylie, a sixth grader, enjoys the camaraderie of her local scout troop, where she's a Cadette. Ms. Rosalyn, the scout leader, asked her and the other members of the group what they'd like to choose for their next community service project. When Kylie's mother, a school counselor, recently gave a talk to the scout troop about Mindfulness, the young ladies were intrigued by how Mindfulness could help them live more in the present and relax. They liked its strong focus on showing kindness and compassion to others.

When Ms. Rosalyn asked for ideas for a new badge project, Kylie suggested working with a local senior center to spend time with the elderly. Scout members could show kindness and compassion to the members by listening to their stories about their lives, playing board games with them, and learning new skills from each other.

The rest of the troop liked the idea, so the scout leader contacted the head of the senior center where seniors exercised daily and enjoyed a snack. The men and women spent their afternoons keeping each other company and talking about their family members, mainly their children and grandchildren. Because all of these relatives had a busy schedule, not many of them took time out to visit their older relatives.

"This is where you come in," Ms. Rosalyn told the girls. "You've already decided to be Mindful listeners when the people at the center tell you stories about their past. You've also said you'd join their exercise class. I hear they're taking Beginner's Yoga and Chair Zumba. Can you think of any other ideas for our badge project? Luckily, the senior center is at its busiest around the same time of day we have our meetings, right after school, so some of your parents could carpool you there."

Kylie overflowed with excitement at the prospect of working on the new badge. "How about if we ask them to write stories and poems about their most interesting experiences? Then they could bring in what they write and share it with everyone."

Zoe, Kylie's friend, suggested the girls bring in their favorite poems or ones they wrote to share with the people at the center. Ms. Rosalyn agreed that would be a good addition to their program.

One of the other girls suggested working on projects like potting plants or cooking since there was a kitchen at the center. That gave Kylie an idea.

"Maybe we could also have them teach us a skill like chess, drawing, or painting."

The other girls agreed they'd like to try these ideas. Jess said, "We could teach them about computers and Smartphones. Some of them would probably like to download and read books on an e-reader. That way they wouldn't have to lug a big book to their doctor's appointments or when they travelled on a plane or train."

"You've all given interesting and workable ideas. This will be a great project that will help the attendees and all of you," Ms. Rosalyn added.

The troop agreed that the most important thing they could do to show compassion to the elderly men and women at the center was to be there and listen. Whatever activities they engaged in with the members should always reflect the spirit of compassion and kindness they learned about in their Mindfulness talk.

Ms. Rosalyn asked the class what they wanted to call the badge since it was a brand new one that wasn't in the handbook. It would be their original badge, and if it worked out, troops around the country might want to add it to their list.

Kylie raised her hand. "Can we call it Showing Compassion to the Elderly?"

"Let's take a vote," the leader said. "Can we have a show of hands."

Every girl's hand shot up. "Showing Compassion to the Elderly it is," said Ms. Rosalyn.

Postscript: The badge project worked out perfectly. The young and elderly learned from one another, and many of them remained friends after the project was over. The girls visited the center on their own and kept in touch with the men and women they met, sending texts, e-mail (taught to them by their girl scout friends), and calling periodically to check in with them.

51. Inspire Your Child to Volunteer

Spencer, age 14, attends an urban magnet school. Mr. Flores, his social studies teacher, asked the students to think of a community service project that would involve volunteering in the local community. Spencer learned about Mindfulness in a school pilot program and would like to incorporate it into his service project. After he learned about Mindfulness in school and explained it to his parents, they thought practicing it would help them become more caring parents and would encourage their son to become a compassionate young man in his dealings with others.

Spencer and his parents, Elizabeth and Daniel, always discuss his schoolwork and home assignments. They don't do his work for him, but listen to his ideas and encourage him about his assignments and how he can best carry them out. Listen to Spencer's conversation with his parents as he discusses ideas for his community service project:

Spencer: Tomorrow Mr. Flores wants us to give him topics for our semester projects. I wanted to see what you thought of a few ideas I came up with.

Elizabeth: You mentioned before you'd like to do something involving that class you took on Mindfulness.

Spencer: You two are always talking about showing compassion to other people. I'm thinking I might do a volunteer project that deals with that part of Mindfulness.

Daniel: There are many opportunities in our neighborhood to show kindness and compassion.

Spencer: That's what I was thinking. Children's hospital is right around the block. Maybe a couple of us could visit the sick kids there and put on a show for them or talk to them one-on-one.

Elizabeth: I like both of those ideas. How would you show the kids in the hospital compassion?

Spencer: The main thing I'd try to do is what you and Dad call Mindful listening. I'd pay close attention to what the kids were saying about stuff they have to go through like procedures, taking medicine, and not feeling like themselves. I'd let them talk without interrupting, and if my mind wanders, I'll bring myself back to what they're saying. In other words, I'd do more listening than talking.

Daniel: You're on the right track. What other ideas do you have?

Spencer: I was also thinking about tutoring younger kids in elementary school. English and math are my favorite subjects, and I think I could get them to like these subjects once they understand them.

Elizabeth: How would you work compassion into that?

Spencer: I think compassion involves kindness and patience. Sometimes parents get annoyed when kids don't catch on to schoolwork. I think kids helping other kids would work out better because the kids teaching them would probably have more patience than family members because they're around their kids all the time.

Daniel: I like both of these ideas for volunteering. Which one will you choose?

Spencer: I'm going to ask if I can do the one at the hospital this semester and work at the elementary school next semester.

Elizabeth: I'm sure your teacher will like that idea. What will you call your volunteer project?

Spencer: That's easy. I'd call it "Volunteering with Compassion."

Chapter Seven

Nurture Kindness

THINK ABOUT THIS

Teaching your children about kindness will help them and others enjoy a happier life. As you would expect, modeling it for them every day by talking kindly about others, even those that you don't feel friendly toward, and by performing acts of kindness, both big and small, will give them the best education in how to show kindness.

You can encourage children to perform an act of kindness each day. Even younger kids will enjoy making a small gift to help a friend or family member feel appreciated. Younger children can also write thank-you notes to someone for help given or for no reason at all, except to say they're thinking kindly about the subject of the letter. Practicing loving kindness in your home on a daily basis will help everyone in your family feel loved and appreciated.

Writing thank-you notes for gifts received has become a lost art. If you teach your child the importance of a hand-written note of gratitude, both the giver and the receiver will benefit. People love to be appreciated for their efforts.

Older children can think about showing kindness with simple gestures and body language, such as a smile or a hug. Even though giving compliments doesn't often come easily to pre-teens and teenagers, doing so can be a tangible way to show friends and relatives kindness.

You can also encourage your children to apologize if they've hurt someone's feelings intentionally or unintentionally. Finally, forgiving someone who has hurt them helps the offending party and them. True acts of kindness come from the heart, and sometimes involve the extra elements of faith and courage in your child and the person on the receiving end.

MODEL A CONVERSATION: NURTURE KINDNESS

52. Prompt Your Child to Take the High Road

Layla, a third grader, tells her parents about a girl in her class who is always in a bad mood and never talks in a positive way. How can she show her kindness even though she doesn't enjoy being around her?

Gloria, Layla's mother, and Wayne, her father, have always modeled kindness for her and her brother. Her parents remind her that being kind isn't always easy, especially when the object of your kindness isn't very pleasant or likcablc. They've always advised her to take the high road and show kindness to everyone she meets, even though they may not show kindness themselves. Tonight, Layla's mother and dad address their daughter's concerns about being kind to people whose company she doesn't enjoy.

Wayne starts the conversation by asking Layla about Jessie, the girl she told them about that she didn't want to invite to a cook-out to celebrate the end of the school year. "You invited all the girls in your class, so it would be hard to leave Jessie out. What are your feelings about this?"

"Dad, it's not just me. None of the other kids get along with her either. She never has anything nice to say about anybody and complains about everything. I don't want to invite her."

"I can understand how it would be hard to be around someone who acts negative all the time. However, maybe if you and some of your friends try paying a little attention to her and show her some understanding, she may get the idea that treating people kindly pays off."

Layla sighed. "We've tried talking to her and inviting her to play at recess, but she still gives us an attitude."

"Mom and I know how you feel. You know our neighbor, Mrs. Gilliam, the one who complained to the township that we left our trash cans on the curb too long?"

Layla smiled. "How can I forget her? She complains all the time and then she lets her poodle dig up our yard."

"One day, when it got to be too much," her dad said, "Mom went to her house and brought Mrs. Gilliam one of her famous blueberry pies. They had a little talk, and things got better. She raved about it for days and said no one ever baked her a pie before, especially a delicious one like Mom made."

"It turns out she was a very lonely lady," Layla's mom said. "Her kids live far away and never bother to call her. She surprised us by apologizing for letting the poodle loose in our yard and for calling the township on us. I guess she felt nobody cared about her and became bitter about her life. Now I try to help her with her gardening and invite her for coffee every so often."

Layla frowned. "Are you saying I should make friends with Jessie even though she gets on our nerves?"

Gloria shook her head. "I'm not saying you have to be friends with her, but it would be nice to show her a little kindness even if you don't like being around her."

"Inviting her to your cook-out is a good place to start," Wayne said, "but of course, that's totally your decision."

"If she sees you reaching out to her in a positive way, you may find her easier to get along with," Gloria said.

"Maybe and maybe not," said Layla. "I do feel bad making her the only one that isn't invited. Let me think about it."

Layla can't decide about inviting Jessie until she begins writing out the invitations. Remembering her parents' advice about taking the high road, she decides to ask her to the cook-out. When Layla hands Jessie the invitation, she smiles and says she'll be there. After school that day, Jessie mentions to Layla that she's always been very shy and it's hard for her to make friends. She says she doesn't know how to act around kids, and maybe that's why she says mean things to her classmates.

Jessie attends the party, but she doesn't mingle much with the kids. Now Layla understands why, and she does her best to make Jessie comfortable by asking her to help her put out the snacks. Layla tells Jessie she'd like to get to know her better.

"Thanks for that," Jessie says. "I know I've been hard to get along with, and I plan to work on that. Now you gave me a reason to try to be a better friend to you and the other kids."

TRY IT OUT: ACTIVITIES TO NURTURE KINDNESS, AGES 6–9

53. Ask Your Child to Practice an Act of Kindness Daily

Samuel's parents, Letitia and Gabe, do their best to live their lives according to Mindfulness practices. They model kindness, one of its most-practiced and beloved principles, for their eight-year-old son, Samuel. Since he entered school, they've encouraged him to practice one or more acts of kindness each day. Every week, the family discusses how their acts of kindness helped the recipients of their kindness and how the kind gestures helped them live more mindfully.

On Sunday nights, the family meets at an ice cream bistro. Over sundaes, they discuss how their acts of kindness help them and others live better lives. Here is what this week's session looked like:

Gabe: So, Samuel, how did your acts of kindness go this week?

Samuel: It went fine, Dad. My teacher asked for a volunteer to help a special needs child with math. I love math and enjoy being a helper, so I said I'd try it.

Letitia: How did it work out?

Samuel: Bobby, the boy I helped, had fun and so did I. He asked me if I'd sit with him sometime at lunch. We decided to meet in the cafeteria next Friday. He said he'd bring in some homemade brownies, my favorite.

Letitia: That sounds like fun. What other acts of kindness did you perform last week?

Samuel: I liked helping Mrs. Lester down the street walk her dog. Sometimes he's hard to walk on a leash because he likes to race ahead, and Mrs. Lester isn't so young anymore. She was happy I asked, and I like her dog Beowulf. He slobbers all over me and almost knocks me over, but he's fun.

Gabe: It looks like you made two friends, Mrs. Lester and Beowulf. Any other kind acts you want to mention?

Samuel: Here's another one I liked doing. Molly, a girl in my class, has her arm in a cast after she broke it playing softball. I help her carry her books and pick up stuff if she drops it. She always says, "Thanks," and shares her dessert with me.

Gabe: It sounds like you're having fun practicing kindness, and the people you help are enjoying it too.

Samuel: A couple kids in my class saw me helping Bobby with his math, and then they asked me how they could volunteer.

Letitia: Practicing acts of kindness can be contagious. The more you practice it, the more it spreads.

Samuel: And helps make a better world for all of us, right?

54. Spread Loving Kindness in Your Home

Mia, a kindergarten student, loves how her parents give small spontaneous gifts to each other and other family members. They told her it's a form of Loving Kindness, a way of expressing love for someone they learned from studying Mindfulness. Along with the little handmade gift, they offer the recipient a short Mindfulness prayer, such as "May you be happy; or May you feel better each day." Her parents write this on the card that accompanies their gifts.

Anthony, Mia's dad, gives his wife a bouquet of colorful cut flowers once a week, while Carmella, her mom, often bakes Anthony a tin of chocolate chip cookies he takes to work and shares with co-workers. She tapes a Loving Kindness note in her own words to the container. Last week it read "May you enjoy work this week."

Last Friday, Mia rushed off the school bus to tell her mother that her teacher, Miss Amy, was leaving to have a baby and that she'd soon have a new teacher. "I want to give my teacher a gift and a Loving Kindness message."

"I think the best gift you can give is one you make yourself, but it's up to you. We can buy something at the gift shop, or you can make one yourself. I can help you write a short Loving Kindness message for the card. What would you like to do?"

"I love handmade gifts. You always make cookies for dad. He said he likes that better than something you'd buy from the store. Can we start making it now?"

"Yes. What do you have in mind?"

"I'm thinking I could draw a booklet of pictures of Miss Amy and the class. I think she'd like that. She loves purples and pinks, so I'd mostly use those colors. I could write what each picture is about. That way she'd see how much she taught me and the other kids. Now all I have to do is think of a Loving Kindness message to write on the card."

As Mia puts the finishing touches on her drawings, she jumps up. "I think I know what to write, but I'll need a little help."

"I'm ready when you are," Carmella says.

"I want to write 'May you and your baby be well and happy.'"

Mia's dad comes into the room and starts making dinner. "I heard about your booklet and your Loving Kindness message. I think it's a perfect gift."

"Thanks, Daddy. Loving Kindness messages are the best because you can pack a big message in a little space."

"That's the beauty of it," Carmella says.

Mia shows her parents her booklet with the pictures and captions. "Do you think Miss Amy will like it?"

"This is a very special gift, Mia." Carmella says, turning the pages of the booklet and admiring the pinks and purples. "I'm sure Miss Amy will treasure it for a long time to come, along with your Loving Kindness message."

55. Encourage Your Child to Write Thank-You Notes

Cole, who attends a cyber school, recently received many gifts from relatives for his ninth birthday. He loves art and building model planes, so they gave him many of his favorite toys. Some family members sent generous checks. His mom and dad, Holden and Elise, have always stressed the importance of showing kindness whenever the chance to display it arises. After Cole showed his parents his gifts, they asked him what he thought would be a kind and thoughtful way to respond to his family members' generosity.

Cole: Maybe I can call them and thank them, or I could send them an e-mail. I already thanked Aunt Suzy in person.

Holden: Can you think of another way?

Cole: I remember you and Mom writing thank-you notes when the people who went to your anniversary party gave you gifts. I'd like to do that, but I don't have time. I'm too busy with homework and sports.

Elise: We were busy too, but we made time to do it, and you can too.

Holden: There's nothing better than a hand-written thank-you note you take the time to write. It means a lot to people to get a personal thank-you note. It doesn't have to be long or fancy.

Elise: All you have to do is write a couple of sentences saying specifically what you like about the gift and how much you appreciate their sending it. If you feel like it, you may want to draw a picture on the note that has something to do with the gift.

Holden: You could also tack on a sticker you think the person would like. We can help start you out to give you an idea of how to send a personal thank-you that would mean much more to the people you're sending it to than a phone call or e-mail.

Cole: Okay. Let's do one now. It sounds like fun, even though it might take a longer time.

Holden: I'll go get a pack of thank-you notes, markers, and some crayons. First, gather all your gifts and see who sent each gift by looking at the card.

Holden: (returns with a pack of thank-you cards and some brightly col-ored markers)

Cole: Here's an origami art set from Uncle Russ. I really wanted one of those. We're learning about origami in art class at school.

Elise: This one will be easy, and so will the rest. Write in your note what you told us, that you really wanted an art set and you're learning about origami at school.

Cole: (Prints this on his note: "Thanks for the origami set, Uncle Russ. I've always wanted one of these. We're learning about origami in school, so I'm going to make a design with it for a school project. Love, Cole." On the other side of the card, he draws and colors a picture of an origami design.)

Holden: That's a thoughtful thank-you note. I'm sure he'll love it. Let's do another one.

Cole: Here's one from Uncle Bobby, a paper airplane book that tells you how to make planes you can actually fly. I can't wait to make some with my friend.

Elise: You're seeing how you can make writing your thank-you notes quick and easy by writing exactly what you're saying about the gift.

Cole: Cool! It won't take me long, and it's actually fun writing these.

Cole: (Prints his note to his uncle: "Dear Uncle Bobby: Thanks for the paper airplane book. I can't wait to start making the planes and flying them with my friend. Love, Cole." On the blank side of the notecard, Cole draws a picture of an airplane and colors it blue, his favorite color. After he's finished writing all his thank-you notes, his mother gives him a book of stamps.)

Elise: Put a stamp on each one and we'll take them to the post office tomorrow.

Cole: Thanks for helping me, Mom and Dad. This was actually fun. I'm going to write thank-you notes every time I get presents.

Holden: It was fun for you to show other people kindness for thinking of you, and it will be great fun for them when they open your thank-you notes.

TRY THIS: ACTIVITIES TO NURTURE KINDNESS, AGES 10–14

56. Explain How to Show Kindness with Gestures

Madison, a caring sixth grader, is taking a Mindfulness course at a school which experienced an uptick in bullying in recent months. Her teacher, Mr. Levy, taught a lesson involving using gestures to reinforce kindness. For homework, he asked his students to think of four instances demonstrating how they could show kindness to others in school and at home by using gestures and body language.

Madison's parents, Chad and Tammy, make themselves available when Madison wants to discuss her assignments. Today, Madison wants to run her ideas by them for reinforcing kindness without using words.

"I think it will be easy to think of examples since you already do a lot here at home to boost your acts of kindness with body language," Tammy said.

Madison thought for a moment. "I think it's important to give hugs to people in our family and to friends. Whether or not you say anything to go along with the hug, it makes people know how important they are to you and that you care about them. So that will be my first example: hugs, hugs, and more hugs."

Tammy smiled. "You certainly don't skimp on hugs, and we appreciate that. What other example comes to mind?"

"When somebody's upset, like my friend Molly was the other day when her cat had to get surgery, a small touch can help. I told her I hope Romeow feels better soon, and patted her shoulder to help her know I cared and was thinking about her."

Chad nodded in agreement. "That's a good thing to do to anchor the feelings you want to get across to her."

"I think so too. Our teacher also told us to be sure the person you're hugging or patting on the shoulder would welcome that. Some people don't, so it's good not to act pushy."

"How do you think you can know about that beforehand?" Chad asked.

"That's easy. I usually only use gestures with someone I know really well. When I'm not sure how the person will take it, I ask if it's okay if I hug them or pat their shoulder."

"You're using good common sense. Can you think of another time you can boost a kindness message with a touch or body language?"

"I can look cheerful by smiling even if I'm not in the best mood. Sometimes I'm thinking of everything I have to do, like homework and band practice, and wondering if I'll get it all done. I might feel pressured and stressed, but if someone wants my help or needs me to listen, I can be mindful of doing it with a smile so they'll know I'm paying attention to what they have to say."

"So, even if you're busy or distracted, you're saying it's good to smile and look friendly when you listen to someone who needs your attention."

"That's right. I also show relaxed body language when I'm listening to someone. That means open, relaxed arms with no crossed arms, and looking at the person but not gaping at him so he feels uncomfortable. I want to make it look like I have a long time to listen and not act like I'm in a hurry to leave and do my own thing."

"It looks like your homework is done, Madison," Tammy says.

Madison gives her mom a hug.

"Three-way hug," Chad says,and they all hug.

57. Show the Value of Giving Compliments

An easy way your children can show kindness to others is by giving compliments freely and sincerely from the heart. Riley, a fifth grader, would like to give more compliments to her family and friends, but sometimes she feels awkward doing it. Her parents, Andrew and Chantel, frequently talk to her and her twin younger brothers, Rex and Torey, about being kind and generous to friends, family, and people they meet along their paths.

Here are Riley and her parents talking about how giving compliments can make people enjoy a happier day:

Riley: Today in homeroom our teacher talked to us about showing kindness to others. She said one way is to give compliments.

Andrew: How do you feel about doing that?

Riley: I don't know. Sometimes it feels weird to give compliments, and I'm not sure if I'll embarrass someone by giving one.

Chantel: How do you feel when someone gives you a compliment?

Riley: It makes me feel like the person appreciates me and notices me. It makes me feel happy.

Andrew: That's exactly how most people feel when you compliment them. Another good thing about giving compliments is that they stay with a person long after you give them.

Chantel: Just the other day, I saw an older woman shopping alone at the mall. She was wearing a beautiful blue jacket. I told her she looked pretty in her royal blue jacket and matching scarf. Her face brightened, and she told me she didn't get many compliments lately, maybe it was because she'd grown older and a lot of people don't notice people her age. I may never see her again, but we had a lovely conversation. She told me what I said made her day special.

Andrew: I think giving a compliment that's specific like that means more than a general one; in this case, Mom mentioned the woman's royal blue jacket and matching scarf. That means more than simply saying, "I like your outfit." It shows you notice someone in a special way.

Riley: I see what you're saying. I like the idea of giving compliments, but kids my age sometimes feel a little uncomfortable saying stuff like that. For example, sometimes I like the poems we're studying in English, but I think if I tell my teacher that after class, some kids might call me a "kiss up."

Chantel (smiling): I must have been the world's biggest "kiss-up" because I once told my high school English teacher, in private, so the other kids wouldn't hear, that I loved studying "Romeo and Juliet" and wanted to read more of Shakespeare's plays on my own. My teacher loaned me a book of Shakespeare's plays, and I read a few of them with a friend, each of us taking different parts. I think that teacher is one reason I became an English teacher.

Riley: I can see how giving your teacher that one compliment influenced you to become a teacher. If you hadn't given her the compliment about what she taught you, she wouldn't have loaned you the book, and who knows what job you'd have now.

Chantel: Yes, compliments can change people's lives in ways you can't imagine when you're giving them one. They can even change yours for the better like that compliment did mine.

Riley: You two make giving compliments sound so interesting, I'm going to try to give more of them. I can start with telling my teacher, in private, like you did, how much I like the poems we're studying.

Andrew: Are there any family members you'd like to compliment?

Riley: The twins get on my nerves when they tease me, but maybe if I give them a compliment about how great they are on the baseball field they'll treat me a little kinder.

Andrew: Sure, that may happen, but you know the main reason you give compliments is to make people feel good about themselves.

Riley: Just kidding, Dad, but I can use all the help I can get with those two guys, and if a compliment helps, I'm all for it.

Andrew and Chantel smile because they know that when Riley's on to something to make her life run more smoothly, and nothing will stop her from trying it.

Riley: I'm thinking I can also gave Gran a compliment the next time I see her. She's always willing to help me with math homework and tells me a lot of interesting stories about growing up in the Sixties. I can tell her how much I appreciate her, without getting too mushy, of course.

Chantel: That would mean a lot to her. While we're at it, I want to say we're proud having you for our daughter. You're kind and caring, and that means a lot in a sometimes cold, impersonal world.

Andrew: I second that.

Riley: You two are pretty special yourselves. See, I did it, and it was easy.

58. Stress the Importance of an Apology

Josh is ten and in the fifth grade at a city elementary school. His father Eli, a widower, is raising him with occasional help from his mother Marsha. Both father and grandmother are doing their best to teach Josh to be a kind, caring young man. Today, instead of greeting his grandmother pleasantly when he walked in the door, he raced straight to his room.

After a few minutes, Marsha knocked on his door. "No hello for Bubbe today?"

Josh slowly opens his door. "Sorry, Bubbe, I'm not having a good day."

Marsha sits on the edge of his bed. "Want to talk about it? I'm a good listener."

"Ms. Warner gave me and a couple other kids detention because we wouldn't stop talking when she was explaining some boring grammar."

His grandmother paused for a minute. "She was only doing her job, and you and your buddies chose to give her trouble. So, did you apologize after class?"

Jake grimaces. "I knew you'd take her side."

"You know I'm taking the right side. When you're right, I take your side."

"I didn't apologize because I didn't think we deserved detention for messing around in class. It's not like we were talking that much. I didn't even think she could hear us."

They both look up and see Eli, Josh's dad in the doorway. "I always walk in at the right time," Eli said with a smile. "I heard the last part, Josh. So, do you want to reconsider apologizing to Ms. Warner?"

"I guess I'll have to if I don't want her to bug me the rest of the year."

Marsha raised her eyebrow. "I don't think you want to apologize for that reason, Josh."

Josh sighed. "I know. I know. I do it because it's the right thing to do."

Eli nodded. "Mom and I always taught you that an apology has to come from the heart. You do it as a sign of kindness, to show you want to make up for what you said or did and make things right."

"Okay, I'll talk to Ms. Warner tomorrow and tell her I'm sorry. I'll try to get the other guys to go with me."

"I hope they do," Eli said, "but you'll probably feel better if you apologize, with or without them."

"I get it Dad. I'll tell her tomorrow at lunch. I shouldn't have messed around in her class, and she deserves an apology."

The next day Josh rushes in the door. "Bubbe, guess what? I apologized to Ms. Warner, and she said to forget detention this time, but if it happens again, I'll get double."

His grandmother smiled. "That sounds fair to me. Did the other kids apologize too?"

"It wasn't easy to convince them, but I told them we should because the teacher was only doing her job even though that stuff she was teaching us almost put us to sleep. They went with me, and after we said we were sorry, she said, 'You're forgiven,' but not before she told us what would happen if we interrupted her class again."

When Eli got home from work carrying containers of take-out cashew shrimp and chicken, Josh's favorite dinner, Josh told him about what happened at school.

"I'm glad you apologized. It's always good to make things right, and the best way is to offer a sincere apology."

"It wasn't as hard as I thought it would be. I guess the best way to apologize is to look at the person you're apologizing to and say, 'I'm sorry. I'll try my best not to do it again.'"

"You can say it short and sweet as you did, and it works just as well as giving a big speech," his grandmother said.

"Giving an apology shows you're a kind person, and that's an important virtue to have in this often-uncaring world," Eli said.

"I'll remember that," Josh said, and they all dug in to their Chinese feast.

59. Promote Forgiveness

Sydney, age fourteen, attends a rural high school. Her good friend Meredith spread gossip about her, saying she was trying to steal a mutual friend's boyfriend, which was totally false. Sydney's Mom and Dad, Dawn and Scott, can tell how upset she is because it's the weekend and Sydney doesn't want to go out with her friends. She told her mother she feels betrayed by her best friend because she spread rumors about her, and now a couple of her other friends won't talk to her.

After Sydney and the rest of the family have dinner, her parents ask her to sit with them and talk about what's bothering her:

Sydney (starting to cry): There's not much to say other than what I told you about Meredith. As you know, we've been friends since grade school, and nothing like this has ever happened before. I don't know why she said those things about me.

Dawn: Have you tried talking to her about it?

Sydney: She won't talk to me. I think she's embarrassed about what she did. One of my other friends said she's jealous because I made cheerleading and she didn't. I didn't act that way when she got a good part in the play. Why is she making such a big deal about it?

Scott: First, try to get her to talk with you about it. Tell her using "I-messages" how much what she did hurt you, especially since you've been friends for so long. You could say something like this: "I felt very hurt when you said I was trying to steal Jen's boyfriend. I'm upset some of the other girls won't talk to me because they think what you said is true."

Sydney: I'm so angry at her for what she did. I don't know if I can be calm enough to tell her how I feel.

Dawn: First, stop for a minute, and take a deep breath. Try using assertive language with her. You could say something like this if she's willing to listen: "I need you to tell the people you spread rumors to about me that none of it is true and you didn't mean to say these things." If you do that, it may not patch up your friendship, but at least you'll have the satisfaction of trying to make things right.

Sydney: I may be able to talk to her if she listens, and it would be great if she'd take back what she said, even though it may be too late to undo the damage.

Scott: Here comes the hard part. If you say these things in your own words, it would help if you could take the next step and forgive her.

Sydney (frowning): After my good friend spread lies about me and hurt my friendship with other girls? No way.

Scott: Forgiving her will help you, Sydney. She was definitely wrong to do what she did. If she agrees to try to correct that wrong, and you forgive her, it will make you feel better too. Would you be willing to take the first step and talk to her about what she did? Forgiveness is a form of showing kindness, especially when other people hurt us and we can't stop thinking about it.

Sydney: I guess so, but I don't like doing it.

Dawn: Let us know what happens.

The next day after dinner, Sydney tells her parents what happened when she talked to Meredith.

Dawn: How did it work out?

Sydney: I told her we needed to talk and she agreed. I guess what she did was starting to bother her too. She listened while I told her how spreading those rumors made me feel, and she actually apologized. She said she thought I was getting conceited because I made the cheerleading squad, which isn't true, by the way. I was happy I made it, but surprised too. She promised she'd tell all the kids she told about my stealing Jen's boyfriend that she made it up because she was annoyed by me.

Scott: That sounds like a happy ending. Did you say anything else to her?

Sydney: If you mean did I forgive her, yes. It wasn't easy, but I took a deep breath and said I was sad about what she did, but I wanted to forgive her because it doesn't help to stay angry and keep it inside.

Dawn: What did she say to that?

Sydney: She was so happy she hugged me and said she still wanted to be friends. I told her that might take a while, and we'd see how things go. I do feel better I forgave her. At least now, we're not enemies and can talk to one another.

Scott: Forgiveness always helps both people feel better. Keep us posted on how things go.

Sydney: Thanks, for listening, Mom and Dad. I feel a lot better now that I talked to Meredith and forgave her.

Chapter Eight

Impart Courtesy

THINK ABOUT THIS

Imparting courtesy in words and action is a form of kindness that will help your children show their generosity to others and will pay off in big dividends for them because people love being around those who demonstrate courtesy. It's especially important for children to treat family members with courtesy by being considerate of their feelings and time. Everyone knows that sometimes kids forget about showing courtesy to their parents and expect them to put their own their needs first, by making demands such a chauffeuring them around at a moment's notice or spending money they don't have for sports, electronic, or musical equipment.

Another aspect of courtesy comes in the form of simple words you'll want your child to use freely and often. Words like "please," "thank you," and "excuse me" often take second place to making a demand, saying "no problem," instead of "you're welcome," and not excusing oneself when coughing, burping, or bumping into someone. Courtesy also manifests itself in simple behavioral gestures such as offering a seat on the bus to an older person, a person with a disability, or a pregnant woman.

Showing restraint is another form of courtesy that a child can practice often. It's hard, especially for children, not to interrupt when others are speaking. However, it's important for children to know they shouldn't always expect instant attention at home or in school. Children also need to respect the privacy of other people in their homes by knocking on closed doors and not eavesdropping on private conversations.

Kids will thank you for teaching them table manners, especially if they're invited to eat at a friend's house. Courtesy also means going the extra mile to help someone whether they're having a problem or need a little assistance.

One of the most important aspects of showing courtesy occurs when a child shows sensitivity to different races and ethnic groups and learns to appreciate differences in people.

Children also need practice in showing concern for those with physical and emotional disabilities. Lastly, it's helpful for kids to show courtesy to people in small ways every day. Courtesy makes a big difference in children's present and future lives as most people prefer associating with someone who shows good manners in words and deeds.

MODEL A CONVERSATION: IMPART COURTESY

60. Help Your Child Honor Family Members with Courtesy

Tristan, a seventh-grade student in a city magnet school for the performing arts, is a highly creative young musician who loves to spend time at his friend Ben's house playing the keyboard and writing music. Sometimes when his parents are tired and don't feel like driving him to see Ben, he complains that it's boring when Ben comes to his house as Ben has all the best musical instruments and accessories, and it's more fun to go there.

How can you as a parent respond when you want to give your children all the advantages to nurture their talents but you have your own life too and it's not always possible to accommodate them with rides to other kids' houses or expensive equipment they say they need to enhance these interests.

In this case, Tristan's mother Shannon tells him it would be hard to drive him to his friend's house tonight because she's exhausted from cleaning the house and still has to prepare her lesson plan for school the next day. Padraic, his dad, is completing his monthly report for work and would also find it hard to drive him. Tristan, a highly emotional youngster, becomes visibly upset when his parents give him the option of inviting Ben to their house or driving him there another time.

He corners his mom after dinner. "I don't see why you can't drive me to Ben's now. He only lives a few blocks away,"

Shannon looks up from clearing the table. "It's not a good time. I'm busy with schoolwork, and Dad's finishing up with his report. How about if we make it tomorrow night? We'll have more time then."

Tristan raises his voice. "You two never have time to help me. This is really important. We're working on some new songs for the school show."

Padraic tries to remain calm, but his patience wears thin. "Why can't Ben come here for once? We'll take you when we can, but tonight isn't a good time for Mom or me."

Tristan crosses his arms. "He has all the good stuff at his house. Our equipment doesn't sound good when we record. I need to go there tonight or we'll bomb at the show."

Shannon puts her hand on Tristan's shoulder, and he shakes it away. "Do you remember when I asked you to clean your room last week and you said you had a lot of homework and couldn't do it until the following weekend?"

"What does that have to do with driving me to Ben's?"

Shannon continues speaking in a calm voice. "Dad and I understood that because you had to finish your homework, you couldn't get to it right away, and we cut you some slack."

"I know, but that was important," he says in a whiney voice.

Padraic moves in closer to Tristan. "That's exactly the point. It was important to you that you needed the time to do your homework, just as it's important to Mom and me that you understand why we want you to wait to drive you to Ben's. If what we'd wanted you to do, in this case, cleaning your room, couldn't wait and was urgent, we would have expected you to act sooner, but we made the judgment that it could wait, even though I did see a few bugs crawling around your bed."

"You're making that up," Tristan says.

Dad raises his right hand. "I'm not kidding. There were big, orange, fuzzy bugs. Ask Mom."

Tristan rolls his eyes. "Okay. I get it. I guess I have no choice. I'll call Ben and ask him to come here tonight."

Shannon smiles. "Thanks for understanding. Just so you know, when someone has to say *no* to something you really want to do, it's an act of courtesy to accept it, even though you may not always agree with it."

TRY THIS: ACTIVITIES TO HELP IMPART COURTESY, AGES 6–9

61. Promote the Use of Courteous Words

Taryn attends second grade at a small religious school. Her parents, Dustin and Amanda, model courteous expressions in all their conversations with her and her brother Rob. Taryn's teacher was so impressed with her politeness that she called her parents to tell them how much she enjoyed having her in class. The principal invited her to have lunch with him and her teacher in his office, and he gave her an award for practicing courtesy and being a good example to her classmates.

Dustin and Amanda make it a point to say *please* and *thank you* when asking for or receiving something. They always say *you're welcome* after someone thanks them. Taryn asked her mom if it would be alright to say *no problem* instead of you're welcome.

"I know a lot of kids use that expression these days, but it's not the same as saying, 'You're welcome,'" Amanda said.

"I agree with Mom. It doesn't carry the same weight," Dustin added. "Some kids forget to say *please* and *thank-you.*"

"I say it because I'm used to hearing it at home, but sometimes I feel a little strange saying it all the time," Taryn said.

Amanda nodded. "Maybe it will rub off on some of the other kids. I'm sure a lot of them hear it at home, but maybe they forget to say what I call 'magic words.'"

"Another thing that would help you show courtesy is talking to your friends' parents. You can say 'hello' when you come in and 'good-by' when you leave. A lot of times parents would like to get to know their children's friends better, and using polite language helps start a good conversation."

Taryn nodded. "Last week I asked a friend's parent how she was doing. She let me know how much she enjoys helping out at our scout group and told me about the fun she had camping when she was in scouts. Then she asked me how I liked scouts. It was fun talking to Olivia's mom."

"If you hadn't asked how she was doing, you wouldn't have gotten to know her," Dustin said. "A few courteous words can go a long way in making friends of all ages."

"When Olivia was here last weekend, she thanked us for having her over and said she loved the tacos I made," Amanda said. "That made me feel appreciated."

"Is there anything else you can do to help spread kindness with courteous words?" Taryn's mom asked.

"I can remember to thank my friends' parents for having me over and say I liked the food they made, like my friend did when she came here."

"You know a lot about using courteous language. No wonder you got the courtesy award and got to have lunch with the principal," her dad said.

Taryn smiled. "It was tuna salad, not my favorite, but I said 'thanks' anyway. The chocolate cake was good, so I really thanked him for that."

62. Encourage Courteous Behavior

Chase, a fourth grader in a progressive elementary school, learns character development, which the school includes as part of every English class. His parents take an active part in his education and make it a point to discuss what he's learning in all his subjects. They have a copy of the syllabus, so they keep up with the daily curriculum. They like the fact that students learn about the value of practicing virtues and read books and study quotes associated with practicing positive qualities like courtesy in their own lives.

Both parents practice Mindfulness and see courteous behavior as an extension of showing kindness, an important Mindfulness trait. Today, Chase's parents, Monique and Shane, ask him to describe what he's learning in school about the importance of courteous behavior. Here's what they said:

Chase: Since kids have been acting more courteous, everybody seems to be getting along better at school. We're learning different ways of being courteous in what we say and do, and we practice it every day in every class. Kids are arguing less in the lunchroom and at recess. I think it's a good thing.

Monique: How can you show courtesy in and out of school?

Chase: For one thing, I can hold the door open for somebody. We all do this for each other at school. It's a nice thing to do for another person. If I'm on the bus going into town with you and it's crowded, I can offer my seat to an older person, someone who has a health problem, or to a woman who's expecting a baby.

Shane: I wish we had that class when I was in school. Everyone would have gotten along better because they would have treated each other with kindness and courtesy.

Chase: Another thing I can do if I accidently bump into somebody is say "excuse me." Before we took this class, kids would push and shove on their way to their lockers or when they raced to the lunch line. That doesn't happen much anymore. Most of the time, they wait their turn. I'm not saying it's perfect, but we're learning to treat each other better.

Monique: I'm impressed with how much this character development class is helping kids get along in your school.

Chase: It really seems to be working. More kids are going out of their way to help each other. When I was having trouble with math, my friend Cara offered to help me with the homework problems at lunch. That made me think of helping Diego, another kid in our class who has trouble speaking and writing English. Even though he takes an English as a Second Language class, it helps when someone his own age practices with him.

Shane: It looks like when one person does a good deed it has a ripple effect and helps someone else practice one. Are there any other tips for being courteous you've learned that you hadn't thought of before?

Chase: Here's one I hadn't thought of. We had a discussion about listening and not interrupting when someone talks to us. It's easy to interrupt because we always think what we have to say is the most important thing and we want to get it in fast. So now I'm trying harder to wait until the other person stops talking before I say what I want to.

Monique: I know what you mean. I interrupt Dad sometimes, and some-times if I'm upset about something you say, I interrupt you. I'm going to try to be more conscious of that.

Shane (smiling): I do it a lot too. I'm going to make an effort to cut down on interrupting, unless you or Mom don't let me get a word in, and I absolutely have to interrupt.

Chase: The teacher said all these ways of showing courtesy are ways to be kind to people. I like the class because kids are nicer now and it helps us relax more.

63. Teach Your Child to Show Restraint

Tiana, a third grader in a gifted program, is talking with her parents, Terrell and Tonya, about courtesy. They model courteous words and behavior in hopes that she and her brother Caleb, a middle school student, will want to practice it with family and friends. It must be paying off since Tiana received the citizenship award at a recent school assembly where teachers and admin-istrators honored students their peers thought were the best example of kind-ness ambassadors.

Today, Tiana's Mom and Dad are talking to her about the meaning of the word *restraint* as it applies to showing courteous behavior, which they've told their children is a form of kindness.

"Restraint is a form of respect for others," Tonya tells her daughter when they're sitting in the family room relaxing after dinner. "What does it mean to you?"

"I think it means being in control and not blurting out something whenev-er you feel like it," Tiana answers.

"That's a big part of it. It also happens when you don't interrupt people and when you don't expect instant attention."

Tiana smiles. "You mean like Caleb did when he kept bugging you about going to that concert with his friends until you gave in and said 'okay'?"

"Now, don't bring your brother into this when he's not here to defend himself," Terrell says gently.

"Sometimes it's hard not to bug you two when something's on my mind. I just want to get it out there and get your answer."

Tonya nods. "I can certainly understand that but practicing restraint and not expecting instant answers makes everyone feel more relaxed and peace-ful."

"Yes, mom. I know how grumpy you two get when one of us keeps bugging you and doesn't stop."

Tonya waits a moment and then asks: "What about family privacy? How does that figure in showing courtesy through restraint?"

Tiana strikes a pose like "The Thinker," and her parents smile. "It probably means knocking before you barge into someone's room, like I did when Caleb was talking on his cell phone sweet-talking a girl on in his class, trying to sound cool."

"Good example," her dad says. "What happened when you didn't knock?"

Tiana frowns. "He threw his big, smelly sneaker at me, but he missed, ha-ha."

"Well, that wasn't what I'd call a restrained response either. But it is important to give everyone their privacy, just like it's important to you that we give you yours."

"I just thought of another example of restraint," Tiana says. "It's not good to listen in on private conversations, like if you and Dad are having an argument or Mom and Grandma are talking about personal stuff like someone in the family having money problems."

"Excellent example," Tonya says. "As in all the other instances, all you have to do is think of how you'd like people to treat you, and treat them the same way."

"What about telling friends or family members what other kids tell you in confidence?" Tiana's dad asks. "Is it ever a good idea to do that?"

Tiana stops and thinks for a minute. "I'd say the only time is when you think someone will get hurt if you don't tell."

"Can you think of any examples?"

"Here's one. My friend told me a couple of mean girls were pushing her at the bus stop, and she didn't know what to do to make them stop."

"What did you tell her?" Tonya asks.

"I said she should tell the teacher, but she was afraid and she wouldn't, so I talked to the teacher after school, and she talked to the girls. They don't bother my friend anymore."

"How did it work out with you and your friend?"

"She was upset I told the teacher because she made me promise I wouldn't tell anyone, but in this case, I felt I had to or she might get hurt. Later, she said she understood and that she was glad I did."

"So, you're saying if someone will get hurt if you don't tell what they told you in private, it's okay to do just that?" her dad asks.

"In most cases, I wouldn't tell what someone says to me in private, but in some cases like this one, it's important to tell."

Tonya hugs her daughter. "This was a great conversation about showing restraint. How do you think it would go over with your brother?"

Tiana laughs. "I don't know if he'd want to sit still for this long."

"Since you sat still and we had this good discussion, I think it's time to bring out some of that Halloween candy you've been hoarding," Tonya says.

"I'm all for that," Tiana says.

Tiana goes to the pantry and pulls out a gigantic sack of candy and they all pick their favorites.

TRY THIS: ACTIVITIES TO HELP IMPART COURTESY, AGES 10–14

64. Foster Courtesy at the Table

Brandon, a sixth-grade middle-school student, was adopted by his dad Marcus, a single parent, three years ago. He's lived in a series of foster homes and has never experienced a sense of stability and permanence until now. Marcus is on a campaign to teach Brandon the social graces, including courtesy at the table.

Many of the homes he's lived in didn't stress this type of courtesy as the parents had their hands full because a few of them had taken in a few other kids and also had kids of their own.

Marcus believes if his son knows how to show courtesy in all its aspects he'll have an easier time adjusting to his new school and to his future endeavors in high school, college, and on the job.

Brandon and his dad are eating at Brandon's favorite restaurant that also features video games for kids. Marcus figures this is a good time to strike up a conversation in a relaxed setting about how to conduct oneself while eating at home or in a restaurant.

Brandon: Thanks for bringing me here. I love this place.

Marcus: You're welcome. After we eat, we'll play a few games and then we'll shoot some baskets at the park if we're not too tired by then. While we're waiting for our dinners to come out, I was thinking we could talk about something that interests me a lot, how courtesy is important in our lives.

Brandon (nodding): We've been talking about it in homeroom guidance a lot. The teacher says if we treat each other with kindness we'll all get along better. She says courtesy is an important form of kindness, one we can easily practice. I think she's right because in my last school all the kids did was fight and curse at one another. A lot of it was because they didn't treat each other with courtesy. If you said "please" or "thank you," kids would make fun of you and call you names, so no one bothered.

Marcus: I'm glad you're discussing it at school. It should give you a better experience this year. Can you think of any ways people can show courtesy when they're eating?

Brandon: That's easy. Don't talk or chew food with your mouth open. That would be sickening. There's this kid at school who does it, and it makes me not want to eat my lunch. I have to admit that I chew with my mouth open once in a while when I'm excited to say something, but I try not to because I know how disgusting it looks.

Marcus: I'm glad to hear that, especially today when I'm going to eat my favorite cheesesteak sandwich. It wouldn't be pretty seeing your tonsils or your uvula.

Brandon (laughing): You're right about that. Even if I don't know what an uvula is, I'm guessing it must be something gross, just by the sound of it. Here's another thing to remember while you're eating: I think it also helps if you offer other people food first if it's served family style. If there are older people like your parents, it's good to offer them food first.

Marcus: I figured you'd know that one since most of the families you've lived with have had a few foster kids living with them at one time.

Brandon (smiling): That's why I'm glad to be an only child now. Here's another important thing we talked about in health class: If you have to cough or sneeze, be sure to block it with the inside of your elbow so the cough and sneeze goop doesn't fly all over and make other people sick. Also, don't forget to say, "Excuse me."

Marcus (patting him on the back): I like your powers of description, son, especially before eating my dinner.

Brandon: Here's an idea, linked in with what you said: Never bring up sickening subjects because it might ruin peoples' appetites. Also, only talk about pleasant topics to make people feel happy and to aid digestion.

Marcus (smiling): Yes, but talking about the sickening ones might help them lose weight because they won't want to eat as much. (The server brings Brandon's cheesesteak and the pizza Marcus ordered.)

Brandon: Thanks, Dad. This is fun, even if my dinner talk wasn't the best.

Marcus: Let's dig in. Your dinner talk didn't bother me a bit. Just don't talk about eating with an open mouth or coughing and sneezing until we finish.

Brandon: That's a deal, but is it okay if I ask you what an uvula is?

65. Endorse Going the Extra Mile to Help Others

Hannah, age 11, belongs to her church youth group. As part of a Courtesy Project, members are looking at big and small things they can do to help others by openly showing kindness and courtesy to others. The youth group leader asked the children to brainstorm with older relatives to help them come up with ideas for projects. The students will choose the ones that most appeal to them and then implement them.

Hannah walked to her grandmother Shirley's house to discuss ideas for her project. Her grandmother enjoys volunteering in her spare time by reading to the blind. She told Hannah that the more she helps people, the more she'll help herself. Here is what they said at their meeting:

Shirley: I've been thinking about your project since you mentioned it on the phone. I'm excited to hear your ideas.

Hannah: I have a few, Grandmom. We're allowed to do more than one project, so we're not locked into one idea.

Shirley: Sounds good. One can be a long-term project and you can do a couple of one-time things. Let me hear your thoughts.

Hannah: A few friends and I were thinking of visiting some people once a week who live in an assisted living home near our school. We could bring them small gifts, like those puzzle and word find books you get at the dollar store. Some of the people who live there don't get many visitors, so we could stay and talk to them a while about things that interest them.

Shirley: I'm sure they'd enjoy talking with you and your friends. The puzzle books would give them something to occupy their time when they get tired of watching TV. Many of the residents can't get out much because of health issues, so they'll be happy to see your happy faces.

Hannah: We were also thinking of having a sing-a-long. We could ask them what songs they'd like to sing and make copies of the words so we could all sing them together.

Shirley: That would make it even more special.

Hannah: I also thought of a couple of projects we could do at school that wouldn't take up as much time as our big one does. One would be to give a student that most others kids ignore a compliment about something she does well, like write poetry or style her hair.

Shirley: That would make someone happy. As you know, being kind and courteous always makes people smile.

Hannah: Our last idea goes along with that. We want to give other kids the chance to show kindness and courtesy, so we could make posters about small acts of kindness that kids could easily do for one another. We could put the posters up in the hallways.

Shirley: I like that idea. Have you thought of any ideas to write on the posters?

Hannah: We could use the one I mentioned and say, "Say something positive to someone about something they do well."

Shirley: Yes, that would be a good one to do and not too hard to carry out. Here are some others: visit a lonely person, and cheer her up in your own special way; offer a friend help with schoolwork he doesn't understand; and walk an older person's dog to give her a break.

Hannah: Good ideas, Grandmom. Was that last one a hint to me?

Shirley: As a matter of fact, it was. Bentley, come out here, boy. Hannah wants to take you for a walk.

Bentley, a supersized, cuddly Australian Shepherd, comes running out and leaps playfully in the air until Hannah puts on his leash and takes him outside.

Shirley (calling from the screen door): See you in a bit. I love your project ideas, and thanks for giving me a break with Bentley.

66. Prompt Your Child to Show Courtesy to Those Who Are Different Than Them

Corey, a fourth-grader in a city school, attends special education classes because of his history of attention deficit disorder. He's made great progress academically and socially and will soon be mainstreamed into a regular class. During homeroom period, students are learning about cultural diversity and extending courtesy to students who differ racially and/or ethnically from them. For homework, the teacher asked parents to discuss with their children ways of showing courtesy to those who are different from them.

Julia and Keith have a strong interest in this topic because they are a mixed-race couple; Julia is Caucasian and Keith is African-American. At a young age, Corey sometimes found himself questioned by curious kids about what race he was. His parents said to say he was half white and half African American, but that he should not respond to any questions or remarks that were rude or discourteous.

Corey and his parents were excited about the assignment because they believe in the importance of showing respect to various races and ethnic groups and wanted to further explore these ideas in their own family so Corey could share these ideas with his classmates.

Corey started off the conversation by saying his teacher used the term *ethnic group*. What was the difference between race and ethnic group, he wondered.

"That's easy," Keith said. "Race is your color. You're a combination of two races, while some people are only one race, such as African American, Caucasian, Hispanic or Latino, Asian, Native American, Middle Eastern, North African, and Native Hawaiian. Your ethnic groups are American, German, and Italian on your mom's side, and Jamaican on my side. Ethnic group includes your roots, where your ancestors came from. A person can have one race, in your case, a mixed race, but can belong to various ethnic groups."

"Thanks for explaining that. I guess one thing we can do to show courtesy to people of different races and ethnic groups is to try to learn something about them, how they're the same as us and how they're different from us. I'm thinking a good way to do that is to have some friends who are different from us. We could sit with them at lunch, play with them at recess, and invite them to our homes. It's more interesting to have different types of friends than all the same kind. It would be boring if they were all the same."

"That's a good way to look at it," Julia said. "Your dad and I have a wide variety of friends from different races and nationalities. We all learn from one another and appreciate our similarities and differences, and that makes it more fun than if we had friends who were all the same."

Corey stopped to think for a moment. "I'm thinking another thing we can all do is speak out if we hear someone saying something that isn't kind to a person who's another race or nationality. We can say, 'I don't want to hear that.' If a person keeps saying mean things, we can tell a teacher or another adult."

Keith patted his son's shoulder. "I'm proud of you for that, son. It's important when you see any kind of injustice to speak out. You don't have to say a lot. Just be sure they get your message that you won't accept any comments like that."

"If you hear anyone talking in a bad way about someone who's different in race or nationality, it's good to tell them you don't like it and don't want to be a part of it," Corey said. "The other day in school we got a new student who's from a different country. A kid in our class made fun of him because he looked scared and talked with an accent. He called the student racist names and used bad words to describe him."

Julia frowned. "What did the new student say to the boy who bullied him?"

"He just looked at him and said he didn't want any trouble and he'd like to be friends," Corey said. "The other kid looked surprised and said he was sorry, but it took him a couple days to apologize."

"Did you and your friends say anything to the boy who said those things?"

"We told him we didn't like what he said and to never say it again or we wouldn't hang out with him. I think he got the message."

"It's a form of showing others courtesy and kindness if we don't accept talk like that about those who are different from us, and that's exactly what you and your friends did," Keith said. "We can honor and appreciate differences in people in many different ways, and if we show them courtesy in the ways we talked about, that's good progress."

"I think you'll have more than enough to talk about in your class tomorrow," Julia said.

"Thanks to you two."

"You did most of the work," Keith said.

67. Advocate Courtesy to the Disabled

Last weekend, Makayla, age thirteen, and her mother Jessica were out shopping for clothes at the mall. They saw a woman sitting on a bench with a service dog at her feet. Makayla, who loves dogs, moved toward the service dog to pet it. The lady told her to please not pet the dog because it was on duty working, and Makayla quickly moved away.

As they walked through the mall, Makayla's mom told her you shouldn't pet a service dog as they are on duty helping someone who has a disability and it could distract the dog from helping the person. This led to a conversation between them later that day about showing courtesy to those with physical and emotional disabilities:

Makayla: When I started to pet that service dog, and the lady told me not to because it was on duty, I started to think more about the problems people with disabilities have and how we can be more courteous to them. We were talking about it in health class the other day because there's a boy in a wheelchair in our class. The teacher asked him to talk to the class about things that are and are not helpful to him.

Jessica: Yes, it's definitely important to treat disabled people with the same courtesy we'd want others to show us. What did your classmate tell the class about how to treat people in a wheelchair?

Makayla: For one thing, he said it's best not to look down at him in his wheelchair like he's a little kid. It's best to sit down so you're at eye level, and if you're standing, just act natural. People with disabilities want to be treated like everyone else. That's the polite thing to do.

Jessica: It's always good to treat people with disabilities, either physical or emotional, with respect. If you talk to them too loudly or slowly, it makes them feel belittled.

Makayla: I've seen people do that, and I can understand why it might hurt disabled people. Another thing I've seen kids do is label people with physical or mental disabilities. One of my classmates used the word *retarded* to describe a person from a Special Ed class. I don't think he was trying to insult him, but he didn't know what to say.

Jessica: That proves that it's not good to label people or to talk about them. It's best to treat everyone with the same courtesy and not use labels, which can be hurtful and insulting.

Makayla: I told my classmate how I felt about the word he used, and he said he honestly didn't know he'd said something wrong, and that he wouldn't do it again. He thanked me for letting him know.

Jessica: That's why it's good to speak out if you see someone saying something that may hurt someone's feelings or promote misunderstanding about a disability.

Makayla: Here's something I'm wondering about: I offered to help an older lady in the grocery story wheel her shopping cart. She was limping, and it looked like it was hard for her to push the cart, so I grabbed it and started wheeling it for her. The lady took the cart from me and told me she was okay with pushing it herself. She smiled and thanked me for my help, but said she didn't really need it.

Jessica: You bring up something important when dealing with disabled people. It's always good to ask first if they want help, and then take it from there. Some people would like your help, but others would rather do things for themselves. It's always polite to ask first and give them the choice. Otherwise, you may make them feel helpless and childlike, something like what the boy in your class was saying when he spoke about how not to talk to people in wheelchairs.

Makayla: I didn't think of that when I tried to help the lady in the store, but I can understand it. I'm glad we talked about this. I'm thinking that there are a lot of things we can do to help people with disabilities and it's not that hard.

Jessica: The bottom line is to treat them with courtesy and respect. With that in mind, you can't go wrong.

68. Urge Your Child to Practice Courtesy Every Day in Small Ways

Drew, a twelve-year-old, is working with a group in his middle school social studies class on a courtesy project. The groups are preparing booklets to distribute to the school about how they can show courtesy every day in small ways. They've brainstormed some ideas that Drew wants to discuss with his mother Brandy, a single parent.

Per the teacher's instructions, all the students are running their ideas by their parents to see if they can expand upon their suggestions. The teacher has found that parental involvement enhances learning and strengthens the home and school connection. Many of the parents, including Brandy, have taken a university-based Mindfulness class at the school and encourage their children to practice kindness and courtesy daily.

Drew and Brandy like the idea of showing courtesy in small ways every day because it doesn't take a lot of effort, and the rewards are gratifying for both the giver and receiver of courteous acts. Here is what they talk about in their brainstorming session:

Drew: Our group thought of some ideas to show courtesy in small ways. If you think of anything else, let me know because our teacher wants parents to be part of this.

Brandy: We've been doing this on our own for a long time, so I'm sure we'll come up with some interesting ideas your group can use.

Drew: For starters, I was thinking that saying one polite thing to a family member every day would be a good idea. Today I can thank you for helping me with this project.

Brandy: You're welcome. I like helping with your projects.

Drew: Our group thought it would be good to ask people who look like they're having a hard time doing something, like carrying packages, if they need help. It's important to ask politely if they need our help and not be pushy.

Brandy: Yes, always ask first, and help them if they accept your offer.

Drew: We also thought about asking someone who looks upset if we could help them.

Brandy: I want to add that being specific is good in these cases. You could say, "What can I do to help you?" For example, if someone forgot his lunch money, you could offer to share your lunch or offer to lend him money. If someone has trouble with science and it's your best subject, you could say, "We can study for the test together, if you want." If you mention a specific way you're willing to help, people will be more likely to accept your offer.

Drew (writing down ideas): I'm going to add that. Being specific is better than just asking if you can help without saying how.

Brandy: Another thing you could mention is spending a little time listening mindfully to someone who needs another person to hear how he feels. You don't have to say anything or give advice. Just be there for a few minutes.

Drew: Thanks for that one. One of my friends got a bad grade on his math test even though he studied hard. He needed someone to talk to. After I listened, he said he felt better and he came up with some ideas, like talking to our teacher about what he can do to understand the subject better so he can bring up his grade.

Brandy: That's an excellent example. Another thing you can add, and this doesn't take much effort, is to simply smile at someone who needs it. Do you remember after I took that Mindfulness class I told you how they taught us to be sensitive to other people's feelings and moods?

Drew: I remember. That's why I never ask you for favors when you look like you're upset about something or not in the best mood.

Brandy (laughing): You are a wise young man.

Drew: Thanks! The other day my teacher didn't feel well. She said she was coming down with a cold. We tried to cut her a little slack and didn't bug her about anything. The next day, she said she appreciated it. I guess it's important to be sensitive about people's moods and try to help them by showing kindness, or even by giving them a smile.

Brandy: It can make a big difference in someone's day, so keep smiling.

Drew: You're pretty smart, Mom. You know that?

Brandy: You've said two nice things in one day—you've exceeded your limit, but I'm not complaining.

Chapter Nine

Foster Respect

THINK ABOUT THIS

Fostering a sense of respect in our children for themselves and others will help them become caring, responsible people. As in all the other ways of living Mindfully, children learn by following your example. Modeling is the most important way to teach children respect and make it stay with them throughout their lives.

It's helpful to share ideas about fostering respect with other parents to get a sense of what they've done that's worked and to talk about what's worked for you. Insisting on respect for you and other family members is a good place to start. Schools can help reinforce the need for kids to show respect by making it a topic of discussion as part of the curriculum or in a character education class.

It's important for parents and schools to work together to promote respect in school and at home. Kids need to show their classmates respect in the classroom, lunchroom, and in the school yard. Lack of respect is the main cause of the bullying and harassment that many kids suffer today.

Since your children spend most of their time at school, you'll want to discuss the importance of showing respect to school staff, which includes teachers, administrators, and those who work in the school community in various capacities, such as custodians and cafeteria workers. It's equally important that students respect all people who are in charge of them, such as school bus drivers, police officers, and security guards in public places, such as malls.

One of the most important qualities parents can foster in their kids is self-respect, which means always measuring what they do against whether they can feel proud about it. If kids care about themselves, it follows they will treat everyone they meet with dignity and respect.

Parents who want to raise respectful kids will also advise their children to treat everyone with dignity, by showing this quality in everything they say and do. To be respectful, kids also need to have zero-tolerance for rudeness of any kind in talk or actions. Likewise, they should show respect to others by not being rude to them. Along the same lines, parents will want to stress the importance of their kids respecting other people's opinions, even if they don't agree with them.

Often, in these fast-paced times, people are less willing to show respect to their friends, neighbors, and family members. Parents can pave the way for a better world for all of us by modeling respect and insisting on respect from their children at all times.

MODEL A CONVERSATION: FOSTER RESPECT

69. Share Ideas About Respect

Two Moms, April and Kim, longtime friends from Zumba class, meet at a coffee shop to talk about their concerns regarding the lack of respect they've seen in their two kids, Ava, age twelve, and Grant, age ten. They want to see if they can come up with ideas to help their kids show them and their husbands greater respect. Here's the main part of their conversation:

> April: It's been difficult with Ava these past few months. She used to be easy to get along with, but now she constantly disrespects her dad and me by mouthing off and walking away when we try to talk to her. I know she's at "that age," but when will she get back to being her sweet self again?

> Kim: I know exactly what you're saying. Grant was the easiest of my three kids to raise, but now he's talking back, even cursing, and telling us in blunt terms what he thinks about us, and it isn't pretty.

> April: I know it's all part of growing up and breaking away, but it's hard to tolerate, especially if you take it to heart as I do. Sometimes I don't like my child, and then I dislike myself for thinking that. Once, in a burst of anger, I told Ava that. Then I really felt guilty.

> Kim: I understand the feeling perfectly. I almost dread when Grant walks in the door from school. He always has some choice words you wouldn't want to hear for me and his father, although I have to say, it's not quite as bad between him and his dad.

April: In my case, Ava's disrespectful with both my husband and me. When she does talk to us, she's usually surly and abrupt, unless she wants something from us. Up until recently she told us she hated us and can't stand being in the same room with us.

Kim: Grant's the same way. He doesn't want to be around us unless he needs us to drive him someplace or wants money. He argues about everything and protests until we give in and do what he wants.

April: I've stopped giving in. If Ava keeps pressing things by whining and complaining, I tune her out, no matter how loud she gets. I simply walk away. I talked to a friend who knows about Mindfulness and she told me to talk to her assertively, rather than passively or aggressively. I tell Ava that I don't want to hear it unless it's something positive, end of message. My friend said to say what I think politely, but make it brief and to the point. The more you talk, the more your child will see you as someone to tune out. From experience, I can say that's true.

Kim: You mentioned you don't pay attention when she starts pestering you about getting what she wants and you're becoming more assertive when you talk to her. The last time we talked, you hinted you saw some improvement because she stopped saying she hated you and couldn't wait to leave. That's progress.

April: I think it's starting to make a difference, but I'll wait and see how it goes. I think it takes time and constant reinforcement on our part. My husband and I are also trying to model more respectful behavior with one another. We used to argue a lot, especially about politics, but now we don't do that as much. I think it became more acceptable for her to treat us disrespectfully when she saw us treating each other that way.

Kim: You make a good point. Sometimes Bob and I say things to Grant and his sister in a harsh way without giving much thought to how it might affect them. I'm going to talk to Bob so we can start working on that.

April: Another thing we're trying not to do is treat Ava like a peer. We're her parents but sometimes we don't always act that way. A psychologist friend told me that our kids want and expect boundaries and they want us to be parents rather than friends to them. She also told us when our kids act disrespectful we should back off from them a little (after telling them disrespectful behavior is unacceptable). We should refrain from giving our kids positive or negative feedback and give them time to think about what they've said or how they acted. Hopefully, they'll eventually come around.

Kim: Eventually, but I hope that doesn't mean too long. I don't know how much more of this I can take. What your friend said makes sense. I'm going to try it too.

April: Geoff and I recently started trying these ideas, but we plan to use them consistently and on a steady basis in hopes we can bring Ava back on track. Obviously, we don't expect perfection; she's a teenager, after all.

Kim: And Grant's a pre-teen. We're trying to get him to respect other people's opinions even if he disagrees. He's listening a little better when we have differences, but he has a long way to go, and so do we in helping him give us respect.

April: It looks like we're both making steady but slow progress. Let's meet again in a couple weeks and compare notes. We'll try out all our ideas and see what works best. I think that in time we're going to make an impression on our kids.

Kim: I can't wait for that day to come. Now, let's drink our coffee and have a couple of these delicious scones.

TRY THIS: ACTIVITIES TO FOSTER RESPECT, AGES 6–9

70. Enlist the Help of Schools to Promote Respect

After a few parents made a request to the principal, third grade students in a city magnet school for gifted children meet in their character education session during social studies class to discuss ways to show respect to family members. This week, the teacher, Mr. Gonzales, who is trained in Mindfulness, talks with his class about granting respect to family members within the context of the Mindfulness techniques he's taught them. Students meet in groups to discuss ideas for showing respect to their immediate families and will present and discuss their thoughts with the entire class.

We'll tune in to one of the groups as they plan their presentation about ways of giving family members respect. Group members include: Jasmine, Maya, Luke, Raj, and Juan.

Mr. Gonzales starts off by saying that while many kids don't think about it, it's important to give their families the same respect they show their good friends. With friends, kids usually act polite, don't scream, complain, or demand things, while sometimes they may not give a second thought to treating family members disrespectfully. He asks the groups to come up with ways to promote respect for their parents and siblings.

Juan, who has four brothers of varying ages, says that for him, dealing with his brothers' changing moods and horseplay sometimes makes it hard to show respect. He gets along well with his parents, and they rarely have disagreements, but he and his brothers sometimes treat each other rudely and argue about the games and sports equipment they share. They also tease each other, which sometimes leads to fights that turn physical. Juan says he's going to make more of an effort to understand his brothers better when he gets upset with them by using the assertive talk tips Mr. Gonzales explained in class.

"I've tried assertive talk with my little sister, who can be hard to deal with sometimes, and it really works," says Maya. "If she starts bothering me, it usually means she wants me to spend time with her. She wants my attention right now and can't wait. Instead of telling her to go away, I tell her I need more time to finish my homework and then I'll play a game with her. I use the 'I-messages' Mr. Gonzales told us about instead of calling her a *brat* like I used to. It works much better."

Luke laughs. "You're right about that. When I'm patient with my little brother, he gives me more space and doesn't follow me around all the time. My friends call him *Luke's shadow* or *Luke's clone*. I'm trying to spend a little more time with him, and that makes him happy. It helps me relax more too because he isn't always bugging me and my friends."

"Assertive talk works when you're talking with parents too," Juan says. If I'm not being clear when I tell them what's bothering me, or I'm being what our teacher calls passive, or too pushy, my parents get annoyed with me. 'Say what you mean,' they tell me. 'We want to understand better, and when you act too meek or too pushy it doesn't help get your point across.' I've started using assertive talk and 'I-statements,' and we get along better.

"Here's an example: I wanted to go to my friend's house and needed a ride. Instead of bugging my parents about it, I said, 'Dad, I want to go to my friend's house to work on a school project. When would it be a good time for you to drive me?' Because I left it open and gave him a choice, he didn't complain, and he drove me when it was convenient for him. I also think it's important to say what you have to and not talk too much for people to get the message. When you talk too much, they tune you out."

Jasmine nods. "I know what you're saying, Juan. I think we can use what you and the other kids said when our group talks to the class. Another thing we can do to show respect to our parents is to avoid name-calling (that goes for brothers and sisters too) and talking back. Sometimes my brothers use bad language on each other. Certainly, if they did that with our parents, they'd be in big trouble. I have to admit that once in a while I get really upset and talk back to Mom. She's quick to put me in my place, and I know I deserve it. I'm going to make an effort not to talk back because it only makes things worse for me because she takes my phone away or I get grounded."

"I like all of your ideas and I think the class will too," Raj says. "I have another one. Timing is very important if you want to show respect to your parents by being considerate to them. Mr. Gonzalez talked about asking your parents whether it's a good time to talk now or would another time be better for them.

"Sometimes bringing up something at the right time can make a big difference if we want to discuss something with our parents or ask them for a favor. A lot of times they're busy and maybe not able to help us when we ask, so we have to be patient and wait. That's why it's wise to ask if it's a good time for them, especially if we're bringing up something that may be a hard subject like whether we can go to a friend's party or we need money for something."

The group presents all their ideas for showing respect to family members to the entire class, and Mr. Rodriguez gives them an *A*. The teacher tells the class to report back in two weeks and to inform their families about their reports to the class. They'll also report to the class about how all of their "show respect to family" ideas are working. They'll talk about what worked and didn't work and go back to their families with more ideas to try.

71. Discuss Treating Classmates with Consideration

Wyatt, age nine, came home from school, crying because one of the older students harassed him on the bus by dumping all the books out of his back-pack. His mother Erin told him to avoid the student and not to respond to him because he sounded like a bully. She said she'd call the principal the next day.

Meanwhile, she felt this was a good opportunity to discuss the importance of treating everyone with kindness and respect, especially since Wyatt had gotten angry at his friend Jim for calling him "stupid" and had torn up Jim's homework a couple weeks ago.

Here's how the conversation went:

Erin: I know how you must have felt when that boy threw your books around. That was a hurtful thing to do. I also know you felt bad about tearing up your friend's work when he called you a name. Both these things are examples of disrespect, just as it was also disrespectful that Jim called you a name.

Wyatt: I know they're all not good things to do, and I told Jim I was sorry.

Erin: I'm glad because that was the right thing to do. I don't know if the kid on the bus felt sorry about what he did to you. Sometimes people don't feel sorry for being disrespectful, and they have to learn the hard way by facing consequences like detention, or by having someone treat them badly and then hopefully understanding how it feels.

Wyatt: It's not easy to respect some kids when they do mean things to you. In school the other day, the teacher stopped teaching because some kids were bothering a girl in the back of the room. They were teasing her by saying she never took a shower and smelled disgusting. She didn't really smell bad, but she was wearing old clothes and looked poor. I guess they wanted someone to pick on.

Erin: That's an example of what we're talking about. It's important to show respect to everyone whether they're popular or not. You don't have to be best friends with everyone; you only have to be polite and respectful. What can you do to respect your classmates and friends outside of school?

Wyatt: I can ask them how they are and try to help them if someone picks on them. I can try not to get angry too fast, especially with a good friend like Jim if he says something that isn't nice. I can say something like, "I don't like what you said," or "Don't say that." I think he'd get the message better than if I tore up his homework. By the way, he said he was sorry and he didn't mean it. He said he wasn't in a good mood that day. We made up and we're fine now.

Erin: I'm happy to hear that. Is there any other way you can show respect to your classmates?

Wyatt: I can be more patient with them and try to understand they might be having a bad day if they say something I don't like. One thing's for sure: I don't think I can be patient with that boy on the bus. I didn't do anything to him and he made me feel bad because he threw my books around in front of a whole bunch of kids, and they all laughed.

Erin: It is hard to know what to do when someone acts disrespectful, and in cases like this one, you did the right thing by not reacting to it. Sometimes when things like this that are hard to explain happen, parents have to become involved and talk to the teacher or principal to make things better.

Wyatt: All the things we talked about are making me think how important respect is, in and out of school. Thanks, Mom.

72. Promote Respect for Authority Figures

Kennedy Elementary, a suburban school, recently experienced some incidents of students acting disrespectfully toward authority figures, such as cafeteria workers and teacher's aides, who guard the halls, playground, and lunchroom and also help out in the classrooms. Additionally, some school bus drivers complained to the administration that some students are noisy on the bus and don't respond when told to quiet down, which creates unsafe conditions for everyone.

Custodians reported students showing a lack of respect for what they do by littering the hallways they've recently cleaned and defacing bathrooms with graffiti that's hard to eradicate. Cafeteria workers noted the increase in food fights in the lunchroom and related stories to administrators about students talking back to them when they made simple requests like waiting their turn in line.

The principal subsequently invited Officer Carlos, a popular local police officer to talk to the students in assembly about showing respect for authority figures. Because of his concern about students' disrespect for authority figures, he gave them an assignment to talk to their parents about the incidents and see if they could come up with ideas to increase respect for these staff members. He said he'd meet with the students the following week to obtain their feedback and would help administrators implement the best ideas.

Last year Officer Carlos conducted a program to encourage student respect for teachers and administrators, and the number of reported incidents among these staff members decreased appreciably. He's hoping to gain the same effect with his program this year. In his presentation, the officer stresses that students need to show the same respect to school workers they show to uniformed police officers.

After dinner, Caden, one of the third-grade students, tells his dad Chris about the assignment.

> Chris: I'm glad Officer Carlos is helping put a stop to disrespecting these workers. They often have a thankless job and contribute a lot to the school. What are your ideas about helping kids become more respectful to them?

> Caden (smiling): All the kids like Officer Carlos and would never be rude to him, especially since he carries a nightstick and gun. Seriously, I'm thinking it might also be a good idea for the principal to have an assembly and introduce the custodian, the teachers' aides, and the bus drivers. He could tell the students what each of them has to do every day and about the problems they deal with. For example, the bus driver has to drive

safely with a busload of kids, who can sometimes be wild and noisy and make it hard for him to drive.

Chris: Yes, and the cafeteria workers have to deal with kids being rude by telling them they don't like the food. Sometimes they have to break up fights before the assistant principal gets there.

Caden: The teachers' aides have to be sure the schoolyard and hallways are safe. Sometimes kids are rude to them if they ask for a hall pass or want to know why they aren't in class. Once I heard a boy tell an aide that was working in our class he didn't have to listen to her because she wasn't our teacher.

Chris: All these workers have difficult jobs, and a little respect would go a long way. I like your idea of the principal explaining what these people do to make the school a better place for everyone. If the students understand what's involved in these jobs, they might gain a new appreciation for the workers who do them.

Caden: I hope so. Another thing we could do is have an appreciation day for school workers and encourage kids to behave for them.

Chris: That seems like a great idea. I'm a member of the Home and School Committee. I'll tell our people about it, and maybe we can arrange a short school assembly honoring these people and give them a reception with refreshments to show our appreciation. We need to recognize these people as valuable members of the school family.

Caden: I like that idea. One more thing we could do is make some signs in art class, stressing respect for custodians, teachers' aides, cafeteria workers, and bus drivers. We could make them colorful and put pictures of these people with positive messages on the signs about how important they are to our school.

Chris: I think you have enough ideas to add to what your class says. I also think the workers you mentioned will appreciate what Officer Carlos and all the students are doing to make their lives a little happier and stress-free.

Caden: A little bit of respect sure goes a long way.

TRY THIS: ACTIVITIES TO FOSTER RESPECT, AGES 10–14

73. Support Respect for Teachers

Sherene, a sixth grader in a city middle school, received one day of in-house suspension for disrupting her English class. She does average work in most of her subjects, but showed disrespect for her English teacher by talking back and refusing to do assignments. Sherene does not like the required reading in English and tells her teacher in no uncertain terms how she feels about the English curriculum. The assistant principal suspended her because she told Ms. Overton, the teacher, that "English sucks, and I hate your class." Then she stormed out of the room and went home, cutting her last class.

Before the assistant principal re-admits her to class, she has to take notes on a mandatory conversation she'll have with her parents about ways of showing her teacher respect. The vice principal directed her to write an essay based on those notes. Her parents, Sean and April, were upset about Sherene's actions in English class and fully support the teacher. The goal of the assistant principal and Sherene's parents in this follow-up to suspension is to reinforce respect for teachers, especially the English teacher, to ensure this doesn't recur.

Here is the essay Sherene presented to the assistant principal on the day he reinstated her:

"Mom and Dad talked to me about how important it is to respect your teachers even if you may not like the subject they're teaching. Mom told me how she disliked science in high school, especially when they had to dissect a cat in anatomy class. She walked away from her group and refused to work on the project. 'After the third day, that poor cat was really nasty,' Mom said.

"The cat that they named Graymalkin smelled so bad that Mom told the teacher the project was disgusting and she wasn't ever coming to class again, and she didn't care if she failed. The teacher told her the dissection was part of the anatomy course, and it was a requirement to dissect the cat. Mom said she kept arguing with the teacher so she gave Mom five detentions for her rude behavior. Mom said she learned her lesson because she missed softball practice and almost got thrown off the team because of talking back to the teacher. Her parents made her apologize to the teacher, which she didn't want to do, but afterward she was glad she did. She told the teacher she didn't mean to be disrespectful but looking at that cat was so gross.

"Dad told me about the time he walked off the basketball court because the coach didn't play him in the game. That was major disrespect, so he got benched for the play-offs. He said he felt worse about not showing Coach respect than not playing in the games because Coach was always good to him and taught him so much about the game that he made the team in high school and college.

"Mom said we may not always like school, but we need to show our teachers respect because all of them can teach us something, things we'll carry with us for the rest of our lives. Dad said teachers deserve respect because they studied hard to get their jobs and went to school for many years. Also, it's not always easy putting up with a classroom full of kids, especially when they argue with you over dissecting a cat, walk off the basketball court, or tell you they hate your class and use a not-so-nice word to describe it. I'm sorry for what I did, and from now, on I'll respect all my teachers, especially Ms. Overton, even though I'm still not wild about those books we're reading."

74. Teach Self-Respect

Keira, a fifth grader in a special education class, is learning about self-respect in social studies. Her teacher, Ms. Patel, has asked parents to give input when their children make posters about the importance of self-respect and ways of practicing it. Children will present their posters to the class and then hang them in the school hallway for all to read.

Misty, Keira's Mom, and Aaron, her Dad, have seen Keira make great progress in school. They model Mindful speaking and listening every day, and because of it, Keira is adept at these Mindfulness practices, so much so that her peers have elected her class representative. Her parents enjoy helping her with projects and assignments, especially one where they'll get to see the finished product, in this case, a poster drawn by Keira, who shows talent in art.

Here's what Keira and her parents have to say about the importance of self-respect and how to practice it:

Misty: I see you've gathered all your art supplies and poster board and are ready to start your project. What do you think self-respect is about?

Keira: I think it means caring enough about yourself to do the right thing. I'm going to write that down, along with all the other ideas we talk about, to write on the poster.

Aaron: Why do you think it's important to have self-respect?

Keira: I think it's important because you can't respect other people unless you respect yourself. That means doing something you're proud of that makes you feel good, not something that would make you feel embarrassed.

Aaron: Can you give an example?

Keira: Sure. A girl I know calls another girl in my class *fat* and says she'd lose a little weight if she didn't eat so much. I heard her say, "You don't see me pigging out on candy all the time like you do. That's why I'm thin and you're not." Maybe she says things like that to make herself feel like she's better than the other girl because she's thin, but I think she feels bad about herself inside. I don't see how she could feel proud of herself saying stuff like that to someone else.

Misty: So, you're saying maybe she doesn't have self-respect if she doesn't say kind things?

Keira: That's what I think it is. I think you have to have self-respect before you can respect other people.

Aaron: Can you think of some other things to put on your poster?

Keira: I also think it's important to accept your faults and the things you can't do perfectly the way you accept your good points.

Aaron: Can you give us an example of that?

Keira: In my case, I take a little longer to understand math and science, but English and social studies are easier for me. I accept the fact that I have a little trouble with these subjects and try my best with them. That's what counts, where you don't get discouraged if you're not perfect and you feel happy about the things you can do well.

Misty: That's another great idea for your project: Accept your faults and good points. I'm sure it will help a lot of kids who sometimes get upset about things that come hard for them.

Keira: I think if you accept every part of who you are, the things you're good at and the things you find hard, then you can have great self-respect. It helps to accept yourself just the way you are.

Aaron: How important do you think it is to have self-respect?

Keira: It's very important to me. If I have self-respect, I don't listen to what other people say about me if it's something that isn't nice. I know I'm a good person. Because I respect myself, I respect other people.

Aaron (looking at Misty): Remember to put that one in big, bold letters.

Misty: I'd say we have a wise daughter here. What do you think?

Aaron (smiling and making eye contact with Keira): She's so wise that she could teach us a few things.

75. Stand Up for Treating People with Dignity

Ravi is a popular seventh grader in a city middle school. His parents, Lila and Sanjay, have become increasingly concerned about the lack of respect they've seen among many pre-teens that they've witnessed in public places. They both try to live Mindfully, practicing mindful speech and loving kindness to everyone they encounter and encourage Ravi to act similarly. This evening, Lila and Sanjay have asked their son to sit for a few moments and discuss the importance of treating people with dignity, which to them, shows a visible sign of respecting people.

Sanjay begins the conversation by talking about some examples of the lack of respect he's seen at the mall among people Ravi's age. He says some young people talk loudly and chase around the mall, almost knocking people over. Others act rude to salespeople. He's even seen a couple of youngsters shoplifting.

Ravi shakes his head. "Dad, I don't think it's only kids my age who are rude. I've seen adults not treat salespeople right and I've seen them call security guards rent-a-cops."

"I don't think we should excuse people of any age for rude behavior," says Ravi's dad, "but it's important that kids learn to be respectful when they're young; that way, they'll continue this good behavior when they're adults."

"Fair enough, Dad. Now I'd like to know more about how you think we can treat one another *with dignity*, as you say."

"One way that helps is knowing how to talk to people. Mom and I like to speak assertively if we have a problem at a store or anyplace else. It's not helpful to become forceful or aggressive. We simply state our case in as few words as possible to help the person understand our problem. That usually gets good results for both of us."

"We also think it's important to act in a respectful way and be considerate of other people when you're in a public place like a mall or movie theater," Lila says. "Your dad and I were watching a movie the other night, and a group of kids started clowning around and talking loudly, so it was hard to hear. That's an example of what we're talking about. When the usher asked them to quiet down, they laughed at him. We missed part of the movie because of their lack of concern for others."

Ravi sighs. "I don't think all teenagers are like that. I've only seen a few."

His dad nods. "That's why we're discussing this, son. A few is one too many. Treating people with respect is important in all the places we go. Here's an example: Mom was wearing her sari at the grocery store and a lady with a young child came up to her and said, 'Why do you dress like that? You're in America now. It's pretty, but you need to get yourself a pair of cool jeans.'"

Lila shakes her head. "Yes, that was a strange experience. I don't know how the woman meant it, but to me it was disrespectful and hurtful, and it also set a bad example for her child. My feeling is if you wouldn't want someone to talk like that to you, it's best not to say what you may be thinking."

"I can understand that, Mom. Some kids at school asked me where I come from. When I tell them America, they don't believe me."

"That's why it's important to be thoughtful when you talk to people, no matter where you are. Treating people with dignity and respect takes so little effort and it helps you make many friends," Sanjay says, smiling.

"I know this would sound weird to some of my friends, but I'm glad you're my parents."

"Thanks, son," Sanjay says. "Now to prove you came from America, we're going to have some apple pie with ice cream for dessert, straight from Mom's kitchen. You can't get more American than that."

76. Help Your Child with Rudeness Issues

Madyson Carter, an eighth grader in a city middle school, was called to the dean's office for behaving rudely toward Faith, a special education student who has Tourette's Syndrome. Madyson's English teacher sent a pink slip to the dean of discipline after she heard her berating Faith by calling her "twitchy" because of her facial tics. Madyson also asked Faith why she made "strange faces and sounds and sometimes said curse words."

As part of her remediation, Dr. Hodge, the dean, had Madyson and Faith meet with her. She wanted Madyson to learn about Faith's experiences with Tourette's Syndrome so she could better understand why her behavior was totally unacceptable.

When the two girls met with the dean, Faith explained how she has no control over the facial and verbal tics she experiences many times throughout the day. She also said it hurts her badly when kids make fun of her and make hurtful remarks as Madyson did. Madyson listened attentively to what Faith said, told her how sorry she was, and promised she wouldn't make fun of Faith or anyone else ever again.

Madyson said she saw her friends making fun of Faith, so she decided to join in or they'd probably give her trouble and start calling *her* names. She admitted that she didn't want to lose their friendship as these girls were her closest friends. Dr. Hodge pointed out that it's important to do what you think is right regardless of how your friends act, and if they acted that way in this situation, she may want to reconsider her choice of friends. Madyson said it was something to think about, and even though these girls were her best friends, what they did wasn't right, which she said she knew all along. She admitted her responsibility for what she did and apologized again to Faith.

When Madyson asked if Dr. Hodge was going to suspend her from school, Dr. Hodge said *no* because she felt Madyson was genuinely sorry. However, in lieu of suspension or detentions, Dr. Hodge sent a note home with Madyson to give her parents, which they were to discuss with Madyson and bring in proof the next day that they did. Here's a copy of the note Dr. Hodge sent Madyson's parents:

To: Mr. and Mrs. Carter
From: Dr. Tiara Hodge, Dean of Students, Oceanview Middle School
Re: Discipline Incident

As you know from our phone conversation, I talked to your daughter Madyson today regarding an incident of inappropriate behavior involving a student in our school who has Tourette's Syndrome. Madyson admitted that she and others (who I will also deal with in my office) spoke rudely to the student and caused her great emotional distress. Subsequently, I've had Madyson and the girl she acted disrespectfully toward meet in hopes that your daughter would better understand the problems this student deals with on a daily basis.

Your daughter apologized profusely, and I believe she was sincere. However, as a follow-up to our session and in place of a suspension, I'd like you to discuss a couple of things with her; namely, the necessity of always granting respect and never showing rudeness to others, the importance of never accepting rudeness from anyone, and the necessity not to give in to peer pressure. Sadly, when Madyson saw her friends ridiculing the student, she felt she had to join in. I've impressed upon her the importance of standing by what you believe and not doing what other kids do in order to keep their friendship.

Thank you for attending to these issues. Please write me a note letting me know you've participated in the follow-up to Madyson's remediation. The school and I want the best for everyone involved.

Sincerely,
Dr. Tiara Hodge, Dean of Students, Oceanview Middle School

In response to her letter, Madyson's parents wrote the following note to Dr. Hodge:

Dear Dr. Hodge:
Thanks for caring about our daughter. We believe what you did will have much more of an impact on Madyson's future behavior than any punitive measures, like suspension or detention, that you could have taken.

We spoke to Madyson and firmly believe she realizes the importance of avoiding rudeness and treating everyone politely. We also reiterated your message about her not accepting rude behavior. You'll probably recall an incident when some kids in her class told her she "sounded dumb" because she had a speech problem. We wish she'd remembered that incident when she chose to hurt another student similarly. Unfortunately, our memories are often short-lived, but we believe she learned something from this experience and won't repeat her mistake.

Please let us know if you have any future questions about Madyson's behavior. We care and want to keep on top of things.

Kind regards,
Travis and Dana Carter

77. Reinforce Respect for Different Opinions

Etan, a gifted middle school student at a private religious school, got into a disagreement with his friend at school about how they should present a joint social studies project. His friend Stan wants to stage a debate between two scientists about whether life exists on other planets, and Etan wants to create a newscast where he will take the role of scientist and Stan will act as moderator. The project is due in a week, and the two can't agree on a format without arguing.

His parents, Zach and Shira, are both familiar with using mindfulness techniques to promote respect for differing ideas. Tonight, the family is sitting down after dinner to discuss compromise and respect for different opinions with their son. Etan told his parents about the arguments he and Stan are having while working on their project that constitutes a good portion of their grade. Now he's worried that because of their stalemate they may not complete the project on time. He's asking for suggestions from his parents so they can move forward with the project.

Zach: We'll all put our heads together so you and Stan can move forward with your project. Mom and I told you about Mindfulness after we took the course at the university. The instructors taught us many good ideas about respecting different opinions that we'd like to pass on to you, if you'd like to hear them.

Etan: I'm willing to try anything at this point. Stan and I both want to get a good grade, but the main thing we want is to keep our friendship going.

Shira: I understand that. You and Stan have been friends since first grade. It would be a shame to end it over a disagreement about a school project. You may want to start by being curious about what Stan has to say. Take a deep breath and hear him out. Be curious about his ideas, and let him talk. See if you and he can work out a compromise after he listens to your ideas. Use some of his ideas and some of yours instead of one or the other.

Zach: When you talk to him, use "I-messages" instead of making him look like he's the bad guy who doesn't want to include your ideas. Here's an example: "I can see why you think a debate might be more exciting than a newscast. I feel more comfortable with a newscast because I'd feel too much pressure doing a debate. A debate is fast-paced and has to follow a certain format. The newscast would make the report more relaxed for both of us."

Etan: I think using "I-messages" would be a lot better than us screaming at each other and getting nowhere. I'm going to try it. I'm also going to listen to what he has to say, like Mom said, even if I disagree with it. I have to admit I haven't given him much of a chance to present his side.

Shira: When you and Stan talk, set up the ground rules; for example, no shouting, no talking when the other person talks, present your case briefly, and talk only to the issue.

Etan: I have to admit we haven't been doing that. Everything seems to turn into a shouting match. It's a good thing we're working on this at our houses on the weekends. If the teacher heard us, she'd be pretty angry at both of us.

Zach: When you disagree, do it respectfully. Don't shout or say things you don't mean, and stay on the subject. When we're angry, we tend to bring in other issues that have nothing to do with the subject we're discussing.

Etan: We're going to meet at the library tomorrow, and we can't be noisy there, or they'll kick us out. I'll let you know what happens. Thanks for the great ideas.

Shira (after the library meeting): How did it go?

Etan: It wasn't easy to stay calm, but we both took your advice and stated our reasons for how we wanted to present our project about whether life exists on other planets. We let each other talk and used "I-messages" instead of getting angry at each other, and we came to a decision.

Zach (looking at Etan expectantly): Don't keep us in suspense. What did you decide?

Etan: Stan said that after I explained how uncomfortable I felt about the debate, he finally understood. He thought I was being stubborn and didn't realize why I didn't want to go along with his debate idea. We agreed to

Chapter 9

let him be the moderator and to cast me as the scientist. I said I'd compromise by presenting my ideas in an interesting way like I was presenting them in a debate but without going back and forth with another person with time limits. The moderator would ask questions about why I believe there's life on other planets, but I wouldn't have to follow the strict rules of debate. We also agreed to bring in some colorful charts about what planets could possibly support different kinds of life. The best part is we're going to make it more exciting by bringing the class into it with a question and answer session at the end.

Shira: I'm glad you two came to an agreement. As you can see, it's always good to listen respectfully to one another's opinions.

Etan: From now on, I'm going to use Mindfulness. It would have saved a lot of time, and we wouldn't have gotten into so many arguments.

Zach (smiling and patting him on the shoulder): You live and learn, and that's good for now and the future. Right, son?

Chapter Ten

Curb Greediness

THINK ABOUT THIS

Promoting generosity in your children will help curb "the gimmies," an insatiable craving and demand for new and better toys, gadgets, and other things they want to acquire. If you model a giving spirit in a variety of ways, kids will quickly catch on that giving often brings more rewards than getting.

Talking with kids about their desire for more and better material things versus the importance of intangibles will help them see how both have their place although their preoccupation with a superabundance of "things" can cause problems now and in the future. Focusing on positive things they enjoy, like going out with friends and things they love to do, will help them put things like getting new and better toys, clothing, and equipment in perspective.

An important part of curbing greediness in kids is setting limits and helping them learn they can't have everything they want. In line with this, it's helpful to discuss the power of advertising on their buying habits and their desire to acquire the latest electronics, jeans, and sneakers.

Although many people these days see "spoiling kids" as an archaic term, to many, the term still has meaning. Parents have different motives for over-indulging their kids. Once they find out what these motives are, they can begin to deal with why they're spoiling their children and think about how to solve the problem.

It's helpful to educate your children about how to tell the difference between wants and needs and how to make wise purchases. Buying shouldn't always be about getting a momentary thrill or indulging a desire for material things solely for the sake of acquiring them. Talk to your children about the importance of avoiding comparisons with what other kids have, and encourage them to think of themselves as individuals with unique wants and needs. Also, explore with your children how to seek satisfaction in a variety of ways besides buying things.

Prompt your children to experience and express gratitude for what they already have. Many times, kids lose sight of the emotional and material benefits they experience each day and need a gentle reminder from their parents.

Buying new things and enjoying them can be an enjoyable experience for kids as long as it doesn't dominate their enjoyment of life to the exclusion of other valuable experiences.

MODEL A CONVERSATION: CURB GREEDINESS

78. Promote Generosity in Your Children

Angela, twelve-year-old Paige's mother, and Bindi, mother of Akshay, who's in the seventh grade, attended high school together in California. They've remained friends over the years and meet frequently at a favorite cheesecake restaurant for lunch. Both of them took a course together in Mindfulness and regularly practice the techniques they learned. The two friends would like to find ways to help their children practice generosity, a virtue they discussed in class.

Today, their topic of conversation focuses on their kids' interest in acquiring new and better things, like electronics and expensive sneakers. Angela and Bindi are both well aware of the effectiveness of modeling to change behavior, and that's what they're discussing now:

Bindi: As you know from our past conversations, I'm becoming more concerned about Akshay's desire to buy every electronic gadget the minute it comes out. He says he should be allowed to get whatever he wants if he's using his own money. I'm trying to show him by example that there are a lot of things his father and I want to buy but that we can't let things dominate our lives. Sure, we enjoy a beautiful home, good food, and trips, but we mainly try to focus on things that bring us joy that don't cost a lot, like time spent with family and simple get-togethers with friends like you and Steven.

Angela: Things have progressed a little in my case, but not for the better. Paige has this penchant for accumulating jeans, the expensive brands. There's not much I can do because she gets a generous supply of money for presents from her grandparents and my sister. As a result, she has enough jeans for the next five years. We've been trying to convince her to wear the ones she has before buying more, but she says all the kids collect a lot of jeans and she doesn't want to feel left out. Her closet, one of those big walk-ins, is bulging at the seams.

Bindi: Maybe you can tell her you're donating some of your clothes to charity and see if she'd like to add some of the ones she no longer wears to the donation bag.

Angela: That may help. I could also try to curb my own habit of recreational shopping. I don't know about you, but I can't resist the coupons I get in the mail from clothing stores, especially those birthday coupons. I have to go out and use them right away even if I don't need anything.

Bindi: That's a hard one for me too. I guess I can't expect Akshay to hold off on buying a pair of new sneaks if I have seven pairs, even though I wear only two of them regularly. Another thing I'm trying to teach him is generosity. My husband and I work at the local soup kitchen when we can. I told him it helps to practice the kindness they stressed in our Mindfulness class by giving your time to someone less fortunate. He took us up on that, and I'm happy to say once a month he helps sort clothes for the consignment shop at our local hospital.

Angela: That's a generous thing to do. You've inspired me to encourage Paige to do some kind of volunteer work. She loves working with kids, so maybe she can help in our church's Sunday school program while the parents attend services.

Bindi: Yes, being generous with your time is one way of showing kids that while material things are fun to have, they're not the most important things in our lives. We can get and give more happiness by sharing our time and talents with others.

Angela: I think our kids are good people, and if we do our best to show them by example there are other dimensions to our lives that bring us better and lasting satisfaction than material possessions, it can help them develop a strong sense of what's important in life. That's not to say it's wrong to enjoy our possessions as long as we do it within reason.

Bindi: I think we both agree on that. Now let's splurge and have some of that decadent cheesecake I spotted in the case when we came in. Just like the kids, we deserve to indulge ourselves once in a while.

Angela: No doubt about that. I'll race you to the case. Whoever gets there last treats.

TRY THIS: ACTIVITIES TO HELP CURB GREEDINESS, AGES 6–9

79. Help Your Child Put Possessions in Perspective

Alexander, a third-grade student in an affluent suburban school district, has many friends whose parents overindulge them by giving them expensive sports equipment, video games, and outings on a frequent basis. For birthdays and other special occasions, they ask their kids what their friends are getting and match or do better than the other parents in giving their children presents. Alexander's parents don't want to buy into this way of thinking.

At a young age, Alexander is starting to get caught up in this out of control wanting and buying. His mom, Shelby, and Ian, his dad, take a few minutes in a relaxed setting to chat with him about the meaning of material possessions in hopes of helping him understand the rationale behind buying and acquiring, rather than always giving in to peer pressure. Here's how the conversation played out:

Shelby: Before we go out to breakfast, Dad and I wanted to talk with you about something that's been on our minds.

Alexander (rolling his eyes): I'll bet I know what it is. When I asked for a new racer bike because my old one's not as good as my friends' bikes, you said we'd talk soon. When you say that, it usually means you don't want to buy it.

Ian: Actually, we wanted to talk about what's behind wanting new things all the time. I'd like to hear a little about how you feel when you get a new bike, video game, or something else you've wanted for a long time.

Alexander: I know you and Mom are psychologists, and you like to understand why people do stuff, but it's not that complicated. I want a new bike. All my friends got one this year and I don't think it's such a big deal. I can help pay with some of my own money. I have a lot saved.

Shelby: See what you think about Dad's question: How do you feel when you get something new, and we'll take it from there.

Alexander: Okay, I'll tell you since you really want to know. I feel excited and happy when I get something new. (His eyes light up.) I can't wait to get that new bike so I can ride around the neighborhood with my friends.

Ian: I hear what you're saying. Now here's a second question: How long does that feeling last after you get something new?

Alexander (smiling): I can see where this is going, Dad. I've been your kid for a long time. Here's my answer: My happy feeling after getting the new bike will last at least a month. After a while, I won't feel as excited about it as I did when I first got it. That's how it goes when I get anything new. It's a big thrill, and then it fades a little, but it's still fun to have it.

Ian: Now let's think this through a little more. After you get over the excitement of getting something you really want, what usually happens?

Alexander: That's easy. I usually move on to the next thing I want and start talking about it until you get tired of hearing me.

Shelby: Bingo! What do you think is the point of dad and I bringing this up?

Alexander: That I'm never satisfied? That I want more and more and bug you until I get it?

Ian: Close, but not quite the message we're trying to get across. The whole idea is that most people feel the same way. They get excited and happy when they get a new bike, video game, or sports equipment. Then they get used to it and the thrill of owning it fades a little.

Alexander: Then they move on to something new. I get it. It makes sense.

Shelby: We're trying to say it's fun to get new things as long as you don't let wanting new possessions take over your life. It's more important to think about lasting things like friendships, people you care about, and helping others. It's also important to feel good about who you are so you don't need a ton of things to make you happy.

Alexander: I see what you're saying. It's not easy having psychologists for parents, but I guess it has its advantages. (Smiling slyly.) Now, when can I get that bike?

Ian: We've already planned on buying you the bike. If you'd like to contribute a little of your money, that would be great. However, before you ask for something new, please think about what we discussed tonight.

Alexander: Thanks. I will, but I won't tell my friends, or they'll say I'm weird for thinking that way, but their parents aren't psychologists—lucky them. Just kidding!

80. Offer Alternatives to Seeking Satisfaction by Spending

Gabriela, age nine, loves going to the mall with her parents and one or more friends every weekend and school holiday. She saves up her money she accumulates from presents and doing chores so she can go on frequent buying sprees. Her favorite purchases are glitzy outfits and accessories to match, like earrings and headbands. Her parents mainly window-shop and buy things only when they think they need them. However, like many of her friends, she can't resist shopping.

Her mom and dad, Luz and Pedro, want her to enjoy pretty things but want her to put shopping in perspective and allow time for other activities that will bring her more meaningful and lasting pleasure. After going to a Saturday movie matinee, the family enjoys hot chocolate and donuts in their cozy kitchen. Everyone is relaxed and happy, and it seems an opportune time for Gabriela's parents to broach the subject.

"Thanks for taking me to the movie. I had a great time," Gabriela says. "You said earlier you wanted to talk to me about something."

Luz gets right to the point. "Dad and I have been thinking how you want to go to the mall every weekend, and you often end up buying things you don't need."

Gabriela smiles. "Yes, it's great fun. I especially like it when I can invite a friend."

Pedro reaches for a donut. "That's what we wanted to talk about. Shopping is definitely fun, but not when it starts to become so important it takes the place of other activities like having fun with family and friends. We'd like to put our heads together and figure out a way you could still enjoy trips to the mall and not get too carried away with buying a lot of things every time you go."

"I didn't think it was that big a problem. I'm spending my own money and having fun looking in all the stores and finding things I like," Gabriela says frowning.

Luz pours Gabriela more hot chocolate. "I understand that, but it's also good to leave time for other things you enjoy doing."

Gabriela thinks for a minute. "Well, what else could I do on the weekends that wouldn't cost much money? I can't think of anything more fun than shopping."

"Maybe we could go on more trips to the park and find activities that don't cost anything, like having picnics and going on hikes. You could invite a friend," Pedro says. "Can you think of any other activities you could enjoy doing with your friends that would cost little or nothing?"

She reaches for her bag from the accessories store that contains sparkly headbands and spreads them out on the table. "We could try new hairstyles on each other and experiment with make-up."

Luz smiles. "I like the hairstyle idea, but I thought we agreed you could start wearing a little make-up when you turn eleven, but only around the house."

"I'm almost ten, Mom. I don't think a year earlier would hurt. How about if it's only lip gloss and blush?"

"As long as you wear it here and not when you go out."

"I think the hairstyles are a good idea, and they won't cost any money," Pedro says. "As long as you don't overdo it with the make-up, that would be fine too. What else could you and your friends do that won't break the bank?"

"Granny bought me those cool new board games for my birthday. She actually looked online to see what games were hot these days. I'm thinking I could play them with my friends, and we could have a family game night once a month with you two and my cousins. There's one she got me called 'Beat the Parents' that would be fun, especially since you always win because in most games, the answers are too hard for me and the cousins."

Pedro smiles. "Excellent ideas for having fun without spending money."

"I still want to shop," Gabriela says, "but I guess it would be good to cut back a little; then I could save money to buy some music I've wanted."

"Good idea," Luz says. "Sure, we'll still take you shopping. It's fun for us too, but we won't do it quite as much. Is it a deal?"

"Sure," Gabriela says, reaching for another donut. "Maybe we could try out that new game tonight."

"Let's play it now before we get too tired from eating all these donuts," Pedro says.

81. Feel Comfortable Setting Limits

At the request of many parents of kids he counsels, Mr. Stein, a school counselor, has agreed to form a parenting group on an as-needed basis. When parents voice strong concerns about behavioral problems with their elementary-age children, and at least four parents express interest in a particular topic, the counselor sets a date for a session.

Within the past week, shortly before the holidays, two couples ask him to discuss setting limits with their kids as things are spinning out of control in their houses. Nicole and Charles are parents to six-year-old twins, Bailey and Payton, while Amber and Brett have a nine-year-old son, Hunter.

The session unfolds as the parents talk about their difficulties setting limits with their children in the area of making purchases, some that they consider unwise.

Nicole: Our twin girls, Bailey and Payton, never seem happy with what they have, and they're very vocal in expressing their anger and dissatisfaction if we don't buy them exactly what they want. Most of the time, they tire of these toys quickly and then begin hounding us for new and better toys and electronic playthings.

Mr. Stein: One thing you can do is put some of the toys away when they tire of them and then bring them out later. In time, they may look at them as they would new toys.

Charles: Believe me, we've tried that, but it only works occasionally, when they're not excited enough about the toy to begin with. Remember, two kids complaining together are a lot louder and demanding than one. They're a strong team when it comes for lobbying for what they want us to buy.

Nicole: I'm embarrassed to say that we usually cave in and they get their way.

Mr. Stein: Don't blame yourselves. Most parents I see have the same issues with their kids when it comes to wearing them down when they want something. It's hard with many parents with both holding down full-time jobs, in addition to the jam-packed activity schedule many kids have, to maintain the energy level it takes to make your point with your kids and stick to it without giving in. Believe me, I know because I'm a parent.

Charles: We sometimes feel guilty because our time with the kids is limited. I manage a grocery store and Nicole's a pharmacist, so we don't have much time to spend with our kids. We often substitute buying them things for the time we wished we could spend taking them places or giving them more attention when we're home.

Mr. Stein: In that case, maybe you both could find a little more time when you're not working to devote to your girls, even if it means giving up some of your own favorite activities, like watching sports on TV or going out with friends.

Nicole: We could try doing that although we have little extra time to spare.

Mr. Stein: It's a good start.

Brett: We have the same problems with our son Hunter. He's only in third grade and he's asking for new and better electronics and toys like his friends have. He shows the same level of anger and dissatisfaction Nicole and Charles' kids show when they don't get what they want. He won't give up once he gets started, and it's exhausting for us.

Mr. Stein (nodding and making eye contact with all four parents): I hear this all the time from many parents. You have to reinforce what you believe is right. The first few times will be hard because in both your cases your kids seem to be strong-willed and don't give up once they get started. However, once you show them by your words and actions you won't be manipulated, they'll eventually come around (albeit grudgingly) to your way of thinking even if they disagree. They'll have no choice if you back up what you say with action; in this case, not capitulating to their demands.

Amber: Hunter sees something on TV, and he immediately wants it. He looks like he's in a trance when he watches commercials for toys and electronics, especially electronic games. He plays them for hours after school with his friends.

Mr. Stein: Tell him you need him to put the game away after what you think is a fair amount of time. If he persists in playing it, take it away until he agrees to use it more responsibly. You have to be willing to hear loud protests from him and to ride it out.

Brett: That's the problem. We're often too tired to deal with his backtalk and complaints if we try to punish him. Sometimes I think he's the one in control and we're at his mercy.

Mr. Stein: It doesn't have to be that way. Try not giving in, let him complain and he'll eventually get the message, but it may take some time, depending on how long you've been giving in when he throws a tantrum.

Amber: It looks like if we don't start setting limits now, we'll have more trouble when he gets into his teen years.

Mr. Stein: I've seen that happen a lot. You also need to talk to him about the power of advertising in persuading adults and kids to buy. Advertising, especially in the form of commercials, can have a hypnotic effect on both kids and adults as it appeals to all the senses. Some experts even believe subliminal advertising plays a part in reaching people's subconscious minds. Nicole and Charles, I would also say your girls are not too young to discuss the hidden persuasive powers of advertising. Be curious and ask them which commercials appeal to them. Also, ask which commercials most influence them to want to buy something new. Have a conversation about it and give them a chance to voice their opinions.

You'll be amazed at their level of sophistication in grasping the psychological power of advertising, even at this young age.

Nicole: It's worth a try. I like all these ideas. I think eventually they will help the girls in their struggle with wanting things. I think It's important for us as parents to keep on top of our kids' endless desire for more and better things.

Mr. Stein: You can see how prevalent it is these days, wanting and acquiring things, that there's actually a name for it, the "gimmies," a funny-sounding word for a serious problem among our children.

Charles: Setting limits on the "gimmies" is our goal as it is with all the parents I know.

Mr. Stein: We'll meet again in a couple of weeks, if you want, to and see how things have improved after you've tried some things we've discussed. Meanwhile, stay strong and don't give in, even if your kids test your patience to the limit. You're in charge from now on.

82. Stop Spoiling Your Kids

You'd be more likely to hear the advice to stop spoiling your kids used by your parents and grandparents when you were growing up than today. The sad fact remains that spoiling or overindulging your children is alive, well, and flourishing. Many parents try to overcompensate for not being available to their kids, due to a hectic work schedule or personal issues, by showering them with expensive material possessions they often don't need. Other parents want their children to have things they didn't have when they were growing up because their own parents didn't have the money to buy them or because they believed giving their kids everything they wanted would make them greedy or selfish.

Eli, a first-grade student in a private school, does not want for anything. He's a bright and precocious child who tested into a gifted class. However, his parents have expressed concern to Eli's pediatrician because he often feels bored despite having a lot of material things to keep him occupied. He also experiences spells of sadness and never seems satisfied no matter how much love and attention his parents give him. His doctor doesn't believe he's depressed although kids of any age can show signs of depression.

After talking to him, the doctor believes he's like so many kids who don't know how to handle always getting what they want. That's why the doctor advises his parents to stop spoiling him and to talk to him about their plan. "I can use the term *spoil* because I'm a grandfather and I've seen it with my own grandkids. Some parents say to give your child all the advantages, but I say don't overdo it, or you'll have an out-of-control child on your hands."

Eli has an insatiable need to acquire new and better toys and gadgets, but once he plays with them for a while, he tires of them and asks for new and better things. All he has to do is say the word, and his parents, Ariel and Ben, respond to his every wish. He recently informed his parents that all his friends have new tablets that are very pricey, and he can't wait a month for his birthday to get it. He wants it now.

In addition to spoiling their son by buying him whatever he wants when he wants it, Eli's parents let him eat sweets whenever the mood strikes him. He helps himself to candy and cookies after he comes home from school because he's "starving" and can't hold off until after dinner. As a result, he has cavities in all his baby teeth and spends hours at the dentist getting fillings.

Ariel and Ben believe it's time to stop spoiling Eli before it's too late to turn things around. He's becoming more demanding each day and won't listen when they try to talk to him about it. They've decided to broach the subject with him on the weekend when he seems more relaxed. This weekend he's in a good mood because his friend's dad is picking him up soon to take him to see his favorite player perform in a pro basketball game.

Ben starts the conversation. "Mom and I want to talk to you about something we've been thinking about."

Eli lets out a long sigh. "What did I do this time?"

"We don't want to talk to you because you're in trouble," Ariel says. "We want to talk to you about something that concerns all of us."

"Is it about bugging you for that tablet all my friends have?"

"That's one thing we wanted to talk about," Ben says. "We plan on giving you the tablet, but not because your friends have it. We think it would help you with your school work, and you could also read some of those books you've been wanting. We've decided to give it to you for a birthday gift."

Eli's voice rises. "That's a whole month away."

"That's right," Ariel says. "I also told you we all need to think about something. It's not just your asking for things all the time that's bothering us. Dad and I have to think about how giving you what you ask for all the time isn't good for any of us."

"What do you mean?" Eli says. "I don't understand what you're saying."

"It means if you get what you want all the time, it's not going to help you grow up to be a generous, caring person. All you'll care about is yourself and nobody else."

"It wouldn't be good for Mom and I to continue giving you what you want all the time, just because you're bored, or sad, or because your friends have it. We want you to grow up thinking and caring about yourself and being considerate of our feelings about what's important to us," Ben says.

Ariel puts her hand on Eli's shoulder. "What's important to us is helping you become a caring, responsible person who shows concern for other people as much as you care about yourself and what you want."

"I think I understand what you're saying. I don't like having to wait for the tablet, but I know it is kind of selfish to expect to get everything I want right away. I guess you're right about how when I'm bored or sad getting new stuff makes me feel better."

"It does with many kids and adults. But what do you think the problem with that is?" Ben asks.

Eli thinks for a minute. "It only makes me feel better for a while. The feeling doesn't last."

Ariel and Ben look at each other knowingly. "Thanks, Son, for getting the message so easily."

"I still want that tablet, but I guess I'll have to wait."

"It's a deal," Ariel says. "Thanks for understanding."

Outside, a car horn honks and Eli races out the door. "See you after the game," he hollers.

"That wasn't as hard as I thought," Ben says.

"I wish we'd had the talk sooner," Ariel answers. "Next on the agenda: the go-easy on the candy talk."

"One step at a time, dear. Baby steps. We'll get there."

TRY THIS: ACTIVITIES TO CURB GREEDINESS, AGES 10–14

83. Encourage Wise Buying

Brooke, a sixth grader in a city middle school, is working on a report about economics for her social studies class. Students could choose any topic dealing with money, and she decided to write her report she'll give to the class about making purchases wisely. Her teacher encouraged students to discuss the topic with their parents before composing their final drafts. It came up in a class discussion that kids and parents often argued about how kids spent money, many times wasting it on purchases that are overly expensive or cheaply made.

Brooke's parents, Natalie and Robert, wcrc glad to take part in the discussion since they had concerns that Brooke needed more help making wise decisions about spending money she earned from babysitting her little sister and an allowance her parents gave her for doing daily chores. Here's part of Brooke and her parents' brainstorming session about her project:

Brooke: I've been thinking of some ideas to make my presentation interesting, and I've decided to bring in a couple things from my closet to show the class to see if they can tell if they were good purchases. I'm going to bring in that fancy pair of jeans I bought to wear during the holidays to show an example of when I thought I wasted money. I've only worn them once and they cost more than I make from babysitting in three months. I'm also going to bring in the pair I wear at least twice a week. I got them on sale and I wear them to school and when I go out with friends.

Natalie: It always helps to use visuals in a presentation because it emphasized your point better than talking about it. Cost per wear is an important thing to consider when you're buying clothes, so you can mention it to the class after you ask them what they think about what you bought. If you wear the jeans a lot, it's worth paying a little more. If you rarely wear them, no matter how great they look and feel, it doesn't pay to buy them if they're going to be tucked away in your closet.

Brooke: I learned about that the hard way. Now I'm out eighty dollars for those jeans I loved when I tried them on in the store.

Robert: Along those lines, sometimes I buy things on the spur of the moment without considering if it's a good purchase for me. I bought a couple of shirts because I liked the color but they're hanging in my closet unworn because they feel uncomfortable around the neck. Now it's too late to take them back.

Brooke: You're right about that. I've bought a fancy dress to wear to a party, but once I got home, I was sorry I bought it. I decided to take it back because it wasn't comfortable, and I knew I'd never wear it. Maybe you could donate your shirts to a charity. They'll even pick them up outside our door. I think donating is a good thing to do if you have clothes you know you won't wear again.

Natalie: Now you have two more good points for your report. The first one is think before you buy. Be mindful about it, and ask yourself if it's right for you. Be sure to try it on in the store; that especially applies to shoes. Walk around in them and ask yourself how they feel. If they're not comfortable in the store, you won't be able to wear them to school or when you go out. The same holds true for all clothes you want to buy. It's important to try things on to see if they look and feel right on you. Another point you made is recycling clothes and other things you no longer need. Someone would love to buy gently used items or those you've never worn if they're a reasonable price, and that's the service charities provide, in addition to making money for their organizations.

Brooke: Another thing I have to work on is looking for the best price before I buy. I bought a shirt last month, and then I saw it in a discount store a couple weeks later for almost half the price I paid. I couldn't take it back because I'd already worn it. Shopping at regular and online stores you know will give you a better discount will help you find better deals. I'm going to add that to my report.

Natalie: Another idea related to shopping stores with good prices is to look for coupons online or in the mail. I see that many department stores offer cash-off coupons and also some with percentages deducted from what you buy.

Robert: I admit that a lot of times I buy things without looking at the price tag first. A couple of times, I caught myself when I went up to the register and put the item back because I noticed the price at the last minute. I saw slacks I liked, but they cost way too much, so I went to a store that offers better bargains and found similar slacks for a lot less.

Brooke: I'd like to end my report on a happy note so kids can still look forward to shopping even when they're trying to shop wisely. I'm thinking of telling the class it's alright to splurge once in a while and to enjoy it and not feel guilty. What do you think of that?

Natalie: I agree that it doesn't hurt to indulge your shopping habit occasionally as long as you don't give into it all the time. I also think it's always good to end a talk with something upbeat.

Robert: I can attest to indulging your shopping habit occasionally. I just bought a set of new golf clubs and I'm going to enjoy using them tomorrow. I feel good about buying them, but in the interest of shopping wisely, I'll have to postpone buying that basketball net I saw in the sporting goods store. You can have too much of a good thing, is the moral of that story.

Brooke: It helped a lot to talk to you two about it. I definitely feel more confident now about giving the report.

84. Promote Mindful Spending

Encouraging your children to be mindful when spending money will help them make good decisions based on their own individual preferences rather than thinking about going along with their peers' buying habits. Being curious, one of the main principles of Mindfulness can lead adults and kids to answer important questions like these before spending money: Do I want this item because it appeals to me personally or because I saw someone else wearing or using it? Will I get tired of it quickly, or will it bring me some measure of lasting satisfaction? Is it worth the money I have to spend?

Needless to say, most kids don't ponder questions like these before they buy something, but asking your child to think about points like these can guide them in gaining more satisfaction from the way they choose to spend their money. Encourage your children to develop their own questions before spending money to help them become wise consumers. They can think of one or two key questions to have in the back of their minds when they want to buy something.

Help them see that spending money mindfully rather than capriciously will help them make purchases based on their own needs rather than going with the crowd. When they decide not to spend money on items others feel they cannot do without, they will have money left to spend on things they really want or can make the choice to save the funds for a future purchase.

Derrick, a recently widowed father, has concerns about his twelve-year-old son Lyle and his strong desire to spend money without considering the consequences. To compound the problem, Miss Bessie, Lyle's grandmother, who lives next door, gives him generous spending money, especially since her daughter's death, thinking it will lessen the pain of his loss.

Lyle and his dad are in therapy because Lyle's mother died suddenly in a car accident, and they're both having trouble coming to terms with her death. Until now, Derrick didn't play a strong role in his son's care, and dealing with this latest problem of his wanting to spend money without giving it much thought prompts an overdue conversation between father and son.

Today, Lyle has just returned home from a trip to the mall with a friend and his parents. His dad has told him about his concern that he's spending his money without giving it enough thought, so he races up to his room with his packages in hopes his dad won't detect the results of his latest buying spree. However, his dad spots the bags from the sporting goods store before Lyle can to sequester himself in his room.

"Let's see what you bought," Derrick says, beckoning Lyle from the bottom of the stairs.

"You're quick, Dad," Lyle says, with a nervous smile. "I can never get past you." He lays the packages on the couch. "I needed new sneakers and sports gear for when we play our next game."

Derrick sighs. "We got you all the clothes you need for your JV game last week, and the sneakers you have are in great shape. We bought them three months ago."

Lyle takes the sneaks out of the box, handling them fondly. "Yes, but Malik has ones like these, and he says they'll help me run faster on the court. Besides, Grandmommy gave me the money and said to spend it however I want."

"I understand that, Son. She's grieving your mom strongly, and giving you money makes her feel better even though to me it doesn't look like it's the best thing for you or for her." He makes eye contact with Lyle and pauses. "Remember how Mom took that course on Mindfulness last year?"

Lyle nods. "That was all she talked about, how it changed the way she thought about everything." He pauses, perplexed. "What does Mom taking that course have to do with my buying new sneakers and clothes?"

"She told me it changed every area of her life, how she looked at us, how she ate, how she enjoyed each day. She also said it changed the way she thought about spending money," his dad says.

"What does Mindfulness have to do with spending money?"

"For one thing, Son, it means spending money because you have a good reason to do so, not because your friend has something and you want the same thing because he says it's better than the one you already have."

Derrick puts the sneaks back in the box. "It made me feel good to buy the sneaks and the clothes. Is that wrong?"

"It's not wrong. I just want you to be curious, as they say in Mindfulness, to ask yourself if you really need what you're buying and why you want it right now."

"I guess you're right, Dad. I didn't need this stuff. My old sneakers were good enough and I have plenty of clothes. I guess I'll have to take this stuff back next time we go to the mall."

"No, that's not necessary, Son. Keep what you bought, but next time, think before you spend. It will pay off because you'll have some extra funds in case you want to save up for something big. Maybe I should talk to Grandma and tell her to save some of that money she's been giving you to buy herself a new furnace. Her old one is not working well and she's very sensitive to the cold."

"I didn't know that or I wouldn't have taken the money. How about if I tell her I can do without the money? I should spend more time with her. She's been really sad since Mom died."

"I'm happy to hear you say that, Son. Let's go over and pay her a visit now and we can talk and then take her out for lunch."

Father and son hug and get ready to visit Grandma.

85. Motivate Gratitude in Your Kids

Showing gratitude is an important part of learning Mindfulness and applying it regularly. It's one of the best antidotes for curing a case of greediness in your child. Studies prove that gratitude helps increase personal happiness and minimize stress in our lives. It also boosts resiliency, an important trait to possess in dealing with the constant stress our kids face every day. If we talk with our kids about practicing gratitude by being thankful for one or two things each day, they'll be more content with their lives and cultivate a more positive mindset.

Hope, a ninth-grade student in a charter school, is learning Mindfulness in her social studies class. She enjoys the incorporation of Mindfulness into the regular curriculum because she's interested in the benefits the teacher said it could bring, like peacefulness, contentment, and an ability to relate well to others. Her parents, Marissa and Brad studied Mindfulness at the local medical center and were thrilled when Hope's school district offered the program as part of the elementary and middle school curricula.

The students learn techniques like mindful talking and listening. They also start their class with a short, relaxing meditation. Hope's assignment is to create a collage of photographs and pictures cut from magazines depicting ways kids can incorporate gratitude in their daily lives. One night after watching a football game together, Hope and her parents brainstorm ideas for her collage:

Hope: I know one thing we do every day that I can put in my collage. When we go around the table with Blake (her brother) and Grammy every night, we say one thing we're thankful for that day. I can get my friend to take our picture tomorrow when she comes over for dinner and use that in the collage.

Brad: I'll be sure to wear a nice shirt and tie, not my undershirt and holey jeans like I usually do. I think practicing gratitude is helpful because it helps you put material things in perspective. If you're thankful for what you already have, getting more and better things doesn't seem quite as important.

Hope: You gave me an idea. I could find a picture in a magazine showing fancy jewelry and post it next to a picture of our cat and write something like this: Which is more fun to have, Furball, this fluffy friend, or a fancy ring?

Marissa: That would get the message across that people and pets take precedence over things. Another idea would be for kids to write personal messages to family members on holidays and birthdays thanking them for specific things they did to make their lives happier.

Hope: They can also write thank-you notes to family members when it's not a special occasion, I can put a sample letter in the collage that goes like this (she stops and thinks for a moment): "Dear Mom and Dad, Did I ever say thanks for being my parents? Even though we don't agree on everything all the time, you're the best parents a teenager could have. I love going places with you and just hanging out. You're the best. Love, Hope XXOO"

Marissa: Now we owe you a thank-you for that kind note! Putting it in the collage will tell people you don't need a special occasion to thank the people you care about. You can do it anytime.

Hope: I'd also like to give kids the message that showing gratitude can help you bounce back when you're having rough times in your life. I could find a picture of someone looking sad and then another picture of that same person thanking someone for doing something kind and looking happy because he felt grateful. I could put a smiley face next to the happy picture because gratitude can make sadness turn into happiness.

Brad: That feeling of bouncing back that being grateful gives is also called resilience, if you want to add that under the picture.

Hope: I like the sound of that word. *Resilience.* It sounds like what it means, being able to pick yourself up and dust yourself off, or what you said before, *bouncing back.* I think gratitude also helps when you're in a sad or grumpy mood. You can't stay that way for long if you think of all the good things that come your way and give thanks for them.

Marissa: I'm excited to see your collage. I learned a lot about gratitude talking about it today.

Hope: I'm always going to try to be mindful of it. It can make your life much happier.

Chapter Eleven

Curtail Conflicts

THINK ABOUT THIS

Kids who learn Mindfulness techniques will find themselves having a distinct advantage when it comes to curtailing conflicts of all kinds. It's easy to arm your children with peaceful and effective verbal and non-verbal ways to respond when they're involved in disagreements with friends or family members. Similarly, using a Mindfulness approach in communicating with your children can help you minimize conflicts and disagreements with them, promoting a more peaceful family life.

Children often tease one another but don't think of the repercussions when teasing turns into unkind behavior. Mindfulness can help your kids know when they or others cross the line from playful teasing into bullying. If they go over that line, Mindfulness can show them the importance of making amends to a friend they hurt.

Sibling disputes abound in many homes and can try even the most patient parents. Striking a balance between not interfering in sibling disagreements and not tolerating the constant bickering that threatens to disrupt a household can prove difficult. Mindfulness will offer you the tools to curtail the severity and frequency of your children's conflicts.

Enforcing household rules, like those that involve bedtime, TV watching, homework, electronics use, and curfews can precipitate arguments between parents and children. Think of how helpful it would be for you not to buy into these disagreements every time they come up, opting instead to resolve them peaceably. If parents use a mindful approach to solving problems without abdicating their authority, kids will listen and cooperate more readily.

Report card day often plays out with drama and unpleasant repercussions for many families. Mindfulness techniques provide a positive framework for discussion about grades, why they're important, and how to turn poor grades into good ones. Similarly, especially with middle and high school students, disagreements arise about children's choice of clothing and hair style. How can you maintain your standards of how your kids should dress and not totally alienate them? Should there be different styles for school and social occasions? Mindful discussions can help.

What time is a good time for your kids to come home? What is a reasonable curfew for your child, while keeping his safety in mind? These issues come up with pre-teens and will accompany you and your child until he leaves home for college or work. Mindful communication can help resolve curfew conflicts as it can all the other ones you'll encounter.

Parents often become anxious and upset when kids start to date. It can bring feelings of a loss of control and fear that your children may encounter new problems when they reach this new stage of their lives. You'll find there are guidelines to consider and different rules to enforce that you've never before encountered. This new playing field can seem daunting because when your kids were younger you had to think only about carpooling your kids to practice or worry about which video games were safe to play.

Conflicts are a painful part of growing up and parenting. You can keep them to a minimum by using Mindfulness as a tool, whether the conflict is between you and your child, your child and a sibling, or with your child's friends.

MODEL A CONVERSATION: TEACH MINDFULNESS TO
CURTAIL CONFLICTS

86. Minimize Conflicts the Mindful Way

Nolan, a popular third grader, usually gets along well with his friends. Recently, however, Brady, one of his best friends, stopped talking to him after an incident at the playground near their houses. Nolan and his friend joined teammates on a neighborhood basketball team for a game with a local team, coached by one of the players' dads. The boys arrived at the playground before the coach arrived.

They started playing and joking around as they always do when warming up for a game. Brady was having a bad day and missed every basket. Nolan jokingly called him "a big klutz." Normally, Brady would have laughed at his friend's teasing and playfully taunted him in return, but this time, the other kids on his team took up the chant "Big klutz."

Nolan shouted, "Knock it off, guys. It was a joke," but it was too late. Brady walked off the court, and Nolan tried to catch up to him, but by the time he turned the corner, Brady had entered his house. When Nolan got back to the court, Coach was there but the kids didn't mention what happened for fear Coach would give them a big lecture. When he asked where Brady was, they pretended they didn't know.

By the time Nolan got home, his regret about the way he treated his friend Brady had intensified. His parents, Bridget and Patrick, knew something was wrong when he slammed the door and ran up to his room. His mom told him he needed to come downstairs and talk about whatever was bothering him. Dinner, his favorite, steak on the grill and French fries, could wait.

He called downstairs to his mom in an irritated voice, "I have to make an important phone call, Mom." Nolan plugged in Brady's number, but his friend's mother said he wasn't feeling well and couldn't come to the phone. Nolan put down the phone, and all kinds of thoughts ran through his mind, mainly ones of sadness and regret. *Now, I've lost a good friend. He'll never talk to me again, and it's all my fault.*

He slowly descended the stairs, dreading telling his parents about what happened, even though they never judged or berated him, especially if they knew he was in emotional pain. They could see he was upset now by observing his body language.

Nolan's parents have modeled Mindfulness for him since they both took the course at the Peace Center. They used the tools they learned in the class to settle their own disagreements and those with their children, Nolan and his middle school sister Genene, who was out to dinner with friends tonight. They both believed the tips they learned in their class could help Nolan resolve his dispute with his friend Brady.

"Do you want to talk about why you're upset, or would you rather wait until later?" Patrick asks.

"I'd rather get it over with. You're not going to like it."

"Tell us what's wrong. We're listening," Bridget says, giving Nolan her full attention.

"Brady's angry with me because I teased him at basketball. The kids on our team made it worse by making fun of him too, and things got out of control. Now he won't talk to me."

"How do you feel about that?"

"I know it was my fault for teasing him, but I don't know how to end the fight and make up with him. I'm also wondering if I should say something more to the other kids. If I don't, they might keep calling him names."

"I'd try using assertive language with the other kids, telling them you made a mistake and it wasn't good to treat a friend that way," Bridget says.

"It's good that you admit you didn't treat him well by teasing him. Kids are going to tease each other, sure, but it's not a good idea because it can get out of control as it did tonight," Patrick adds.

"You're right about that. What can I say to make things better? I don't want him to hate me."

"When he feels like talking, which may not be for a while, you can tell him you're sorry."

"That's all I have to say to make things better?"

"See how it goes," his mother says. "Notice how he reacts. Watch his body language and what he says after you tell him you're sorry. That can tell you a lot. If you think he needs to hear more from you about what happened, then feel free to tell him."

"Remember how we talked about 'I-messages'? You can use those when you talk to him to get your point across," Patrick says.

"You mean say something like, 'I'm sorry. I didn't mean to call you those names. I don't know why I did, but I'll never do it again. When the other kids started saying mean stuff, I wish I could have stopped them. I tried, but it didn't work.'"

"Something along those lines would help him know your true feelings about what happened. It would help him understand better. However, it's up to him whether he's willing to forgive and move on."

"The most important thing," Bridget says, "is that you listen to what Brady has to say. Let him talk without saying anything until he's finished. He's needs to tell you how he feels about how you and the other kids treated him. When you talk to him, be specific, letting him know his friendship means a lot to you and that you want to stay friends."

"I'll try what you and Dad said. I want us to be friends."

"I know it won't be easy, but talking to the other kids would definitely be a good idea. You may want to talk to one you find it easy to talk to and ask him to talk to the other kids," his dad says.

"I can use the same 'I-messages' I'll use when I talk to Brady and say, 'I made a mistake. It wasn't good to treat a friend that way. I'm sorry about how I treated Brady, and I hope you and the other guys are too. If you think it's a good idea like I do to apologize, I'm hoping you'll apologize to him too. We're all friends, and I think you want to keep it that way. I know I do.'"

"That's a good idea too. It's important the other kids know what you think. I'm hearing that you feel responsible for what happened, and also that you've found a good way to make things right. Let us know how it turns out. If you need more ideas about how to handle things with Brady and the other kids, we're here," his mom says.

"Thanks. Can we eat soon? I'm feeling better already," Nolan says, going up to his room to try calling Brady again.

TRY THIS: ACTIVITIES TO CURTAIL CONFLICTS, AGES 6–9

87. Decrease Parent/Child Disagreements

Parent/child conflicts erupt in many homes all too frequently with kids of all ages. Reasons for disagreements can range from dawdling over getting ready for school, not doing homework, TV watching, bedtime, and curfews. How you handle these conflicts makes all the difference. You know that "Because I'm the parent," "I said so," and variations on this theme don't work anymore as they rarely did during your own growing-up years. Making threats you'll never carry out like, "No TV for a month if you don't stop watching it now" also fails to get your kids' attention.

On the other hand, permissiveness doesn't help you maintain your authority as a parent or help your children learn to deal with frustration and learn to live in the real world where things won't always go their way. A mindful approach to solving parent/child conflicts often works better than an authoritarian or permissive approach. Listening without judging, assertive communication using "I-messages," and speaking positively rather than negatively will help you get your point across and gain better cooperation from your children.

Micaela, a fourth grader, has frequent conflicts with her parents, Ana and Kevin. These disagreements are usually more pronounced with Ana, since Ana works from home and mother and daughter spend more time together. The main issues here involve neglecting homework assignments and complaining about a nine o'clock bedtime on school nights. Micaela's parents recently attended a Mindfulness seminar offered by their school district, and they're ready to try implementing some of the principles they've learned to help solve their communications problems with their daughter.

Micaela's parents have chosen to talk to her on a Saturday afternoon before her friend comes over to ride bikes. She's well-rested and content, and they want to discuss bedtime and homework, the main topics of their disagreements, when they think she'll be most receptive.

Ana: Dad and I were thinking about some of the problems we've had lately about homework and what time you need to go to bed.

Micaela: I don't like it when we fight. I wish you two would understand the way I feel once in a while. If you'd at least listen instead of saying, "We're the parents. This is the way it is, take it or leave it," I'd feel as if you'd at least heard me. Right now, it's like what I think doesn't matter.

Kevin (listening mindfully and trying his best to put himself in Micaela's shoes): Mom and I are willing to listen, but we need you to be open to what we say too.

Micaela: You mean it? Even if you don't agree? You won't start yelling and telling me to go up to my room if I say something you don't want to hear?

Ana: Dad and I will listen. We may not agree, and we'll tell you if we don't. We'll also give you a reason why we want you to do something. We'll start with your not caring about getting your assignments in on time. Your teacher called last week and said your math grades are dropping because you haven't been doing the homework. That means you don't know what you need to study when a test comes up. If you have trouble doing certain problems, that's what you need to concentrate on.

Micaela: I hate math. Mr. Blume makes it so boring.

Ana: Math wasn't my best subject, but it was important to do the assignments to help me understand it better. If you ask your teacher, he'll be glad to help you during recess. We've already talked about it with him. All you have to do is bring in the work you don't understand, and he'll explain it. He said when he looks at the problems you get wrong on the homework, he can tell what's giving you difficulty in the tests.

Micaela: I'll try to do better about doing homework. I don't know if I want to talk to Mr. Blume. It's boring enough to hear about math in class. I don't know if I could stand hearing about math during recess. I need that time to relax.

Kevin: I hear what you're saying. Tell you what, get all your assignments in on time, and we'll see how you do on the next test. If you pass, you won't have to miss recess. If not, I think it's best to get the extra help if you want to pass the course so you don't have to go to summer school.

Micaela: I definitely don't want to spend the summer learning math because I was too lazy to do the homework. It's a deal.

Ana: Good. We have a few more minutes before your friend comes over. We're making progress. Nobody's raised their voice or said an unkind word. Let's move on to bedtime. You say you want to stay up until ten, but we think we're being generous giving you a 9:00 bedtime on school nights. Your dad and I both feel strongly that you need your rest. You need to wake up at 7:00 to make it to the bus stop on time, and kids your age need about ten hours sleep.

Micaela (sounding frustrated): I can't fall asleep early. I toss and turn in bed if I go upstairs early, and I don't need as much sleep as most of my friends.

Kevin: I have noticed that you seem to be a night owl, that you feel better going to sleep later and waking up a little later. I'm that way too, but Mom's definitely a morning person. Here's what I'm thinking, but Mom will have to give her opinion too: Let's try a 9:30 bedtime. If you can't sleep, read for a few minutes, and then turn out the lights. If you feel very tired the next morning, then we'll go back to 9:00. We're trusting you to tell us if you think you can handle the later bedtime.

Ana: I like Dad's idea and think it's a good compromise. What do you think? Would you be willing to let us know how it works for you, and if it doesn't, to go back to our original time of 9:00?

Micaela: I'd definitely like to try it. It's only a half hour earlier than what I've been bugging you for, and I like the idea of reading in my room if I can't sleep.

Kevin (smiling): As long as you don't read for too long, it works for us.

Micaela: Thanks. I'm going to get my bike helmet. Moira will be here any minute and we're going to ride around the park. She and her parents are always arguing. I'm going to tell her how we worked things out so we're all happy.

88. Help Settle Sibling Disputes

Adrian and Seth find their sons' constant fighting intolerable. Cooper, age nine, is a year older than his brother Ross, and both boys are strong-willed. Once in a while, their parents have to physically separate them because they're ready to fight physically, which could be especially hazardous to Ross since he's slight in build compared to his brawny brother.

The brothers fight about everything, like mutual possessions, especially their sports equipment, who gets to sit in the front seat of the car, and whose turn it is to watch a favorite TV program. Their parents, Adrian and Seth, feel they must intervene every time the boys argue or they may hurt each other physically or psychologically during one of their fracases.

Since it's Sunday, both boys have invited friends over to play ball, which creates the perfect scene for another disagreement between the boys. The boys both received softball equipment their parents told them they must share. Unfortunately, there isn't enough equipment for both boys to use with their two groups of friends.

Unbeknownst to Ross, the older boy, Cooper, invited his friends over first. Scenarios like this happen often because one child doesn't keep the other informed since they don't talk much to one other. When Cooper heard that Ross wanted to use the equipment to play with his friends, he stormed into the house screaming for Seth to arbitrate the dispute in his favor. Seth is crouched over his computer trying to finish some work he brought home that's due the next day.

Cooper: Dad, my friends are coming over soon to play ball, and Ross invited his dumb friends without telling me. I get to use the equipment because I invited them first. Besides, I'm the oldest, and that should mean something.

Seth (looking up from his work): You two need to work it out. I'm tired of being a referee.

Adrian (the boys' mother, who comes in the door carrying a bag of groceries): What now? Tell me you two aren't arguing again. I heard what you said to Dad.

Cooper: I hope you two can set Ross straight before my friends come over. I don't want him pestering me and messing up our game.

Adrian: (Calls upstairs for Ross to come down.)

Ross: (When he comes down, he looks disgusted and won't make eye contact with Cooper.)

Adrian: I want you two to work this out. Dad and I are tired of your fighting. What can you do to make it okay for both of you? I want ideas now.

Cooper: Make him disappear and never come back?

Seth: We don't talk like that in this house. You know that. We want you both to settle this before your friends come over. It's bad enough when you fight in front of us. I'm sure you wouldn't like your friends to know how you treat each other.

Cooper: It's nothing new to them. They fight with their brothers and sisters too.

Adrian: That may be true, but we hold you to a high standard. We don't want to see any more of this fighting, especially when it gets out of control.

Seth: Ross, you haven't said anything yet. Do you have any ideas about how to solve the problem so you're both okay with it?

Ross: If I'd known Cooper invited his friends, I wouldn't have asked mine. I don't like fighting, especially since it's no fun when he takes it out on me. In case you haven't noticed, he weighs fifty pounds more than I do.

Cooper (getting in his face): Are you saying I'm fat?

Ross: I'm saying I'm tired of you bullying me. Look, I don't want to fight. Let's try to think of a way to solve this problem that's fair to both of us.

Adrian: That's the best thing anyone said today. I'm sure you two don't enjoy what's been happening around here lately. You need to find a way to get along or none of us can relax.

Seth: Mom's right. Instead of arguing, I want you both to brainstorm ideas before your friends come over. First, we'll set up some ground rules. No name-calling and no arguing.

Cooper: How about since I asked my friends first, you and your friends can play another game like basketball or video games?

Ross: Why do I always have to give in because I'm the youngest? I didn't know your friends were coming over, and we were looking forward to playing baseball.

Cooper: I've got an idea. Why don't we all play ball together. We can form two teams.

Ross: The only way we can do that is if we divide each team into half my friends and half yours or it won't be fair.

Cooper: I guess we'd better split up our players because you're younger and a bunch of puny runts.

Ross: And you're a big gorilla.

Seth (assertively): Boys, remember the ground rules. No name-calling and arguing.

Cooper: Okay. Sorry Dad. (Looking at Ross.) So, we break up into teams the best way we can to make it even, and then we play to win.

Ross: Why are you so nice all of a sudden?

Cooper: Let's say I'm sick of fighting too. I know we'll fight again, maybe even tomorrow, but when we can't agree, I think we should brainstorm like we did today.

Ross: Another thing before we shake on it: I don't want you hitting me anymore. You have to promise that.

Cooper: I'll try, but it won't be easy—just kidding! Okay, it's a deal. (They shake and go upstairs to get ready before their friends arrive.)

Seth: I guess the secret is to let them have a role in handling their own disputes. We've gotten too involved and made things worse by not letting them dream up some creative solutions for themselves. We still have to be involved, but in a different way, as facilitators rather than by being in total control of the situation.

Adrian: I agree that being too involved is as bad as not intervening at all. Let's see how long it lasts. If they go back to their old ways, we'll remind them of the good job they did today, using their own ideas and resources.

89. Enforce Rules Calmly

Practicing Loving Kindness, a deep concern and consideration for others, is an important precept of Mindfulness. When your kids press your buttons by not abiding by your rules, they test your impulse to demonstrate this kindness. If you can step back from your feelings of anger and use Mindfulness principles to calm yourself before reacting when your children don't cooperate, they and you will feel calmer and more relaxed. You'll also be more likely to gain their cooperation without having to bear the dissension that usually accompanies your kids not cooperating.

Imani, a fourth grader in a city magnet school for gifted kids, struggles with her weight and deals with on-going health issues because of it. Her mother, Risa, does her best to help Imani resolve her problem by modeling healthy eating habits for her daughter although Imani doesn't embrace her mother's message. Risa works as a nurse in the local hospital and lost her husband in a car accident when Imani entered first grade. Since her father's death, Imani has struggled with depression and objects when her mother tries to help her regulate her weight. She also argues with her mother frequently and wants her own way, even when it's not the best thing for her.

The psychologist recommended that Risa take a Mindfulness course, hoping that she could elicit better cooperation from Imani if she learned about the assertive communication, active listening, and Loving Kindness that the class promoted. Risa found learning about these techniques, in addition to practicing stepping back from her feelings of anger and taking a deep breath, very helpful in theory. Would they work in Risa's interactions with Imani? She could only hope.

Now that the time has come to implement these ideas, she makes up her mind to embrace an optimistic mindset. After all, didn't the Mindfulness instructor say that Mindfulness was all about looking on the bright side, no matter how difficult your situation appeared on the surface?

Presently, an immediate issue Risa faces with her daughter is that Imani wants to visit her friend Rachel's house. Rachel and Imani are good friends, but Risa's concern stems from Rachel's lack of parental supervision regarding food choices. Her parents allow her to eat sweets and unhealthy food, like sugary cereals and fruit pies, anytime she desires them.

This brings us to the long-range challenge Risa has of encouraging Imani to eat wisely to help her lose enough weight so she can begin to address her health problems. With both issues, Imani's reluctance to embrace a healthy lifestyle and her desire to visit a friend whose family indulges her with unhealthy foods, precipitating conflicts, Risa thinks it may be helpful to use Mindfulness to solve the problem. Mother and daughter have reached an impasse about Imani watching her diet, and this new disagreement about visiting Rachel makes things come to a head.

Imani comes downstairs to the kitchen in an angry mood because Risa told her she can't go to Rachel's house. "It's bad enough some kids make fun of me at school for being big. I told you how those girls called me 'cow' and 'king size.' Now you won't let me have friends."

Risa takes a deep breath and composes herself before responding. "I hear you, and the counselor is working with those girls that are bothering you. I know you and Rachel are good friends. The main problem in going there is that her parents let her eat whatever she wants. You need to watch what you eat or it will hurt your health."

"Please let me go over. She's my best friend ever. We're planning to paint our nails with that turquoise polish you bought me. Then we were going to play some of those games she got for her birthday."

Risa reminds herself that Imani doesn't give up, and she takes another deep breath. She recalls the assertive language she learned in her Mindfulness class and also remembers the importance of being brief and concise since she knows Imani will take her more seriously if she speaks directly to the point without rambling on. "I want you to ask Rachel to come over here today. You can still polish your nails and she can bring over some of her games."

"It's not the same. Her mom's cool because she always gives us home-made caramel cookies. Sometimes she even makes vanilla fudge, my favorite. Whoops! I shouldn't have told you that."

Risa smiles. "It's a little hard to compete with those treats when all I have to offer are strawberry yogurt pops and blueberries."

"Seriously, Mom, it's boring here. I want to go to Rachel's. She called a little while ago and asked when I'm going over."

Without skipping a beat, Risa says in a firm but friendly voice, "I want you to call Rachel and tell her she's invited for dinner. You two can help me cook. We'll have tacos with all the trimmings and low fat, but yummy, apple crisp for dessert."

"I have to admit, that does sound a little tempting. Can we make the whole dinner? Rachel loves to cook."

Risa takes a deep breath of relief. "Sure, I'll stay out of the kitchen. It will give me a break for a change. Thanks for understanding."

Imani smiles. "I'm glad we finally agreed on something. I'm going to call Rachel now. Then I'll start peeling the apples. Oh, and I'll need the recipes before we start. Thanks, Mama."

She hugs Risa and runs to her room to call her friend.

"I never thought it would be that easy," Risa says aloud, looking upward to the heavens. "Thank you, Mindfulness."

TRY THIS: ACTIVITIES TO CURTAIL CONFLICTS, AGES 10–14

90: Enjoy a Peaceful Report Card Day

Sawyer, a freshman in a competitive suburban high school, dreads going home because of getting a report card filled with Cs and a D in English. His parents grounded him for a month last marking period for getting only two Cs. What punishment would befall him this time?

As he ruminated about whether to go straight home or to go to the park to think about how he'd make excuses to his parents for his mediocre grades, he dreaded the anger and disappointment he'd face when he showed his parents his transcript. Both his parents would be home because his dad managed his own business from home, and his mother had Fridays off from her job as a retail manager.

As Sawyer rode the bus home, he remembered how his parents reacted the last time he brought home what they called a below-average report card. His dad said, "You'll never get into college with those grades." His mom added that college admissions officers look at all report cards from ninth grade on, including it as part of a student's total grade point average. "If your grades are unsatisfactory, or average, they may not admit you to college."

Why were his parents such a pain? Why didn't they understand he hated school except for seeing his friends and sports?

This time, Melanie and Bradley, Sawyer's parents, weren't surprised when they saw his report card. They'd gotten calls from all his major subject teachers, telling them what to expect since they'd asked for frequent progress reports. They'd hired a tutor for English, the main subject that gave him trouble, but that hadn't helped him raise his grade in that subject. Before he got home that day, his parents made a pact to take a different approach since the previous punitive one didn't work and only made things worse.

Their friends, who took a Mindfulness course, told them about Mindfulness techniques that helped with their own kids. They advised practicing active listening by accepting and validating what Sawyer said even if they didn't always agree with what he said. Negativity wasn't helping, and grounding didn't make his grades improve. In fact, frequent arguments about grades seemed to be eroding their relationship with Sawyer.

They decided to listen more and talk less to see if they could gain an understanding of his motivation for not trying harder in school. They also wanted to get their point across that whether or not he chose to go to college after graduation, he should at least leave the possibility open by doing his best in high school.

Sawyer's parents are waiting for him in the living room, when he walks through the door:

Bradley, Sawyer's Dad, starts the conversation, which he believes will either improve the report card issues between parents and child or worsen it. In his view, there will be no middle ground. He knows the outcome depends on how he and his wife handle the discussion. This time, they both want their approach to work.

"We already know about your report card. We've been in touch with all your teachers. We'd like to talk to you about it."

Sawyer's fears about his grades disappear as he faces his dad head-on. Since he's probably in trouble anyway, he might as well say what he thinks. "What's there to talk about? You know I hate school. You're lucky I didn't fail anything."

"It matters to us how you do in school, but it's what you think about it that matters most. Mom and I don't enjoy every part of our jobs, but we do the best we can for our own satisfaction, not just because of the raises and promotions we may earn. We take pride in what we do, and we'd like you to have that feeling too, even if school isn't always fun or exciting."

"I understand how you'd feel that way about your jobs, but school's another story. Most of the subjects I take have nothing to do with real life. What is Shakespeare going to teach me about being a police officer? That's what I want to be, you know. I don't have to go to college for that. So, why do you make such a big deal about grades?"

"We know you've been talking to Officer Lombardi about joining the force when you graduate," Bradley says. "He told us when we went out to dinner with him and his wife last week. Mom and I respect that job choice, but you still need good grades to get into the police academy. You may decide to get a college degree in law enforcement, which may open more opportunities to you. Many police officers now complete two to four years of college. Whatever route you choose, you'll need grades that will make you stand out."

"I never thought about that. I figured as long as I passed everything, I'd be okay getting into the academy. Officer Lombardi did say I'd have to pass written and oral tests to get in, so I guess it's a good idea to start preparing now by trying for better grades."

"What would it take for you to want to work up to your ability?" Melanie asks, building on the opening her son gives her. "We know you can do better. When the counselor tested you, she said you have an excellent ability to perform well in all your subjects."

"Maybe if you and Dad stopped pushing me so hard, I'd want to do better. The more you ground me or say mean things about me, the more I feel like not trying. I guess it's a way of getting back at you." Sawyer looks down and pauses. "To be honest, I don't like acting that way."

"I understand. That's why Dad and I have decided to try looking at things your way and take it from there. You say you don't enjoy going to school, except for friends and sports. At the same time, we know it's important for you to make the most of school and get good grades so you'll have more choices when you graduate."

"Thanks for saying that. It's the first time you understood where I'm coming from. I think if I try harder, it will be pretty easy to bring up my average. I'll spend a little extra time studying for tests, and stop skipping assignments, even though they're boring. I have to admit that I've been slacking off. I want to do better. You may not know this, but it makes me feel lousy to get this kind of report card."

"I'm sure it does," Bradley says. "We're going to do our part by being more positive. What can we do to support you in trying to get better grades so you'll have more options open to you? We believe that what you do now has an influence on what you'll be able to do in the future."

"If you do what you're doing now by standing by me and helping me, that's the best thing you can do. I'll try harder and do my best not to disappoint myself. Maybe we can get that English tutor back to help me decode Shakespeare. That's the one subject I find hard. Otherwise, I'll be okay if I study harder."

"You have the right idea," Bradley says. "It's important to do your best for yourself. Obviously, we'll also feel better if you do, but it's most important to 'be true to yourself,' as your friend Shakespeare says. You can actually learn something from the ancient bard if you open your mind to it. I think that's the secret to success in anything, opening your mind to it."

"I'll be in touch with the English tutor," Melanie says. "Meanwhile, if we can help in any way, please ask. This was a good conversation. I think we got a lot accomplished. The best part is there was no shouting, no name calling, and no hard feelings. I think you're on your way to solving your own problem."

"With a little help from you," Sawyer says, smiling, "and me."

91. Reduce Disputes about Appearance

Reagan, a sixth grader, loves to wear ripped or distressed jeans to school and wants to dye her hair purple like her best friend Claire. Her parents, Gina and Mario, encourage her to express her individuality in what they envision as constructive ways, like writing poetry or going to ballet class. Reagan doesn't understand what's wrong with dressing like all the others kids, although she admits she and her friend are the only ones who crave purple hair.

Parents and daughter get along well in all other respects. Reagan is always willing to babysit her little sister Cara when her parents want to enjoy dinner or a movie on weekends. She also does well in school, and her classmates elected her student council president. Her parents would like to minimize the conflicts about clothing and hairstyle so the family can once again enjoy a peaceful life style.

Reagan's parents know the arguments over clothes and hairstyles usually happen when she's tired and irritable from a long day of school and homework. That's why they decide to talk with her during the early evening of a teacher in-service day when she doesn't have school and will feel rested from sleeping late. They decided ahead of time not to stoke the flames of a longtime argument. This time they plan to listen to what Reagan has to say and to present their case calmly in hopes of reaching a compromise. They also want to encourage her to use her own ideas to end the stalemate.

Gina: Daddy and I want to talk to you about what we discussed the other day.

Reagan: I figured that. My one day off and we're going to get into another fight.

Gina: I don't want that either, believe me. Daddy and I are tired from work. We want to settle this issue and put it to rest. It's getting on all our nerves.

Mario: Especially when I picture you parading around in purple hair. Scary!

Reagan: Daddy, that's not funny. Purple, pink, and blue hair look cool. All the kids love it on Claire.

Gina: As you know, we have different opinions about that. We also don't like you to wear those ripped jeans and distressed denims to school, even if, as you say, all the kids wear them that way.

Reagan: The student council asked the principal to add them to the dress code and she's okay with it. Why can't you be?

Gina: I think it's fine to wear them when you go out with friends. However, every family has different ideas about how you should dress and present yourself at school and elsewhere. Daddy and I think more casual styles are better worn in a casual setting, like movie dates with your friends or going to the mall. School's a more formal setting, where it looks better to wear a nice pair of slacks or jeans.

Reagan: School's not like it was when you were growing up. Kids are more relaxed and laid-back now. They want to feel free, not boxed in to certain dress and hairstyles. A couple of my friends have belly button piercings and tattoos. Their parents don't bug them about it.

Mario: We don't know what their parents say behind closed doors, but that's not the point.

Reagan: Then, what is the point, Daddy? I make good grades. My friends aren't wild like some kids at school. Why do I have to dress like they did back in the olden days when you two were in school?

Gina: We're not asking you to do that, and besides, it wasn't all that long ago. We're not the old fossils you think we were. We dressed casually for school and even more so when we went out with friends, but we thought it was important to us to look presentable for school. Our parents wouldn't let us out of the house if we didn't.

Reagan: Now I can see why both of you are that way. But you have to remember that you grew up back in the day when kids didn't have much say about what they wore or how they did their hair.

Mario (smiling): It wasn't all that long ago. I have to admit I tried to look like one of the cool kids with my long, shaggy hair. Now that I look back on it, I looked like one of the Beatles. My parents didn't think it looked great, and they made me go for the tamed look when I went to school, so I gelled my hair back so it looked slick. On the weekends, I could let loose with the flyaway look.

Gina: A lot of girls wore their hair long and straight back then, but mine was a wild, unruly mane, so I figured I'd let it hang loose. At school, though, I usually swept it back in a sleek ponytail or bun so people could see my face; otherwise, I'd be invisible beneath that big mop of hair. I admit we put highlights in our hair with that spray that washes out, but purple or pink would have mortified both my parents and me.

Reagan: But that's the style now, Mom.

Gina: I don't know if you can consider it the style if only you and your friend Claire want to dye your hair purple. Not everyone likes it. It would make you stand out, that's true. But think of how you want people to perceive you. Would you want to be identified mainly by your hairstyle or by the things you accomplish at school, like honor roll, student council, and the poetry you write?

Reagan: I guess you're right. It would look pretty bizarre for me to all of a sudden go from dark brown to purple, but I still want to try it.

Gina: Here's a solution. See what you think. If you still want to go purple by the time summer rolls around, why not try a temporary rinse instead of a dye that lasts a long time? By the time school starts, you'll have tried your purple hair and probably be ready to go back to beautiful brown.

Reagan: What if I still like it and want to keep it?

Gina: I'll bet you a new pair of ripped jeans you won't.

Reagan: I'll go for that. Now what about the jeans? Do I still have to wear my regular jeans to school after I paid all that money for the other ones?

Mario: Yes, you do. However, on the weekends, you can wear the ripped and distressed jeans if you want when you go out with your friends.

That's fine with us. We both feel strongly that you need to look present-able for school but that it's okay to wear a more relaxed look when you're with your friends. What do you say?

Reagan: I guess it's a good compromise, even though I love those jeans and want to wear them all the time. So, okay, I'm in.

Gina: What do you think about our idea for trying out the purple hair in the summer?

Reagan: Maybe by the summer I'll want pink or blue hair, or maybe I'll just want my own color. You know how I love to change my mind. I agree that wearing purple hair to school would call too much attention to something I don't want to stress, so I won't wear it to school.

Mario: I'm happy we can all agree, and not once did we raise our voices. It's a miracle. Remind me to tell you sometime about how we dressed back then and what kind of music we liked.

Gina: Sometime Daddy and I will take you roller skating. That was the big fad back then. I also have an old mood ring from the seventies. It changed colors according to the mood you were in.

Reagan: My friends would love that. Can I borrow it?

Gina: I'll get it for you right now. You can start a whole new fad. Maybe Claire won't care about purple hair anymore.

92. Find a Solution to Curfew Issues

Trey, a bright and popular ninth grader in a city high school, frequently argues with his parents about his curfew. His mom and dad, Vanessa and Owen, have told him he has to be home by nine on school nights and ten on weekends. He believes he should be allowed to come in at ten on school nights, except when he goes to sporting events that run later, and eleven on weekends. He loves going to concerts, but many of these events last past eleven, so he'd like them to make exceptions when he attends them.

Trey is gearing up for a weekend party with his friends. They told him it would last until eleven and hoped he could stay until the end because they knew he had an earlier curfew than they had. His friends don't tease him because he has to be in earlier than they do, but they say things like, "Your parents are living in the dark ages. Tell them to get with it, man, or we can't have any fun."

Trey doesn't respond when they say things about his parents and their rules, but he seethes inside. Why can't they be more flexible? What are they trying to prove by making him look like a little child in front of his friends, whose parents understand them better?

After dinner, Vanessa and Owen broach the subject of curfews since they know Trey plans to attend the party tomorrow. They know he's in a good mood because his JV team just won the city championship. They've learned throughout the years with all three of their children that timing is very important when talking to their kids about a sticky issue. Vanessa starts the conversation:

"Now is a good time to talk about what time you need to come home from the party tomorrow. Dad and I want to hear what you have to say, but we also don't want to compromise our values. Given those conditions, what do you think is fair?"

"We're not saying we'll do what you think, but we want to hear your ideas, and then we'll decide," Owen adds.

Trey stops for a minute to consider their offer. "I'm thinking nine-thirty on school nights instead of nine. I asked for ten, but I think both of us could live with nine-thirty, except for games, which you're okay with my coming in later anyway."

"How about if we try it your way for a while? Nine-thirty on school nights sounds like a good compromise, and later, of course, if you go to games," Owen says.

Trey's mother moves closer to him. "Let's try it out, and if you seem tired the next day for school with the later time, we can always re-evaluate it."

"Okay, I'm in," says Trey. "Now, what about the weekends? There's that party tomorrow. I also told you my friends and I are planning to go to a concert next month. It would be embarrassing to leave the party or concert earlier than my friends."

"I can understand that," Owen says with a faraway look. "I remember when I was your age my parents wouldn't allow me to go to concerts. I felt left out and foolish. If you want to talk about over-protective, you should have seen the rules your grandma and grandpa made for me and my sisters."

Trey rolls his eyes. "I can believe it. They still treat you like a baby. Grandma's always reminding you to wear your heavy coat and asking you if you've had enough to eat."

Owen smiles. "I guess we'll always be little kids to our parents, but in some ways, that's a good thing. Shows us how much they love us. Nobody loves you like your parents, son."

"I know that, Dad. It's just that I don't want to be the only one who has an early curfew, especially on the weekends when everything fun's happening."

Vanessa nods. "We understand. That's why we're having this talk, so we can come to an agreement that everyone can live with. I'm thinking if Dad's okay with it, we can move up your weekend curfew to eleven for the party, and see how it goes. If we all feel comfortable with it, we can try it for a while. If it works out, we can make it permanent."

"That sounds fair to me," Owen says.

"Thanks," Trey says, surprised things are going so smoothly. Maybe his parents weren't as old-fashioned and rigid as he thought. "Now what about the concerts? Can we move up the time for those, depending on when they end?"

"We can do that on a case by case basis. If we think one will end way too late, we'll still have the right to tell you to come home at a reasonable hour. We looked up the one you're going to next week online and saw that it would probably end at twelve. That would be okay, if you didn't make a habit of keeping those late hours."

Trey smiles and hugs his parents. "Thanks, you two, for understanding. It's so much better than arguing."

Owen pats him on the shoulder. "I won't disagree with you on that. It's always best to solve problems peacefully whenever you can."

93. Come to an Agreement About Dating

Daisy, a very mature-looking eighth-grader, finds she's romantically attracted to Christian, a bright and respectful ninth-grader in her Spanish class. Daisy's father is not in the picture, and her mother Marla has been in and out of drug rehab because of an opioid addiction. Daisy's grandparents, Ruby and Glenn, have taken care of her since she was a toddler. With Marla's approval, Daisy's grandparents brought her to live in their home, with the option she'd return to live with her mother when she was able to care for her. Recently, Marla moved to a halfway house in hopes that she'll eventually make a full recovery.

Last week, Daisy told her grandparents that she'd like to date Christian, but they believe she's too young for dating, especially in view of what happened with her mother Marla. To her parents' dismay, after dating Daisy's father for a year, Marla became sexually involved with him in the tenth grade. He abruptly left her when he discovered she was pregnant. Daisy's father made it clear when he left that he wanted nothing to do with his child, and the family has been unable to contact him for help with child support.

Marla's parents supported their daughter financially and emotionally during and after her pregnancy, but she fell in with a wild crowd after she dropped out of school and, in her despair, turned to drugs.

Daisy has a good relationship with her grandparents. Dating is the first issue they've fought about. They're distressed that Daisy has threatened to see Christian behind their backs if they don't allow her to go out with him. They found that ultimatum so unlike her. They also know they can't control what she does when she's out of their sight. This argument made her grand-parents see the need for a serious discussion about dating.

When she got home from softball practice, Daisy told her grandparents she'd like to go to a movie with Christian this weekend. She promised that his parents would drive them and stay with them at the movie. They'd prob-ably take the two teens to an ice cream parlor after the movie. Here's how the conversation went:

Ruby: What you're saying is that you'd like to date this boy from school. We both think you're too young. We think you need to wait another year to gain more maturity.

Glenn: I have to agree with Granny. Eighth grade is too young to go out with a boy, even if his parents drive you and stay with you at the movie.

Daisy: We're not going to make out or anything, especially in front of his parents. You already told me about what you call "the birds and the bees," so I won't be getting into any trouble. You know you can trust me.

Ruby: It's not that, honey. At your age, you should be going out with your girlfriends, doing one another's hair and make-up, and going shopping. Boys can wait. Pop and I weren't allowed to date until we were sixteen.

Daisy: I don't think there's any magic age for having a boy for a friend, plus he's not even my boyfriend yet, just a friend. It doesn't mean I'm going to marry him. Anytime I see him, his parents, or you and Pop, will be close by, so there's nothing to worry about.

Glenn: The main thing we're concerned about is that one thing will lead to another. If we let you go out to the movie, the next thing you'll want is to go out with him in a car with some of his friends who drive.

Daisy (frustrated): None of his friends drive, and he can't drive for at least a year, so no worries there.

Ruby (shaking her head): I'm beginning to wonder if Pop and I are too old to be your guardians. You need younger parents who aren't too tired to keep up with your quick answers.

Daisy: You're the best grandparents, and I'm glad you're taking care of me. I wouldn't want to live with anyone else, even Aunt Patsy, who keeps asking me to live with her. She's a terrible cook and she can be grumpy sometimes, even though I love her.

Glenn: Well that settles it. You're stuck with us. Do you want to say anything else about your requests before we decide?

Daisy: I hate to break it to you now, but I guess it's as good a time as any. Christian's ninth-grade graduation dance is coming up, and he asked me to be his date. He asked what color dress I'm wearing so he can buy me a corsage. You don't have to buy me a new dress if I go. I can wear the pink one we bought for the awards ceremony at school.

Ruby (frowning): Just when I thought we only had to deal with going to the movies, now we also have to think about your going to a graduation dance.

Daisy: Well, let's talk about the movie first.

Ruby: Pop and I need to go into the other room to discuss this privately. We'll be right back. (They move into the kitchen to talk.)

Daisy: What's taking them so long? Why is it such a big decision for them to tell me if I can go to a movie with his parents sitting right next to us? (Daisy is about to give up on her efforts to convince her grandparents she'll be perfectly safe going out with Christian to the movies with his parents in tow, and going to his graduation dance with teacher and parent chaperones in attendance. Ruby and Glenn return to the living room.)

Ruby: We've decided to let you go to the movies with your friend and his parents. If you want to see him at our house or theirs, there always has to be an adult close by in the house.

Daisy: Thanks, Granny. Now what about the graduation dance?

Glenn: As long as you're not embarrassed to let us be chaperones, it's fine with us.

Daisy (laughing): Do you have to?

Glenn: Got you going there for a minute, didn't I? Just kidding!

Ruby: We also want to buy you a new dress for the dance. Your friends can't see you in the same dress you wore to the awards ceremony. That would be very embarrassing, right?

Daisy: Thanks, Granny and Pop. I'm glad we agreed without arguing.

Glenn: I'm glad too, but wait until you want to go out in a car with a boy. That may be an entirely different story.

Ruby: Let's take it one step at a time, Glenn. So far, so good.

Chapter Twelve

Deliver Meaningful Consequences

THINK ABOUT THIS

As you can see, parenting is a balancing act. You want your kids to know you love them and to show that love toward them unconditionally. However, you also need to do your best to make sure they learn self-discipline and know their limits because practicing self-control and acceptable behavior is an important factor in helping them living their best possible lives. Sometimes, the balance shifts one way or the other. In the end, if children know they're loved and you demonstrate it with your words and deeds and discipline them in the best way possible when you have to, they'll have their greatest chance for living happy, well-adjusted lives.

We've all known parents who stress giving their children all the material advantages and giving in to their every whim at the expense of creating uncaring, selfish adults. You are the main people your children turn to for guidance about how to behave throughout their formative years. Let your children know when they cross the line of good behavior and respect for you and others. In the long run, you'll enjoy a better relationship if you hold them to high behavioral standards.

These days many parents hesitate to correct their children when they misbehave because they fear alienating them. We've all observed children acting out in public places like stores and restaurants, causing inconvenience to other patrons and embarrassment to their parents. Some parents hesitate correcting their children for fear of hurting their feelings or making them feel unloved. Other parents are exhausted from work and try to make up for time away from their kids by overindulging them with gifts and overlooking episodes of acting out and rudeness.

Ironically, setting high standards for behavior and enforcing them by giving children appropriate consequences will help create a strong bond between you and your children. Consistency in discipline helps reinforce the behavioral standards you set and makes it easier for your kids to know exactly what you expect from them every time.

When your child rebels and tests your limits, consider using calm reasoning, assertive talk, and appropriate consequences to reverse his behavior. However, if you don't believe you can handle a discipline issue alone, you can turn to school and community resources for help, or you and your child can use a private counselor to help remediate the problem. There is always hope and help, no matter how serious the situation.

It takes courage to discipline your child and to follow through with consequences. It's often easier to overlook a breach in behavior than to take the time and effort to deal with it before it mushrooms into a bigger problem that will prove more difficult to handle. Thinking of the right consequence for misconduct often requires creative thinking on your part.

A challenge often presents itself when you're trying to make the consequence fit the misdeed so the punishment you give will help your child grow and learn from the experience. Sometime, if you see fit, you can ask your child what he thinks would be an appropriate consequence for his misbehavior. Kids can surprise you with the creative consequences they invent. It's interesting to note that they are sometimes harder on themselves than you would be in creating and meting out a consequence.

Delivering meaningful consequences can also involve using incentives for good behavior. Using incentives doesn't necessarily mean giving material rewards, although it doesn't preclude it. Mainly, it means offering your child extra perks and privileges for continuing to abide by your rules. Children often respond well to incentives being added to the mix because it's a form of positive reinforcement. In line with this, it's important to ensure that your consequence motivates change in that it makes your child think about the positive results that will come from behaving the right way.

One of the most important things you can do to inspire your children to behave well is to be role models for them in practicing positive behavior traits, such as honesty, kindness, and industriousness. The best thing you can do to model and promote self-control is to teach your kids self-discipline by example. If your children see you practicing self-discipline, rather than merely giving it lip service, they'll be more likely to embrace your values.

Often, older relatives, such as grandparents, aunts, and uncles, can influence children more strongly and easily than their own parents can because kids tend to listen to them more than they do their parents. These relatives aren't as close to kids' daily problems and acts of misbehavior, so they tend to listen more objectively and patiently than parents do.

Using Mindfulness principles can help you restore discipline and order to your home. It can boost your parental powers by giving you techniques like flexibility, thinking before you act, and assertive speech to help manage your children. Ultimately, using discipline mindfully will help your children in all areas of their lives: at home, in school, and in the world of work.

MODEL A CONVERSATION: DELIVER MEANINGFUL CONSEQUENCES

94. Show Firmness and Strength When Disciplining

Ethan, age fourteen, attends a private school and is failing two of his school subjects, due to not applying himself. Clayton and Julie, his parents, have experienced serious behavior problems with Ethan. He has become increasingly rebellious to the point that they feel they're losing control over him. Recently, his parents found out he attended a party where the attendees drank alcohol, unbeknownst to the parents, who stayed upstairs in their room and didn't check on the kids celebrating in the basement rec room.

Clayton and Julie knew the parents of the boy who hosted the party and thought they were responsible until they discovered they didn't properly supervise Ethan and the other youngsters. After this episode, which they discovered when Ethan arrived home with alcohol on his breath, they grounded him for a month, but he became more defiant than they'd ever seen him and said he wanted to move in with his friend Carlton's family. When his parents refused, Ethan had little to do with them, taking his meals alone after they left the table and rarely talking to them.

Shortly after the party episode, Mr. Lawrence, the dean of discipline at his school, called Ethan's parents after he was suspended for cutting two of his classes that happened to be the ones he's failing. The school counselor met with Ethan's parents to discuss Ethan's case after their son's reinstatement to school following his suspension. He suggested that the parents meet with Mr. Lawrence to see how they could work as a team to help Ethan. Mr. Lawrence studied Mindfulness extensively and finds it helpful with kids like Ethan, who are rebellious and have serious behavior problems. Here's what happened at their session:

Mr. Lawrence: Welcome, Julie and Clayton. Please feel free to call me Douglas. I'm hoping I can help you with Ethan's behavior problems. I know you must be at your wit's end with one thing after another happening.

Clayton: We've had some problems with Ethan in the past, and they've grown worse. This year has been very hard for us.

Julie (visibly upset): I know the counselor told you about the party episode, and we found evidence that he's smoking despite his asthma. He rebels against everything we want him to do at home and school. As you know, his grades have plummeted. His social studies teacher says he talks incessantly in class and won't follow instructions. Also, he the cut those classes, causing his suspension.

Mr. Lawrence (nodding and putting himself in their place): I can see how upsetting this is for both of you. I'm thinking I could model some Mindfulness techniques for you to help get Ethan back on track. Mindfulness can prove very helpful in solving behavior problems if your child is open to it. If you don't see satisfactory progress in a reasonable period of time, I hope you'll seek psychological help for your son.

Clayton: We want to help our son in any way we can. If things don't improve, we'll seek help for all three of us. We see it as a family problem and not only as a problem with our son. Perhaps our main shortcoming in raising Ethan is that we've been too permissive and overlooked too many things. Sometimes, when he was much younger, we'd laugh at his misbehavior, thinking he was clever or cute. As he grew older, he started testing us more by not listening and talking back. We reached the point where we felt overwhelmed and didn't know if it was too late to regain control.

Mr. Lawrence: In some cases, even though the pattern is set, you can help a child change his behavior. In others, it may be too late. You will know soon enough by the way he responds to your efforts. Now let's get started with our modeling exercise to see if we can help Ethan. Clayton, I'd like you to take the part of Ethan. I'll pretend I'm you talking to Ethan using "I-messages" and communicating assertively. Julie, you can be yourself. Try to use some of the Mindfulness techniques of validating, empathizing, and putting yourself in your son's place that I sent to your home last week in the packet.

Clayton (acting as Ethan): Dad, I'm tired of you two telling me what to do all the time. I want to go live with Carlton. His parents don't bug him all the time. They said I could stay with them as long as I want.

Mr. Lawrence (acting as Ethan's dad Clayton): Moving in with your friend's family would have to be something we'd approve of, and we don't. We're your parents and we want to help you. Living with your friend isn't going to solve our family's problems. I know you feel we boss you around, but the truth is we're concerned about a lot of things that happened, like your drinking at the party, smoking, and cutting classes. If you were us, wouldn't you be concerned?

Clayton/Ethan: I guess I would, but I'd probably handle it a different way.

Julie (listening, acting curious to find out more): What would you do if you were Dad and I?

Clayton/Ethan: I'd try to understand where you were coming from. I'd also back off more and let you make your own decisions.

Mr. Lawrence/Clayton: We're willing to do that if you prove yourself responsible over a reasonable period of time.

Clayton/Ethan: What does that mean? What would I have to do?

Julie: You'd promise yourself and us to stop cutting class and stick to it. If you find it hard, you could use self-talk, a helpful Mindfulness technique. All you do is say something to yourself in your mind like, "I feel like cutting today, but if I do, my grades will drop again. I'll get suspended, and it's not fun staying home with no TV and video games. Maybe I'll rethink cutting and go to class."

Clayton/Ethan: I've never heard of self-talk, but I guess I do it sometimes when I want to make excuses for myself. This kind of self-talk is different from what I've done. Maybe I'll try it, but only in my mind, of course, or my friends would think I've lost it if they heard me.

Mr. Lawrence/Clayton: You could also use self-talk to help you stop smoking. I'd like to see you start turning things around, not only for your mom and me, but mainly for you. Here's another example of how you can help yourself with Mindfulness: When you make a change by saying what you mean by using assertive language instead of arguing and talking back, we'll be able to talk to one another and get somewhere.

Clayton/Ethan: You're saying if I'm annoyed about something or think what you want me to do is unfair to say it straight up? That's a switch.

Mr. Lawrence/Clayton: That's right, but you need to say it without placing blame or demanding that we change our standards for behavior to meet yours. Then we'll come back to you with our position. Naturally, since you're still a minor, under our care, we'll have the final say. The difference is that we'll listen to you more than we did before and try to understand your point of view.

Clayton/Ethan: I don't know if I'm going to like what you say, but okay, I'll try using your assertive communication.

Julie: You may not be aware of it, but you used it now. You said what you thought without arguing. You got your point across.

Clayton/Ethan: What if these things don't work?

Mr. Lawrence/Clayton: We'll deal with that if and when it happens. For now, we've made a good start. If we can talk to one another civilly, we're on our way.

Julie: I agree. I think we can do this if we all try our best.

Mr. Lawrence: You folks did an admirable job with this exercise. I'd like you to go home and try using the Mindfulness techniques we modeled today with Ethan. In a week or so, please call and let me know how he's progressing. Thanks for coming in today. After today's session, I'm hopeful we can reach Ethan. All he has to do is want to respond. That's a big order, but I'm optimistic, given your willingness to reach out to him.

TRY THIS: ACTIVITIES TO HELP YOU DELIVER MEANINGFUL CONSEQUENCES, AGES 6–9

95. Have the Courage to Discipline in Public

Savannah, a bright, engaging child, who recently started first grade in a parochial school, often acts socially immature and younger than her age when she's out in public with her mom. It doesn't happen when she's with other family members or friends, only with her mother Mallory. Her mom, a divorced single parent, has total custody of Savannah and has raised her alone since she was a toddler.

When Mallory takes her daughter grocery shopping, Savannah often tosses candy and cookies into the shopping cart without her mother's permission. To Mallory's embarrassment, Savannah throws loud temper tantrums when they get to the check-out counter if her mother tells the cashier not to ring up the goodies that Savannah puts in the cart. Her mother usually gives in to her child's demands, due to customers giving her disapproving looks.

When mother and daughter go to a restaurant, Savannah sometimes leaves the table and crawls around on the floor under the tables, disturbing neighboring patrons. If Mallory tries to stop her, she creates a scene. When they visit the mall, Savannah runs around the store touching the mannequins and displays, and it's hard for her mother to catch up with her. Recently, in one of the major department stores, Savannah got separated from her mother who naturally became frantic. A few minutes later, Mallory heard this announcement over the loud speaker: "Savannah's mother, please report to the security desk. We have your daughter." By this time Mallory had broken out in tears, more out of relief than anger.

Mallory has tried everything with her daughter, including reprimands, time-outs, and trying to reason with her, but nothing seems to work. Her friend Lacey, who studied Mindfulness, suggested talking to Savannah with assertive language and "I-messages" to let her know she won't tolerate her misbehaving in public. If this doesn't solve the problem, Lacey advises immediately leaving the store or the restaurant in order to help Savannah learn proper public behavior.

Mallory and her friend meet at a local coffee shop on Mallory's day off from her job as a paralegal in a local law office. After they order their coffee and scones, Lacey initiates the conversation about Mallory's difficulties dealing with her daughter when they're out in public.

"I know how upset you've been about Savannah's behavior in public. It's hard for me to imagine since when I'm at your house, she's a model child."

"That's what everyone, including her teachers, tells me. She only acts out when we go to restaurants or malls. At home, she rarely gives me problems. Sometimes, I think she's crying out for attention because of how intense she gets when she has these episodes. If it keeps up and I can't find a solution, I may take her to a child psychologist."

"That might help. If you'd like to try a few things first, I'll be happy to suggest some ways I've used Mindfulness when my own kids test my boundaries."

"I know that I overlook a lot of things Savannah does when we're in public, and even though her actions anger and embarrass me, I cut her a lot of slack because she's basically a good kid and she has only me. As you know, her father bailed out a long time ago and doesn't visit her or support her financially."

"I understand how hard that must be for you and her. However, we're here to see if we can get Savannah to show good behavior whether she's home or out."

"What do you suggest? You mentioned something about talking to her a certain way."

"First, let me know what you do when she puts the candy in your shopping cart and creates a scene when it's time to check out if you don't give in and allow her to have it."

Mallory lowers her eyes. "I don't say much until we get home because I want to get out of the store as quickly as possible. Everyone is looking at us, shaking their heads and rolling their eyes. Sometimes they even make comments about parents who can't control their kids, which makes me feel really bad. In the car, I tell Savannah I'm not proud of the way she acted and that she'll be punished when we get home. It's usually no TV for the rest of the day or I take away her video games."

Lacey touches her friend's hand and makes eye contact. "The main thing is to deliver the consequence as soon after the action as possible. You need to say something in the store, not wait until you get in the car. You could say, 'We have candy at home and we're not buying this. I need you to stop screaming now.'

"Talk assertively and briefly. Then, if she doesn't stop screaming and demanding that she gets her way, apologize to the cashier and ask if she could get another worker to return your groceries to the shelf. At that point, if Savannah doesn't stop her tantrum, the best thing to do is lead her bodily out of the store, even if she is kicking and screaming. Look your daughter in the eye and say firmly, 'We are leaving now' and follow through."

"I've never tried talking that way to her, but it sounds like a good idea. I usually respond one of two ways, by telling her in a loud voice to behave or by overlooking it and dealing with it when we get home. If I do make a threat, I usually don't carry it out. I know I'm what Mindfulness people would call a passive communicator."

Lacey smiles warmly. "I'd like to see you try using assertive speech with Savannah. You won't know if it will work unless you try it. Here's another example: When you take her to the mall, use assertive speech like this: 'I need you to stay close by me at all times. If you break away or I have to find you in the security office, you'll stay home with a babysitter next time. You won't be allowed to go shopping or out to lunch at your favorite restaurant.' If she doesn't follow your rules for staying near you when shopping, enforce the consequence you gave her and don't back down. That will give her a strong incentive.

"Now, I'd like to see what you would say to Savannah if she starts misbehaving in a restaurant when you're out with her. Imagine she's running around and crawling under the tables, disturbing other diners."

Mallory takes deep breath. "First I'd go over to her and lead her back to our table. I'd grab her hand and physically take her back. I'd say, 'I don't like when you do this. I want you to stop it now.'"

Lacey gives her a thumbs-up. "I like how you used the 'I-message' and talked briefly, using assertive language. Now here's the true test: What would you say and do if she doesn't do what you ask?"

"I'd say, 'You're bothering other people who are trying to enjoy their dinner. You chose not to move when I asked you to come back to the table. I'm going to tell the hostess we have to leave. We'll eat the leftover lunch-meat I have in the 'fridge.'"

"Good response. The next time you have a problem with Savannah be-having, see how using assertive talk and action works for you. Remember to follow through with what you say you'll do, or it won't work. Please call me the next time you have a problem and let me know how it works out."

"I hope I can get her to behave in public by using assertive talk with 'I-messages' and also by letting her know I'll follow up with a consequence when she doesn't cooperate. If it doesn't work, we'll take the next step."

Lacey hugs her friend. "I agree. Take one step at a time. I'm hoping for the best. Fingers crossed . . ."

96. Make the Consequences Fit the Act

The same old punishments, taking away TV, electronics, and time-outs, aren't working anymore with Avi, a third grader in a public magnet school for gifted children. He behaves perfectly in school and scores high honors on his report card. However, he misbehaves regularly at home by bullying his little sister Ruth and by leaving his games and books strewn all over his room despite his parents' strong attempts to get him to modify his behavior.

One counterproductive thing Elisa, his mother, and dad, Aaron, do is make threats they don't carry out. For example, when he called his sister Ruth names, like "piglet" and "stupid," his mom told him he couldn't use his video games for a week. However, she caught him using them openly many times; he didn't try to hide his disregard for the consequence.

When Avi's parents discussed his non-compliance with their punishment, they concluded that maybe the punishment didn't work because it had nothing to do with calling his sister names. Another problem they saw was repeatedly using the same punishment, like taking games and visiting friends away from him. They felt the punishments had lost their meaning and they knew they had to come up with something new—but what?

On a couple of occasions, Avi pushed Ruth for touching his belongings, and she fell to the ground. Although she wasn't hurt physically, her parents could tell that she suffered emotionally because she loves Avi and doesn't understand why he treats her this way. After Avi pushed Ruth the second time, his parents told him he couldn't visit his friend for two weeks. It didn't seem to make an impression on him because he spent a lot of time those two weeks texting his friend and playing video games with him online.

Avi's parents began to see that their consequences had lost meaning for him. His mom enjoyed reading books about Mindfulness and decided to try applying it to her continuing problems with Avi. Her husband agreed it was worth a try, since nothing else seemed to work. Now that Avi is asleep, his parents meet in the living room to discuss their next step.

Aaron: Things are really getting out of hand. The other day Avi told Ruth she was a "chunky loser" and shoved her, all because she touched his precious tablet. She was so upset she wouldn't even come down for dinner. We have to do something now before it gets worse.

Elisa: If I hadn't gotten between them, Ruth might have fallen again when he shoved her. We can't have this happening. I told him to apologize to his sister, but it was barely audible and very feeble. I don't think Ruth was convinced he meant it.

Aaron: You told me something that you read in your mindfulness books about practicing Loving Kindness. It sounds like that may be something we're looking for to help Avi look at his sister in a new and caring way. Could we try to use it with Avi when he treats his sister unkindly?

Elisa: I like that idea. How about if the next time he shows disrespect to Ruth, we have him make a list of five things he can do to show her kindness? We'll let him know before he writes his acts of kindness, that he'll have to carry all of them out in a week's time. He'll make up a check list that states each one and then check them off as he does them.

Aaron: That's creative thinking. Hopefully, it will help since it's directly related to how Avi treats Ruth.

Elisa: This is the main problem we want to solve, but I'm wondering what we can we do about the smaller problem about how he leaves everything around his room. It looks like a fire hazard, and I'm afraid someone will trip in there with all his possessions thrown all over.

Aaron: I'm thinking along the same lines you just did when you came up with things he can do to show kindness to Ruth. I'm thinking that again the punishment must fit the misdeed. If it's unrelated, and if you repeat it too many times as we did, it's not going to work. How about every time he leaves things around his room, we gather them in those big trash bags and don't give whatever's in the bag back to him for a week? If he backtracks, the clothes and toys go back in the bag again.

Elisa: Let's try it. I'm sure we'll hear a lot of complaints if we do that, but it will be worth it if it motivates him to keep his room presentable.

Determined to help their son overcome his mistreatment of his sister, Elisa and Aaron implement their new plan. It seems to be working well. At this point, they aren't as concerned about the other challenge of keeping his room habitable because they're giving the problem with Ruth priority. They'll tackle that problem once they solve the major one.

Here's a list that Avi made up the last time he called his sister names. He posted it on the kitchen bulletin board and checks off each act of kindness as he does it.

Things I can do to be kind to Ruth
by Avi

1. Share my candy with her, giving her first pick.
2. Tell her thanks for not touching my videos.
3. Do a project with her, like baking cookies.
4. Watch a TV show with her that we both like.
5. Say "I'm sorry" when I slip and say something mean to her.
6. Never push her, no matter what.

97. Ask Your Child to Create a Consequence

Sometimes when your child's been misbehaving and you're looking for an innovative way to help her change her ways, try something different and ask her to suggest a consequence. You'll be surprised at the creativity and ingenuity kids are capable of when you ask them to think of a disciplinary action they think will work for them. Obviously, it's helpful to have this discussion when you aren't experiencing anger or annoyance about something your child has recently done that she shouldn't have. It's best to talk about it after you and she have cooled down rather right after she does something that warrants your disapproval.

Often, children follow a pattern, displaying one or more discipline problems over a period of time. You know what kinds of infractions to watch for in your child; so, you'll know which ones to discuss with her, along with her ideas for consequences, when she's most receptive.

Caroline, a popular fourth grader in a suburban school, puts up a fight whenever her parents ask her to do simple chores, like feeding the cat or setting the table. Talking back and arguing are a frequent occurrence lately. She also complains when her parents don't let her go to a friend's house the nights she has homework. Caroline wants her parents to treat her like a teenager by giving her more freedom even though she's a tween. Her parents would like her to know that gaining more freedom involves taking more responsibility for her actions. If she shows maturity by her actions, they'll be willing to listen to her requests.

Her parents, Trevor and Holly, would like to find ways to involve Caroline in the remediation process. They're talking to her mindfully on a school holiday when she's relaxed and looking forward to inviting her friend Jayla to a movie with the family:

Holly: Before we get ready to go out, Dad and I would like to talk to you about what I mentioned the other day.

Caroline: Every time we talk, it turns into a fight, so can't we forget it and have a good day for once?

Trevor (validating and using assertive talk): I understand what you're saying and accept it, but we need to discuss how to deal with it when you talk back or argue with what we say. We want to involve you in the process. So, will you sit with us for a few minutes and give us your ideas about what you think are good consequences when you don't cooperate?

Caroline: You're asking me to tell you what I would do if I were the parent? Did you really say that?

Holly: We're asking for your ideas because some of ours don't seem to be working. We want to give you more of a say about consequences because we think it will help you be more responsible for your actions. If you come up with a good consequence, you'll be more likely to think before you misbehave next time.

Caroline (considering what they say): Picking my own punishment sounds a little weird, but, okay, maybe it is something to think about. Those time-outs, yelling at me, and taking away things I like don't seem to help much, so maybe we can try this. I like the idea of your trusting me to think of something the next time I give you problems, and you know I will. (She smiles.) I can't help giving you grief sometimes. After all, I'm practically a teenager, and teenagers can be a real pain with their parents.

Trevor (listening and accepting): I know you like to think of yourself as a teenager, and, if that's the case, we expect you to try your best to act more grown up when it comes to cooperating and talking to us with respect as we usually talk to you.

Caroline: Except when I stress you out, which is pretty often these days.

Holly: I think if we all make an effort to treat each other better, we'll live happier and more peaceful lives. Dad and I don't like arguing with you, and it can't be fun for you.

Caroline: I'd like us to get along too. Okay, how about if I give you my idea about what to do when I talk back?

Trevor (acting curious): Can you think of anything you can do to stop yourself before you talk back to us?

Caroline: That would be even better. I could stop and take a couple of deep breaths like the school counselor told us to do when we get upset. Then I could try my best to be calm when I talk.

Holly: You're on the right track. Once you start talking about what's bothering you, you could explain it clearly and briefly without getting worked up. That's called assertive speech.

Trevor: Now can you think of a consequence if you forget to pause and take a deep breath and start talking back?

Caroline: I could write you a letter of apology. You know that writing isn't my favorite thing, so that would be a good consequence. Then I could offer to do a couple of chores I don't usually do and add it to the chores I already have. Maybe I could empty the dishwasher and fold the laundry. I could do the extra chores for a week. If I *really* talk back, we could make it two. Of course, I'd still write the apology.

Holly (smiling at Caroline): That sounds like a punishment to fit the crime. You're writing something personal about what you did and want to make up for it, and you're doing something to help us to make up for saying hurtful words.

Trevor: What consequence would you give if you argue when it's time to feed the cat or set the table?

Caroline: I need to think about that one.

Holly: Take your time. We like how this is going, and we're willing to wait.

Caroline: I've got it! If I argue about feeding the cat, I won't be able to play with him for a couple of days, and you know how much I love watching him catch his squeaky toys when I throw them. If I don't set the table or take my time doing it, I'll have to scrape and stack the dishes in the dishwasher for a week. That's one job I can't stand.

Trevor: I must say you're harder on yourself than we'd probably be with you.

Holly: I'd like to add that in all the cases we've talked about, the consequence does fit the deed. I say we should try your ideas. What do you think, Trevor?

Trevor: I'm in. Let's see how it works out: taking a couple of deep breaths and calming yourself before you say something to us you don't mean, and if you don't do certain chores, using the consequences you suggested. We'll give your ideas a fair chance.

Caroline: I like this idea. I'm going to tell Jayla about it when her mom drops her off for the movie. Maybe she can do it when she gets in trouble too. Thanks for listening to my ideas. (She runs upstairs to get ready. Her parents give each other a high five.)

98. Use Incentives to Encourage Good Behavior

Giving incentives is an effective way of encouraging desirable behavior in your children as long as it doesn't look like a bribe. A bribe will look something like this: "You can have an extra piece of candy if you go to sleep right now." An incentive, on the other hand, is a motivator that sparks consistently good behavior in your child. Enlist your child's cooperation in dreaming up incentives that interest him and ask what he thinks would be a good way of keeping track of his progress in giving incentives for behavior issues he wants to work on with you.

Harley, a first grader who loves to play rather than do his homework, is having trouble adjusting to school. He comes home tired and irritable and throws tantrums when his mother Ali won't give him candy and cookies before dinner. He doesn't care for most healthy snacks and demands sweets.

He has outbursts of major proportions over this issue, and once he fell when his mother caught him kneeling on a countertop, sneaking candy from a high kitchen cabinet. He got startled when his mother saw him and fell onto the hard linoleum floor, banging his head. His mother rushed him to the drugstore clinic because he screamed so loudly that she worried he may have had a concussion. Luckily, he wasn't hurt seriously, but he complained loudly for the rest of the afternoon about how mean his mother was for not letting him have sweets after school. He also made her feel guilty by saying she caused him to fall by not putting the candy in a place he could reach it.

Harley also whines and protests loudly when it's time to do his homework. "I don't want to go to school. I want to stay home with you," he says to Ali, who works from home. His teacher, Ms. Wilson, says that after being tested the counselor found that he has normal intelligence and is capable of doing first grade work. Ms. Wilson believes that he's experiencing a hard adjustment to the routines of first grade with no naps and only one playtime.

The teacher reassures Ali and her husband Jon that he'll probably grow out of his negative feelings about school before the second report period closes. However, his parents have great concern about his disruptive behavior at home regarding his desire to eat sweets whenever he wants them and his reluctance to cooperate about doing his homework.

When Harley's parents, Ali and Jon, meet with the school counselor about his school problems, they mention his behavioral issues at home. The counselor says she's seen incentives work with some children when using consequences alone didn't help much. She suggests they sit down with Harley and discuss what types of incentives would motivate him to cut down on temper tantrums and work up the motivation to do his homework.

That night, after dinner, Ali and Jon tell Harley they want to talk about a new way of helping him deal with being upset about not having sweets when he gets home from school. They tell him they think this new way of helping him might also make it easier for him to want to do his homework so he's well prepared for school the next day and won't feel as frustrated about school.

Harley doesn't look thrilled about not having his sweet snack after school, but he wonders what they'll have to say, so he sits down on the sofa with them. "I don't like the snacks you give me. Why can't I pick the things I want to eat? I'm starving after school, and it makes me feel really grumpy. That's why I scream and say mean things to you."

"I know how you feel," Jon says. "When I come home from work, I'm so hungry I could eat a big hot fudge sundae with whipped cream or that coffee cake your mom hides from me, but you won't see me doing that."

"Why not?" Harley says. "You're an adult. You can eat anything you want."

"I'll tell you why. I might crave it, but I know it's best for my health to eat a good dinner first with you and Mom. If I want a snack and I can't wait for dinner, I'll grab a piece of fruit or maybe a chunk of cheese." Harley frowns. "I don't like fruit or cheese."

"What kinds of healthy snacks do you think you'd like?" Ali asks.

Harley rubs his chin, in thinker mode. "I like strawberries. Maybe I could have them with a sprinkling of sugar. I also like fruit smoothies. I could make one for myself with fruit, honey, and crushed ice."

Jon nods in agreement. "You've thought of two good things to eat for snacks."

"I don't know if I could eat them every day. How about if I eat healthy snacks three days a week and have cookies or candy the other two? That would be during the school week because weekends you usually let me have a couple of sweet snacks between meals."

Ali considers his ideas. "Let's say healthy snacks four days a week after school and a small amount of sweets any one day you choose, maybe one cookie or a fun-size candy bar. I think that would be a good compromise. If you eat the healthy snacks four days a week, I'll give you a star for doing that on a chart we'll set up on the kitchen bulletin board. You can paste your own star on the chart and when you have fifteen stars, you can pick a reward."

Harley gets excited at the prospect of choosing his own rewards. "How about this? If I get fifteen stars I'll be allowed to stay up a half-hour later on a school night or an hour later on the weekend for two days that week?"

"That sounds like a good incentive to me," his dad says.

"Now what about doing homework without making a big fuss? What kind of incentive would you choose for that?" Ali asks.

"I've got an idea," Harley says. "If I do my homework without complaining, I'll get to paste a star on the chart each time. When I do that for two weeks in a row, I'll get a reward. I'll get to play video games for an extra hour on the weekends. You know how I love playing video games and how you're always telling me to stop playing and read a book."

"I still think it's better to spend more time reading than playing video games, but I think it's a good reward you chose for doing your homework without complaining. Do you agree, Jon?"

"I think so too, but with the promise that Harley will read more books."

"If I read more books, can I get to pick more rewards?"

Ali laughs. "It has to stop somewhere. Let's keep it the way it is with rewards for eating healthy snacks and for doing homework without a hassle. Reading will be its own reward."

"I think I'm okay with that. I found a couple of books at the book fair I'd like to read, so I won't need a reward for that because I'm excited about reading them."

"Now you're talking, son," Jon says. "Remember that the rewards won't go on forever. Eating healthy and doing well in school will give you their own rewards."

"Let's make the chart now. I can't wait to get started," says Harley, running to the cabinet to find paper, markers, and stars.

TRY THIS: ACTIVITIES TO HELP YOU DELIVER MEANINGFUL CONSEQUENCES, AGES 10–14

99. Teach Self-Discipline to Promote Self-Control

Consequences and incentives can definitely help modify behavioral problems, but the best long-term solution to remedying these issues lies in helping your child acquire a strong sense of self-discipline. When a child displays self-discipline, she can control her feelings and overcome her inclination to give in to negative behavior.

Parents can teach children self-discipline in many ways. The first and most important way is modeling behaviors associated with it. For example, if you tell your child it's important to pay your bills and you get the job done in a timely manner instead of postponing it for another day, you're showing self-discipline. If you're preparing for a big family dinner and you buy the groceries and prepare some of the dishes ahead of time instead of racing around at the last minute, you're displaying self-discipline.

You can foster self-discipline in children of any age. In Arabella, a ninth grader's case, her mother Jacqui used logical consequences to help her daughter wake up to catch the school bus in time. Giving consequences worked for a short time, but after a while, Arabella was late waking up at least three days a week.

Jacqui and her husband Cory knew they had to teach their daughter to gain the self-discipline to motivate herself to wake up on time each day to arrive at school before the late bell rang. Additionally, a lack of self-discipline in studying for tests also caused Arabella to face possible failure in her Spanish class. She didn't study the new vocabulary and grammar each night and ended up cramming, which resulted in low test grades.

Her parents knew it was time to have a serious talk about Arabella's problems when she received detentions from the school disciplinarian for lateness to school and also a failing notice from her Spanish teacher. Here's a replay of the conversation between parents and daughter:

Jacqui (using "I-messages"): I can see you're feeling regret about those detentions for being late and that failing notice because of poor test grades. Dad and I would like to help you, but we're at the point where we've done all we could. We've tried giving consequences to help you do better in both areas, but it looks like they didn't help you change your behavior.

Cory: Now we realize that in both these cases, you have to want to change your behavior. It has to come from you, not us, if you truly want things to work out with getting to school on time and passing your Spanish course. That said, we believe the most important trait you can have to succeed in anything is self-discipline.

Jacqui: I wish I'd been more consistent in showing how to practice self-discipline, but sometimes we adults slip too. As you know, I decided I wanted to lose five pounds, so I started going to the gym and watching what I ate. I was doing well, until a month ago, when I stopped going to the gym because I got bored by pedaling those in-door bikes. When I got discouraged for not staying with the program, I consoled myself by eating a few treats when I watched TV at night. As you would expect, I gained a couple more pounds because I wasn't active and was eating more. Now I'm practicing self-discipline again, and I'm making progress. I've found an exercise I enjoy, Zumba, and I'm cutting back on the sweet treats. As a result, I feel better in every way because I'm using self-discipline to meet a goal. I have to say that Dad has always been self-disciplined. If he has a work project due, he gets it done in advance. He also set a goal for himself to watch what he eats, and he lost three pounds last month.

Cory: It isn't always easy, but I've found that having self-discipline is the best way to live. I set goals. I do my best to take action on the goals, and then I reach them. If I don't, I modify my goals in staying with I can realistically accomplish, and then I set out to do my best. Self-discipline helps me succeed every time.

Arabella: I like that idea and want to try it. What do I have to do to be self-disciplined so I get to school on time and don't get failing notices? I want to make things better and to be more responsible for myself. I shouldn't need you to punish me like I'm a small child to do what I know is right for me.

Jacqui: You can write notes to remind yourself to study for Spanish. Use large lettering so you won't overlook them. Display them in a place where you won't miss them, next to your phone or your computer, for example. Also write a personal message in large letters on your reminder to motivate yourself like, "Study for Spanish exam. I need to pass." I recently wrote myself notes like this to push myself to keep going to Zumba class, and it worked. Now that it's working for me, I feel I can be a role model for you.

Arabella: I'm going to try writing notes to remind me I have to study Spanish so I can try to pass, even though it's late in the semester.

Cory: It may not be too late if you start now. Do you have any ideas about helping yourself wake up on time to make the bus? If you think of your own ideas, you'll be more likely to carry them out.

Arabella: I usually set the alarm for 7:00 o'clock, but as soon as it rings, I shut it off. I can make the decision to wake up and start getting ready when it rings. I can also ask Mikey (her little brother) to come in when he wakes up to make sure I'm awake, and if I'm not, to barge into my room and act like his usual wild, noisy self.

Jacqui: I like your ideas. It looks like we're going to be a family who practices self-discipline from now on. The best thing is that you won't get consequences from us and you'll gain the benefits of not getting late-to-school detentions and failing grades. That should be an incentive in itself. When do you want your self-discipline program to take effect?

Arabella: How about tonight when I study for my Spanish test and tomorrow morning when I wake up in time for school?

Cory: That's certainly soon enough.

Jacqui: If this works out, which I think it will, you won't have to tell your friends you were grounded because you didn't wake up for school on time or because you failed Spanish. Most of all, you'll be able to meet any challenge you'll face in life by using self-discipline.

100. Enlist Family Members to Inspire Positive Behavior

Often other members of your family, such as grandparents, aunts, and uncles, can get kids to cooperate more easily than you can. Because your children aren't with them all the time and because they often give them special attention, they're more likely to listen with open minds to what these relatives have to say. Also, it's common knowledge that many older relatives, such as grandparents, are great listeners who listen mindfully when their grandchildren talk. They tend not to hurry their grandkids or interrupt them as parents who have busy schedules sometimes do. They give them unconditional love that motivates children to take their advice to heart.

Older relatives usually practice patience and empathy while these traits are, understandably, often in short supply when kids start pushing their parents' buttons. These treasured family members seem to know intuitively about Mindfulness and how to use it to help their younger family members. They model positive traits and also know how to talk with children about the importance of positive behavior characteristics such as honesty, industriousness, productivity, and loving kindness without sounding preachy or bossy.

Darlene, the grandmother of Logan, the young man in this story, took a Mindfulness course at one of the city hospitals. She thought the course would help her deal with her adjustment after a recent retirement from her job as a human resources manager. After taking the course, she also decided to play a more active role in her grandson's life and found that Mindfulness was the perfect tool to help him with his behavioral issues.

Logan's parents, Sharon and Carlo, found out that Logan lied to them a couple of times by saying he was visiting one friend, when in truth it was another friend, who was known to bully a couple of classmates. His parents also find it impossible to motivate Logan to study for tests. As a consequence, he's not doing well in a couple of his classes.

Sharon, Logan's mother, has asked her mother Darlene to talk to her son about some problems she's had with him lately. Here's a conversation between Logan, a high school freshman, and his grandmother:

Logan: I got your text. What do you want to talk about, Gran? Has Mom been talking to you about me?

Darlene (smiling warmly): You know you're one of our main topics of conversation. Actually, I wanted to talk to you about the fact that your mom's concerned about you although she didn't give me the specifics. You and I always have a good way of discussing whatever's on your mind, so feel free to let me know how you're feeling about what's happening with you.

Logan: I know you wouldn't approve of my lying to Mom and Dad about going to one friend's house, when I went to another kid's house, but that's what I did, if you want to know the truth.

Darlene (acting curious so she can understand better): Why don't your parents want you to be friends with this boy?

Logan: He bullies a couple of kids in the class, but he's really not as bad as people think. He's a great baseball player, and that's why I like going to his house. We like to practice together since we're both on the team. Sometimes, I think those kids he bullies ask for it because they kiss up to teachers and act like they know everything.

Darlene: I don't think anyone ever deserves to be bullied, and I know you never did either.

Logan: I guess you're right, but I hate it when Mom and Dad tell me who I should have for friends. I'm in high school now and should be able to decide for myself.

Darlene (using empathy and "I-messages"): I can understand how you feel. However, when you make this kind of decision, you need to do it based on what you believe is right, and I honestly don't believe you think bullying someone is right under any circumstances.

Logan: When I think about it, no, I don't ever believe it's okay. Maybe I should spend more time with my other friends, but I don't like Mom and Dad always telling me what to do, and so I went behind their backs and saw Damon.

Darlene: That's a different issue. Most people, especially young people, don't like being told what to do. I know I didn't when I was a young girl. However, I think you're saying you agree with your parents more than you disagree with them on this issue.

Logan: Yes, and because I do, I probably shouldn't look the other way when Damon bullies those kids. I still feel annoyed with Dad and Mom for bossing me around about everything. That's probably why I lied about seeing Damon. I realize that now.

Darlene: Why not talk to your parents and tell them how you feel? They're reasonable people. When you talk to them, try to talk Mindfully. That means not being pushy or mean like you'd be if you talked aggressively, or not being passive and talking around the issue. Also, be willing to listen to what they want to say because in the end, they have the final say. Work with them and they'll be more willing to work with you. I know they won't compromise on having Damon as a friend unless he changes his ways. That's only right.

Logan: Okay, I'm willing to try it, but I'm only doing it because you asked me.

Darlene: Thanks for saying that, but I hope you're mainly doing it for yourself because you know it's the right thing to do.

Logan: I'm wondering if Mom told you anything else.

Darlene: I'm sure you know they're also concerned about your grades. They said they try to get you to prepare for your tests, but they can't get you to do your work so you'll pass those courses.

Logan: That's because I don't like those subjects. When will I ever use algebra? Who cares if I know the difference between an adjective and an adverb?

Darlene (accepting, validating what he says): A lot of kids feel that way, but I doubt things will change. Schools have taught the same subjects for years even though they may need an update in content and presentation. You have to live with it, so try to make the best of it. Besides, algebra helps you think logically, and you definitely need to know about adjectives to make your descriptions more vivid when you write. It's good to know about adverbs, but don't use them too often. Take it from me. I've written many reports in my day. Adverbs drag down your writing. Strong verbs rule.

Logan: My teacher never told us that. Gran, you're one smart lady.

Darlene: Besides the practical knowledge studying math and English give you, they exercise your brain. You want to keep that in tip-top shape, right? You never know when you'll have to use it to outsmart Gran, right?

Logan: You're one person I can never outsmart. I'm going to try harder to do better studying for tests, and like you said, I'm going to try it for me, because I'm the one it hurts if I don't study and pass everything.

Darlene: Anytime you want to talk, I'm here. I'm going to check in with you to see how things are going, and I'll always listen to what you have to say without judging you. When I don't agree, I'll say that too.

Logan: I'm cool with that. Thanks, Gran.

101. Use Mindfulness Techniques to Boost Desirable Behavior

Living Mindfully means being a good listener, giving Loving Kindness, talking assertively rather than passively or aggressively, and showing concern if a person needs help or has a problem. Mindfulness also promotes accepting a person's feelings without necessarily agreeing with that person's viewpoint, growing spiritually by living in the moment, and taking time to meditate each day.

As you've seen, this book emphasizes the importance of modeling as a child-raising tool. As you would expect, many other factors intervene, like your children's temperament and ability to regulate their own behavior through self-discipline. For many children, modeling Mindfulness helps build their sense of an internal conscience and gives them peaceful ways of responding and interacting with others.

When you model Mindfulness for your children, it eliminates many potential behavior problems since your kids will be more likely to act the way you do and become more caring and responsible without needing a lot of external controls imposed on them through consequences and other disciplinary techniques you use with them.

Two friends from work, Kerry and Rosa, took a Mindfulness class together. In the beginning, they did their best to practice Mindfulness every day. However, as time went on and the obligations of daily life intruded, they went back to their old ways of living, mainly in the future or the past, rather than in the present moment. Now that their children, Blair and Andres, are in high school, they think modeling Mindfulness for them may help them with the peer pressures they're facing.

Both Kerry and Rosa, psychiatric social workers, have seen Mindfulness help many of their clients, and now they'd like to help their sons cope with pressures they face in school by showing them how Mindfulness can work in their own lives.

Today, the two friends discuss specific things they can teach their sons about Mindfulness to help guide them to right action. Their mothers can also model this behavior so that it will be easy for the boys to learn it. Here's what the two friends said during their lunch break:

Rosa: I know our kids are facing a lot of pressures, especially when they go to parties. I've heard that a few of their friends smoke and drink beer, especially when they get together at parties. I believe that assertive speech can help get them out of sticky situations when they feel pressure to do something they think is wrong. Assertive speech is brief and to the point, so they could say something simple like this when someone offers them a cigarette or a drink: "No thanks." They don't have to go into detail as it would make them look weak or ambivalent.

Kerry: I believe assertive speech is the best way to get your point across. I've been modeling it for Blair and his younger sister. When I want them to do something I'll say, "I want you to do your homework now," or "Stop fighting and set the table." If I use passive talk or a question, like "Would you like to do your homework now?" or aggressive talk like, "You'd better get started on that homework or you're going to fail," they're more likely to tune me out.

Rosa: I see the same thing happening at my house. I also like how Mindfulness uses "I-messages." I used it yesterday with Andres when he talked back to me about cleaning the table. I said, "I don't like when you talk to me like that. I need you to show the same respect I show you." It actually worked.

Kerry: The other thing I'm trying to do is pick a good time to talk to Blair if I see something's bothering him. I say something like, "I'd like to talk more about your problems in science class. Would you like to discuss it now, or should I check in with you tomorrow?" Timing can make all the difference in a child's receptivity to your message. Blair could use that technique when approaching his science teacher to talk about his grades. He could ask the teacher when would be a good time for him to talk, and he could discuss his concerns about his grade when the teacher was ready to listen and wasn't preoccupied.

Rosa: I also remember what they told us in our Mindfulness course about accepting whatever someone has to say and listening to that person before reacting or responding. Too often, I pounce all over Andres because he wants to do something I don't approve of, like meeting up with his friends at the arcade on weekends. I'm making an effort to listen and let him finish what he has to say before I give my opinion. I notice he often doesn't listen to me before jumping in and giving his point. Maybe if I tried harder by showing him how it's done, he'd get the message.

Kerry: Speaking of listening, I'm trying to show more empathy when I listen to my kids. I'm going to look at them more and stop thinking of what I'm making for dinner or what approach I have to use with the next client in my caseload tomorrow. I'm going to use the same mindful body language I use with my clients with my children, by nodding when they talk and showing them I understand, whether I agree or not.

Rosa: You know how we're Mindfully curious when we talk to our patients? I'm starting to do that with Andres again by being curious and asking him questions to draw out his feelings about things he's thinking about. I'm trying not to interrogate him like he's on the hot seat, but I want to clarify the issue we're discussing before I respond to him.

Kerry: I'm going to try that too. You're right. I use these techniques on my patients, but I often forget about using them with my own family. They really work, so I'm going to remember what you said. I'm also thinking about getting back to practicing Mindfulness Meditation again. I felt greatly relaxed and handled stress better when I meditated regularly. I'd like to teach Blair how to meditate because he's feeling nervous about a couple of his classes, and it may help him. I could teach him the type of meditation we learned in class, the one where you're conscious of your breathing. I'd leave it up to him how long he wanted to do it each day. I don't know if he could sit for ten or fifteen minutes at a time like I do.

Rosa: Thanks for reminding me. Meditation was my special time to unwind and relax. I'm going to start up with my practice again and encourage Andres to try it too.

Kerry (looking at her watch): It's time to get back to work, but we need to do this again. I'm glad we made the time to talk today. It's much easier coming up with solutions when we pool our ideas. I may not be the perfect parent, but parenting mindfully helps me with whatever issues come up with my children, every single time.

About the Author

Catherine DePino has written seventeen books about bullying, grammar/ writing, spirituality, and women's issues. She recently published *Cool Things to Do If a Bully's Bugging You*, which offers practical, hands-on tips for kids who face bullying. Her self-help book, *Fire Up Your Life in Retirement: 101 Ways for Women to Reinvent Themselves*, helps women deal with the challenges they face in retirement. Her bully prevention book, *Blue Cheese Breath and Stinky Feet: How to Deal with Bullies*, has been published in many different languages. Bully prevention programs value it as a treasured resource. She recently wrote *Helping Kids Live Mindfully: A Grab Bag of Activities for Middle School Students*.

Her background includes a BS in English and Spanish education, a master's in English education, and a doctorate in curriculum theory and development and educational administration with principal's certification, all from Temple University. She worked for thirty-one years as a teacher, department head, and disciplinarian in the Philadelphia School District, then at Temple as an adjunct assistant professor and student teaching supervisor.

Catherine has also written articles for national magazines, including *Christian Science Monitor* and *The Writer*. She views her most important accomplishment in life as being the mother of three and the grandmother of five. She was on the board of the Philadelphia Writers' Conference for many years and and holds membership in the Association of Children's Book Writers and Illustrators. Visit her website at www.catherine depino.com.